THE UNTOI
OF THE GC
HEIGHTS

Inspiring, passionate and intellectually engaged, this collection of essays (some originally written in Arabic) focuses on the political and cultural agency of Syrian Arabs in the Occupied Jawlan (Arabic for Golan); their experience of everyday colonization by Israel of Jawlani society; and their determined, non-violent, ceaseless assertion against it. This book goes beyond the politics of the region, and speaks to the possibilities for democratic resistance everywhere, under fascism, majoritarianism and occupation."

NIVEDITA MENON, *Jawaharlal Nehru University, India*

This book, the outcome of a collaborative research project, tells the neglected story of the occupation of the Golan Heights, by focusing on the political and cultural agency of its inhabitants. Through considering the interplay between everyday colonization and the politics of the governed, the book offers an original and eclectic understanding of agency and power in prolonged settler colonial contexts, what it authors term lifeworld colonization. The book, with its sensitive prose, illustrations and its moving reflections, is vital for scholars interested in understanding dispossession and survival more broadly. More specifically, its critical approach is a unique contribution to the growing interdisciplinary field of Palestine Studies."

DINA MATAR, *SOAS, University of London, UK*

The Untold Story of the Golan Heights is one of very few books about this region. But what distinguishes this volume is the fact that it is a collaborative endeavor authored by Jawlanis and their allies, thereby giving readers a chance to learn from the truest of experts."

LISA HAJJAR, *UC Santa Barbara, USA*

THE UNTOLD STORY OF THE GOLAN HEIGHTS

Occupation, Colonization and
Jawlani Resistance

**Edited by
Muna Dajani,
Munir Fakher Eldin and
Michael Mason**

I.B.TAURIS
LONDON • NEW YORK • OXFORD • NEW DELHI • SYDNEY

I.B. TAURIS
Bloomsbury Publishing Plc
50 Bedford Square, London, WC1B 3DP, UK
1385 Broadway, New York, NY 10018, USA
29 Earlsfort Terrace, Dublin 2, Ireland

BLOOMSBURY, I.B. TAURIS and the I.B. Tauris logo are trademarks of Bloomsbury Publishing Plc

First published in Great Britain 2023

Cover design by Toby Way
Cover image: *Shouting Hill. The Golan.* © Alaa Armoon, 2021.
Courtesy of the artist.

A catalogue record for this book is available from the British Library.

A catalog record for this book is available from the Library of Congress.

ISBN: HB: 978-0-7556-4451-3
PB: 978-0-7556-4452-0
ePDF: 978-0-7556-4453-7
eBook: 978-0-7556-4454-4

Typeset by Deanta Global Publishing Services, Chennai, India
Printed and bound in Great Britain

To find out more about our authors and books visit www.bloomsbury.com and
sign up for our newsletters.

CONTENTS

SECTION V A JAWLANI POLITICAL ECOLOGY

ILLUSTRATIONS

Figures

Maps

CONTRIBUTORS

Jumanah Abbas is a Palestinian architect, writer and researcher from Safed. She holds a master's degree in Critical, Curatorial and Conceptual Practices from Columbia University.

Amal Aun is a Palestinian citizen of Israel and an independent researcher and holds a master's degree in Public Administration, with a focus on Human Rights, from Cornell University.

Ali Aweidat is a Syrian researcher and activist from the occupied Syrian Jawlan.

Muna Dajani is a senior research associate at Lancaster Environment Centre, Lancaster University, and a Palestinian researcher from Al-Quds (Jerusalem).

Munir Fakher Eldin is the Faculty of Arts Dean at Birzeit University and a Syrian academic from the occupied Syrian Jawlan.

Diaaeddin Horoub is a journalist and researcher interested in oral history and a master's student at Birzeit University.

Alaa Iktash is a Palestinian researcher from Al-Quds (Jerusalem) and a PhD student at the London School of Economics and Political Science.

Yasser Khanjar is a poet from the occupied Syrian Jawlan.

Michael Mason is the director of the Middle East Centre at the London School of Economics and Political Science, UK.

Nadine Musallam is a journalist and holds a master's degree in International Relations from Birzeit University.

Bassel Rizqallah is a master's student in Israeli Studies at Birzeit University.

Aram Abu Saleh is a Syrian writer and activist from the occupied Syrian Jawlan.

Wael Tarabieh is an artist from the occupied Syrian Jawlan and an activist in the field of culture and education.

Omar Tesdell is an assistant professor in the Department of Geography at Birzeit University.

Abdel Qader Thweib is a master's student at Birzeit University.

ACKNOWLEDGEMENTS

The editors and publisher gratefully acknowledge the permission granted to reproduce the copyright material in this book. Photos are credited immediately below the photo in question on the relevant page. Full credit lines for copyrighted material are as follows:

Cover art: *Shouting Hill, the Jawlan*, painting by Alaa Armoon ©Alaa Armoon, 2020. Reproduced with the permission of Alaa Armoon.

Figure 1.1: Kamal Kanj trial, Israeli military court, Majdal Shams, November 1971 © Israel State Archives. Courtesy of Dan Hadani Collection, The Pritzker Family National Photography Collection, The National Library of Israel.

Figure 2.2: Ruined Al-Kushniyah Mosque, 2019. Courtesy of Michael Mason.

Figure R1: Jawlanis discard Israeli ID cards, Ein Qiniya, 5 April 1982, by Yosi Elmakis © Israel State Archives. Courtesy of Dan Hadani Collection, The Pritzker Family National Photography Collection, The National Library of Israel.

Figure R3: One of the first Jawlani demonstrations in support of the Syrian revolution, Majdal Shams, March 2011, © Atef Al-Safadi. Courtesy of Atef Al-Safadi.

Figure 4.1: *A Quote*, drawing by Randa Maddah, © Randa Maddah, 2012. Reproduced with the permission of Randa Maddah.

Figure 4.3: Unnamed (2020) statue by Ayman Al-Halabi, June 2020, © Nabih Aweidat. Courtesy of Nabih Aweidat.

Figure 6.2: A view of the orchards of Majdal Shams and the Jabal al-Shaykh southern foothills, January 2021, © Wesam Sharaf. Courtesy of Wesam Sharaf.

Figure 7.1: Donald Trump 'presents' the 1981 National Document of the People of the occupied Syrian Golan. Digitally manipulated image, Golan Youth Movement, 26 March 2019. Courtesy of the Golan Youth Movement.

Thanks to Jumanah Abbas for permission to reproduce the following artwork and graphics:

- **Figure R2**: 'Solidarity with the Jawlan' (2021), by Jumanah Abbas.
- **Figure R6.1**: A perspectival map positioning and visualizing Jawlani sculptures in dialogue with each other (2021), by Jumanah Abbas.
- **Figure R6.2**: A map highlighting the Jawlani summer camps for young people (2021), by Jumanah Abbas.
- **Figure 7.2**: A counter-cartography of Jawlani identity politics and resistance (2021), by Jumanah Abbas.

Particular thanks are extended to the Jawlani photographer Fares Al Welly, who has kindly permitted the reproduction of a number of photos from his personal archive:

- **Figure 2.1**: Israeli police disperse protestors opposing municipal elections, Majdal Shams, 30 October 2018. Photo by Fares Al Welly, © Fares Al Welly 2018.
- **Figure 3.1**: Protest march in Mas'ada, 14 March 2004. Photo by Fares Al Welly, © Fares Al Welly 2004.
- **Figure 4.2**: 'The March' (1987) statue by Hassan Khater, Majdal Shams, April 1987. Photo by Fares Al Welly, © Fares Al Welly 1987.
- **Figure R4**: *Al-Masirah* ('The March') statue under construction, Majdal Shams, March 1987. Photo by Fares Al Welly, © Fares Al Welly 1987.
- **Figure 5.1**: Protest march of Jawlani school students, Majdal Shams, March 1987. Photo by Faris Fares Al Welly, © Fares Al Welly 1987.
- **Figure 6.1**: Syrian-flagged Jawlani bulldozers reclaiming land, Mas'ada, 2010. Photo by Fares Al Welly, © Fares Al Welly 2010.

We are also very grateful to the poet Yasser Khanjar for allowing us to publish five of his poems in this book, both in their original Arabic and in English translation. Raya Publishing House and Al Mutawassit have generously allowed re-publication of three poems. The new English translations in this book are by the poet and literary scholar Dr Ghareeb Iksander, to whom we extend our gratitude. Two of the poems – 'Tranquility' (2021) and an untitled poem (2020) – are published in Arabic and English translation for the first time. The three previously published in Arabic are:

'As for Me', poem by Yasser Khanjar © Raya Publishing House 2014. Published in English translation from Arabic original with the permission of Raya Publishing House.

'Complementarity', poem by Yasser Khanjar © Al Mutawassit 2019. Published in English translation from Arabic original with the permission of Al Mutawassit.

'Dawn', poem by Yasser Khanjar © Al Mutawassit 2019. Published in English translation from Arabic original with the permission of Al Mutawassit.

Reflection 8 includes lyrics from a song by Samih Choukair (1990) *Zaher Al Rumman* ('Pomegranate Blossom'). Lyrics and music by Samih Choukair, extract used by permission of Samih Choukair.

Every effort has been made to trace copyright holders and to obtain their permission for the use of copyright material. The publisher apologizes for any errors or omissions in the above list and would be grateful if notified of any corrections that should be incorporated in future reprints or editions of this book.

NOTE ON TEXT/ TRANSLATION

Readers will encounter several different terms referring to the territory covered in this book. Adoption of the term 'occupied Syrian Golan Heights' follows United Nations usage for the area of Syrian territory occupied by Israel since June 1967 (e.g. United Nations Security Council Resolution 497 (1981)). 'Occupied Golan' or 'occupied Golan Heights' is sometimes employed in the book as a shorthand for 'occupied Syrian Golan Heights'. The use of the term 'Jawlan' by contributors (from the Arabic for the 'Golan') signifies its adoption by the local Arab population, who identify as 'Jawlani', hence also the terms 'occupied Syrian Jawlan' or 'occupied Jawlan'. As discussed in the book, *Jawlani* is an identity adopted across a range of political, cultural and ecological practices to signify indigeneity. At the same time, this is a relational and dynamic identity – fusing place attachment, Arab Syrian nationality, the Druze faith and/or secular ideas – defined against its Israeli 'othering' as non-Jewish. The Israeli classification of the Golan as part of 'northern Israel' is a unilateral designation made in violation of the international legal principle prohibiting the acquisition of territory by force. The majority of Jawlanis have rejected Israeli citizenship, choosing to be 'non-citizen residents' of Israel despite the political and economic disenfranchisement that this entails.

Translators are credited at the start of chapters, reflections and other pieces originally written in Arabic. In the text, transliteration into English of Arabic terms follows the transliteration system of the *International Journal of Middle East Studies*, Cambridge University Press. However, transliteration of Syrian place names (both existing and destroyed localities in the occupied Golan Heights) follows Jawlani pronunciation. Arabic sources in the bibliography are, for convenience of the reader, translated into English.

ABBREVIATIONS AND ACRONYMS

ASD	Arab Society for Development
IDF	Israel Defense Forces
INPA	Israel Nature and Parks Authority
LSE	London School of Economics and Political Science
NIS	Israeli new shekel
OECD	Organisation for Economic Cooperation and Development
UN	United Nations
UNDOF	United Nations Disengagement Observer Force
UNGEGN	The United Nations Group of Experts on Geographical Names

1 INTRODUCTION

REPRESENTING THE OCCUPIED JAWLAN/GOLAN

MUNA DAJANI, MUNIR FAKHER ELDIN AND MICHAEL MASON

The 'Shouting Hill'

The cover image of this book reproduces a painting – *Shouting Hill, the Jawlan* [Golan] – by Jawlani artist, Alaa Armoon. It depicts two women, in white headscarves, waving over the fortified fence that marks the United Nations (UN) Purple Line, the de facto border between Syria and Syrian territory occupied by Israel since the June 1967 Arab-Israeli War. The women are waving from the occupied Syrian Golan (Map 1.1). Israel occupied the western two-thirds (1,200 square kilometres) of the Golan Heights and, while capturing further Syrian territory during the October 1973 (Yom Kippur) war, a separation of forces agreement in May 1974 saw combatants pull back to the Purple Line, with a United Nations Disengagement Observer Force (UNDOF) established by UN Security Council Resolution 350 to maintain the ceasefire and supervise the disengagement of Israeli and Syrian forces along a buffer zone. UNDOF was established for an initial period of six months and the Security Council has regularly renewed its mandate ever since.

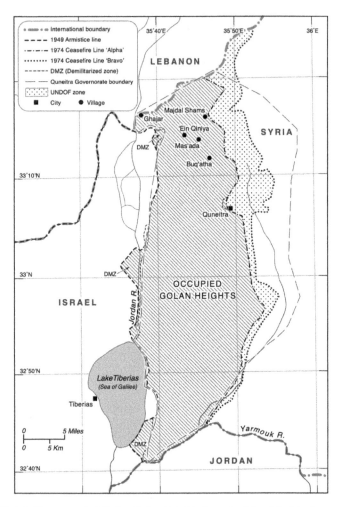

MAP 1.1 The occupied Syrian Golan Heights (map by Mina Moshkeri).

In the painting one of the women is waving a veil of white muslin, which, like the white scarves, is traditionally worn by religious Druze women in the Jawlan/Golan. They are waving to be seen, probably by relatives – sisters, brothers, sons, daughters and their spouses – on the other side of the ceasefire line, who, barely visible, are shouting from an assembly point built by the Syrian government. As a result of the 1967 war, some 127,000 inhabitants (95 per cent of the population in the conquered Syrian territory) fled or were forcibly displaced to Syria, while depopulated villages were systematically demolished under the supervision of the Israel Land Administration. Israel decreed the occupied territory as a closed military zone with no one allowed to leave or enter: Military Order No. 57, issued in September 1967, banned those forcibly displaced from returning to their homes. Strict restrictions on movement and communication remained, with occasional family reunifications and visits at the discretion of military and later civil authorities (Russell 2018). Only a small population of the indigenous Syrian inhabitants remained, in five mostly Druze villages clustered on the south-eastern slopes of Jabal al-Shaykh (Mount Hermon) and the Alawite village of Ghajar further west on the Lebanese border. One of the Druze villages, Sahita, was razed by the Israeli military in 1969, although the four other Druze villages – Majdal Shams, Mas'ada, Buq'atha and Ein Qiniya – remained. By 2020, these four villages, and Ghajar, contained 26,600 residents. The tenacity of these communities, in the face of over half a century of resource dispossession and economic de-development, is at the heart of the untold story of the Golan Heights.

Located 3 kilometres east of Majdal Shams, next to the 1974 ceasefire line (UNDOF Line 'Alpha'), the Shouting Hill (*talat al-ṣurākh*) first emerged as an area where people gathered to communicate with relatives and friends over the border fence. During the 1974–81 period, families met in UN tents across the ceasefire line, but Israel put an end to it after passing the 1981 Golan Heights Law, which applied Israeli law, jurisdiction and administration to the territory – an annexation in all but name. Kept 500–600 metres apart by mines and other security structures, people resorted to megaphones to make themselves heard and used binoculars to see more clearly their interlocutors. The valley became an arena for political gatherings, but quickly also became an intimate public space for separated families to reconnect, sharing news of everyday events and practical matters, of births, illnesses and deaths. Over time, the act of shouting across the ceasefire fence acquired a ritualistic quality, as the overlapping cries stubbornly performed kinship and community in the face of enforced separation: the political and the private converged. In the 1980s and 1990s, thousands gathered from both sides on 17 April to celebrate Syrian Independence Day and on 14 February to mark the anniversary of the declaration of the 1982 Jawlani general strike against the 1981 Golan Heights Law (Mara'i and Halabi 1992: 91; Phillips 2015). The arrival of mobile phones and internet access in the late 1990s reduced the scale and incidence of these gatherings, but the hill retains symbolic significance as an arena for communal celebrations and political demonstrations.

The six months general strike that commenced on 15 February 1982 was a monumental event that impacted the lived geographies of the Jawlanis and reconfigured their relations with land. On 17 April 1982, at the height of the strike, the Jawlanis went out to the streets to commemorate the 36th anniversary of the Evacuation Day (*Youm Al Jalaa*) – a Syrian national day commemorating the evacuation of the last French soldier and the declaration of Syrian independence and the end of the French mandate on 17 April 1946. Nearly 6,000 of them marched towards the ceasefire fence. On that day, the Jawlanis also declared their commitment to steadfastness (*sumud*), to protecting their land and agricultural livelihoods. In a statement published that week, they announced ('On the Anniversary of the Colonial Defeat'):

Land is the symbol of our sumud and our principal foundation to strengthen our existence and to continue our struggle to reach our human and national aspirations. The decision is to work in a collective and organised manner so that the production can be for the public good. This way we can continue with the strike.

'Shouting Hill' has become a mainstream – typically outsider – label, popularized in Israeli 'alternative' tourist guides for those seeking the frisson of a visit to the ceasefire line. Among the Jawlanis, the charged terms of 'Crying Hill' (*talat al-tabkī*) and 'Valley of Tears' (*wādī al-damūʾ*) capture more fully the insider perspective of separated families and friends, an emotional and psychological wrenching that is counted in generations rather than years. The Jawlani women in the painting are also in an allegorical sense waving to be seen, to reveal a story that is untold and largely unknown by the outside world. For Israel, the existence of the Jawlanis *as Jawlanis* is dismissed: their lived experiences are distorted or erased in mainstream histories and geographies of the region. This book therefore contributes to the social history of the occupied Jawlan. It seeks to transform our imaginary of the region, of the people who remain and of those who have been displaced.

So far, the only scholarly book in English on the Golan Heights is a political and settlement history, by Israeli author Yigal Kipnis, focusing on Jewish colonization since 1967 (Kipnis 2013). By 2020, facilitated by the Israeli state, 34 Jewish settlements, with 26,250 inhabitants, had

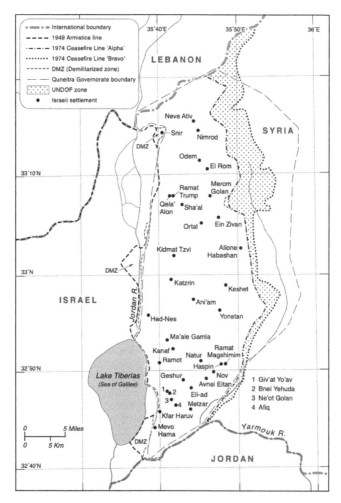

MAP 1.2 Israeli settlements in the occupied Syrian Golan Heights (map by Mina Moshkeri).

successfully been established in occupied Syrian territory (Map 1.2). Kipnis claims that his account of the Golan Heights is objective and fact-based (2013: 3), yet the remaining Arab population is absent as an historical actor after 1967. There is nothing on the land and water confiscation from the northern Syrian communities, nothing on their resistance to occupation or the coercive measures employed against them. Tellingly, Kipnis also does not discuss international humanitarian law pertaining to belligerent occupations, despite unequivocal statements by the UN (e.g. UN Security Council Resolution 497 (1981)) that this law applies to the occupied Syrian Golan. For example, population transfer into the territory, as driven by Israeli government policy (Kipnis 2013: 68), is in direct breach of Article 49 of the Fourth Geneva Convention, 1949, which was ratified by Israel in July 1951.

In this volume, we reveal the untold story of the Golan Heights – the political and cultural agency of the remaining Syrian Arabs, paying particular attention to events since 1981, when the territory was effectively annexed under the Golan Heights Law. The dual conceptual focus of the book is on processes of *everyday colonization* and the *politics of the governed*. From the lens of 'everyday colonization', we are interested in the daily experiences of, and reactions to, the Israeli occupation as manifest in Jawlani society, culture and land use. How are settler colonial processes of dispossession, segregation and misrecognition bound up with wider processes of state rule and economic exchange? By 'politics of the governed', we mean the various ways in which the Jawlanis engage with the political field of settler colonial power. Annexation in 1981 sparked a movement of non-violent resistance deploying diverse forms of political opposition, including a general strike, communal rejection of Israeli citizenship and, more recently, boycotts of Israeli local elections and protests against Israeli wind farm development (Fakher Eldin 2019). Contributors to this book show that an anti-colonial politics suffuses Jawlani cultural expression, is renewed by youth mobilization and solidarity with Palestinians, and also generates a singular political-ecological identity based on the collective defence of land. However, they also reveal that Jawlani politics is not simply oppositional but rather a myriad of tactics and manoeuvres among very unequal power relations and dependency: the demands of everyday living necessitate frequent exchanges with Israeli actors and institutions – interactions that may bring material and other gains to individuals, although short-term benefits may restrict future options for community self-determination (e.g. rents from leasing agricultural land for wind turbines).

Indigeneity in the post-1967 Jawlan

On the eve of war in June 1967, the administration of the Golan Heights mainly fell under the Syrian province of Quneitra, with the eastern third of the plateau part of Dera'a province. Of 160,000 inhabitants across the

Golan, the great majority of the population was Sunni Muslim (including over 9,000 Palestinian refugees from the 1948 war), with significant Christian, Druze and Alawite minorities. The non-Arab population comprised smaller numbers of Circassians, Turkmen, Armenians and Kurds, who were Sunni Muslims. While the villages across the region tended to be differentiated across ethnic-religious lines, these communities had a long history of coexistence, despite occurrences of communal strife in the late Ottoman era and French colonial rule (Kipnis 2013: 56–7; Mara'i and Halabi 1992: 78).

Israel completed its 1967 invasion of the Golan Heights within two days (9–10 June) and moved unsparingly to deepen the depopulation, forcibly displacing civilians in the wake of those who had already fled and undertaking the widespread destruction of Syrian villages and farms. Murphy and Gannon (2008) claim that these acts constitute war crimes, including grave breaches of the Fourth Geneva Convention, which prohibits the forcible transfer of a civilian population (Article 49) and the destruction of private and public property (Article 53). There are different figures available for the number of destroyed Syrian settlements in the occupied Golan Heights, for some smaller sites were left abandoned rather than demolished. Davis (1983: 5) notes that 131 villages and 61 farms were destroyed. Map 1.3, using data published by Al-Marsad (2021), shows 341 Syrian villages and farms destroyed.

As the war ended on the Golan Heights front, the Druze villages remaining were disconnected from each other and the outside world. Jawlanis recall how during the first days and weeks of the occupation, they were not aware how many villages remained intact, who was controlling what area and the situation in the nearby city of Quneitra. Slowly, with the presence of Israeli army in their villages and the imposition of military rule, it became evident to the Jawlanis that familiar worlds of experience were vanishing. The Israeli occupation caused a devastating physical and existential rupture, also disrupting the socio-economic and political lives and disconnecting the remaining inhabitants from their Syrian homeland. It was nonetheless considered by the remaining population as a 'temporary' phase of military rule that was to be tolerated until political interventions and negotiations rectified the situation. For the Jawlanis, the 1967 war and its aftermath are considered a point of rupture in their lived experience. Similar to the *Nakba* (catastrophe) experienced by Palestinians in 1948, the Jawlanis experienced an abrupt disintegration of their social and political everyday life.

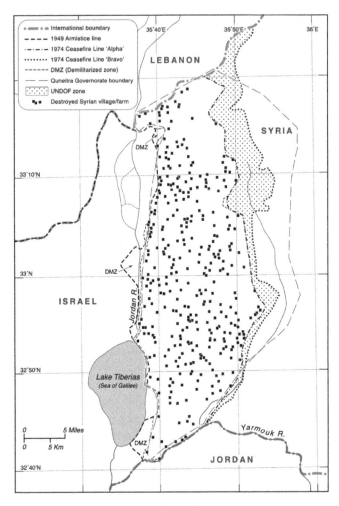

MAP 1.3 Destroyed Syrian communities in the occupied Syrian Golan Heights (map by Mina Moshkeri using data from Al-Marsad (2021)).

Shortly after the end of the 1967 war, Israeli archaeologist Dan Urman was appointed the Israel army staff officer in charge of antiquities in the Golan Heights. As Head of Surveying and Demolition Supervision for the Golan Heights, he coordinated the first round of demolition of Syrian villages (90 depopulated villages from a list of 127), preceded by surveys of sites deemed by the Israel Archaeological Survey Society to be of interest (Shai 2006: 100–1; Suliman and Kletter 2022: 57–62). The archaeological surveys, under Urman's direction, focused on evidence of Jewish settlements during late antiquity and claimed that there were sixty-five such sites, double previous estimates (Urman 1995), although some of his claims about Jewish presence were later rejected by other Israeli archaeologists (Maòz 2010). Given that the Golan Heights were regarded at the time by the leading Israeli politicians and the Zionist right as being *outside* the map of the 'Greater Land of Israel' (Kipnis 2013: 229), efforts to construct archaeological evidence of Jewish indigeneity were central to those supporting settler colonization, notably the religious Zionist settler movement Hapoel Mizrachi. However, the first Jewish settlement established in the Golan Heights was the non-religious Kibbutz Merom Golan, and most of the settlements that followed were either kibbutzim or moshavim. From the mid-1970s, the right-wing Orthodox Jewish settlement movement, Gush Emunim, added further momentum to this construction of the Golan as part of Greater Israel, supporting new settlements (Kipnis 2013: 161–7). The archaeological surveys of the Golan in 1967–8, led by Urman, supplied biblical and Talmudic justification for settlers summoning a Jewish presence in the depopulated territory.

The remaining Syrian villages disrupted the Zionist notion that the conquered Golan was a land emptied of its non-Jewish inhabitants and history. The Druze communities in the northern Jawlan date back over 300 years to the flight of the Yamani tribal-political faction after the battle of Ain Dara in 1711 (Hitti 1928: 8; Kirrish 1992: 126). In his comprehensive survey of the 'Jaulân' conducted in the 1880s for Ottoman authorities, the engineer Gottlieb Schumacher observed the 'fine large villages' of the Druze in the north-east, living peacefully alongside their Bedouin and Circassian neighbours (Schumacher [1888] 2010: 59). However, in 1925–6, under the French Mandate for Syria and Lebanon, the local population joined the wider Druze-led revolt against occupation and Majdal Shams became a rebel stronghold, defeated by the French in April 1926, who razed the village as collective punishment. As Mara'i and Halabi (1992: 80) note, in June 1967 the uprising against French rule was within living memory of older members of the Jawlani population, motivating community members not to flee. Also significant was the assumption by the occupying forces that the Syrian Druze in the occupied Golan would, like the Druze communities in the Galilee, ultimately acquiesce to Israeli sovereign authority, including the ascription of 'Druzeness' as a non-Arab ethno-religious community. Early in the occupation, there was even an unsuccessful attempt by the military administration to convince

FIGURE 1.1 Kamal Kanj trial, Israeli military court, Majdal Shams, November 1971. Courtesy of Dan Hadani Collection, National Library of Israel.

a prominent local leader, Shaykh Kamal Kanj, to consider a Druze buffer state between Israel, Syria and Jordan – a proposal championed by Israel's Minister of Labour, Yigal Allon, that was soon dropped. Kanj feigned interest and was imprisoned by Israel (Figure 1.1) for informing Syrian intelligence about the proposed partition state (Kipnis 2013: 94–5; Mara'i and Halabi 1992: 80).

In its treatment of Syrian Druze communities, the Israeli occupation of the Golan Heights has replicated the handling of other non-Jewish populations subject to Zionist settler colonization, as observed in the Naqab (Negev), Galilee and occupied Palestinian territory (Dajani 2020b; Khalidi 2020; McKee 2016). The occupation of the Jawlan has always been framed as a case of 'subtle' or civilian occupation (Ó Cuinn 2011), that of a 'refined' settler colonial rule (Gordon and Ram 2016), further sidelining the Jawlan as a case of a 'forgotten' occupation (Al-Marsad 2018). However, it is subject to the same settler colonial regime, based on a spatial Judaization in which the control of land introduces a wide set of differential social relations over property, citizenship, resource extraction and cultural production (Falah 1996; Mamdani 2020: 288–94; Mbembe 2003: 25–6). The discriminatory consequences of this field of sovereign power, where state interests are inseparable from those of Jewish society, are undeniable. Spatial Judaization creates 'permanent minorities' of non-Jewish communities, whose indigeneity is at the same time erased:

'In Israel, the non-Jew ceases to be a genuine native, no matter how long she or her ancestors have been in the territory' (Mamdani 2020: 254). Of course, this is not an exceptional situation: many other peoples across the world are marginalized by the structural power of settler colonialism, whether or not the territorial conquest and settlement took place centuries ago or in the last hundred years (Elkins and Pedersen 2005; Veracini 2010, Wolfe 1999). However, the coercive workings of Israeli settler colonialism, which can be observed in real time, jar against the international humanitarian and human rights standards with which democratic states claim legitimacy.

If elimination of the native, through various registers of physical and symbolic violence, is at the heart of settler colonial rule (Wolfe 2006), those remnant populations that survive ethnic cleansing and displacement have to navigate their 'othering' as non-native by the settler state. The misrecognition characterizing the annexation law involved the imposition of Israeli citizenship on the remaining Jawlani population, which sparked outrage and protest in the Jawlan and across historic Palestine. The Israeli army distributed leaflets on 10 March 1982 in the Jawlani villages, announcing the end of the military occupation and the enforcement of civilian law. It stipulated that the military identity cards would expire by the end of March and individuals were required to have a civilian Israeli ID, to be distributed by the army during a curfew on the villages (Israel State Archives 1982).

The annexation law and the enforcement of Israeli citizenship came in a critical time following the arrest of the political activists, community leaders and religious figures, who were working for the Syrian government and protesting against the Israeli occupation. This political repression included the expulsion of teachers from schools because of their anti-Israel sentiment and support for Syria (Mara'i and Halabi 1992; Qassem 1984). The 1982 general strike organized by the Jawlanis included 3,500 students refusing to attend the Israeli-run schools. The strike resulted in the withdrawal of forced citizenship and the issuing of Israeli travel documents to the inhabitants of the occupied Golan Heights, stating 'undefined' under nationality, becoming isolated therefore as 'non-citizen residents' of Israel. The denial of recognition, in the face of a continuing policy of normalcy and Israelification, continues to the present day.

As the contributions to this volume demonstrate, the 'normalization' of the occupation through the application of Israeli law and administration is routinely rejected through the affirmation of an indigenous

'Jawlani' identity across a range of political, cultural and ecological practices. However, this is a relational identity – a dynamic hybrid of place attachment, Syrian nationality, the Druze faith and/or secular ideas defined against its othering by political Zionism and not without internal differences (Mason and Dajani 2019). In the context of everyday occupation, a cultural fixation 'on 'indigeneity' risks becoming an essentializing category that reproduces the racializing, binary logic of settler colonialism (Tatour 2019), although the accounts in this book demonstrate, we argue, that Jawlani identity is consistently expressed as a struggle for self-determination against colonial domination.

This is evident from how the Jawlanis have forged political solidarity with Palestinian and Syrian national movements. In this book we reveal that this encompasses associations forged by Syria and Palestinian political prisoners from the late 1960s to more recent coalitions. For example, on 15 May 2011, as part of coordinated border demonstrations across Egypt, Jordan, Lebanon, Palestine and Syria commemorating Nakba Day, thousands of pro-Palestinian protestors from Syria massed on the ceasefire line near Majdal Shams. About a hundred crossed the barbed-wire and mined border fence, to be welcomed by local Jawlanis, although five were fatally shot by Israeli soldiers (Wessels 2015b: 279–80). Similarly, the Jawlanis have adopted the Palestinian idea of sumud as a collective strategy of non-violent resistance and benefited from Palestinian legal advice on how to protect their lands from confiscation. Books by Abdul Sattar Qassem (1984), Nazeer Majalli (1982), Nawwaf Al-Batheesh (1987) and Muhammad Muslih (1993) were among those who wrote in Arabic extensively about the six-month strike and occupation of the Golan Heights in general. These accounts reflect how Palestinians were also shaping ideas of sumud together with Jawlani counterparts and companions, noting that the general strike of 1982 preceded the First Intifada, where civil disobedience, strikes, non-violent and community mobilization reflected many of the tactics employed by the Jawlanis in their strike. Similarly, the concerted expansion, over decades, of Jawlani orchards, as supported by agricultural cooperatives and shared water infrastructure, mirrors Palestinian efforts to defend their olive groves from dispossession and destruction. Our approach in this book is to learn from these connections, documenting and narrating local writings and experiences, and re-imagining what sumud actually entailed and how Palestinian and Jawlani struggles are intertwined and cross-pollinating.

Collaborative writing

The outcome of a collaborative research project, *Mapping Memories of Resistance: The Untold Story of the Occupation of the Golan Heights*, this book provides an original survey of Jawlani politics and culture. It offers new insights on processes of everyday colonization and community-based resistance to Israeli rule, paying particular attention to events since Israel passed the Golan Heights Law in 1981. The collaborative project was part of the Academic Collaboration with Arab Universities Programme, run by the Middle East Centre at the London School of Economics and Political Science (LSE) and funded by the Emirates Foundation. Running from September 2018 to April 2021, the project featured collaboration between the Department of Geography and Environment at LSE, the Israeli Studies MA programme at Birzeit University in Palestine and Al-Marsad – Arab Human Rights Centre in the Golan Heights. Alongside this book, the project also produced an online curriculum (in Arabic and English) for teaching about the Jawlan (Mason et al. 2021) and also the development of an online public database containing primary sources on the Jawlan since 1967, including archival material, interviews, posters, photographs and newspaper articles.

Jawlani and Palestinian researchers were at the forefront of knowledge production for this book, which embraces a 'decolonizing' research strategy and pedagogy. At the start of the programme, five Palestinian Birzeit University students from the Israeli Studies MA programme, along with four Jawlani students, were involved in selecting and carrying out interdisciplinary research projects on aspects of Jawlani life under occupation. Their research training as co-investigators anchored the wider collaboration project, which then widened to include several other students and, through the generous interest and assistance of the Jawlani community, also encompassed the direct participation of activists, planners and artists. True to the aim of inclusive knowledge production, much of the content of this book was originally written in Arabic: translators – often undervalued as cultural producers in their own right – are credited at the beginning of relevant material. The commitment to diverse voices from those subject to occupation/annexation is evident from the innovative format, which includes shorter 'reflections' following, and linking to, longer chapters. As with the chapters, the reflections were both peer reviewed by the project team and subject to external peer review. While following professional norms of academic research, we have sought to relay a diversity of Jawlani voices. They reveal that the book is a collaborative, necessarily incomplete, effort both to speak truth to power and to convey faithfully the ways of living and knowing of the Jawlanis.

The book is divided into five sections, composed of chapters, reflections and selected poems by the Jawlani poet and activist Yasser Khanjar. Following the Introduction, it begins with a theoretical investigation of everyday colonization, reflecting on the shock of annexation and the 1982 general strike that followed (Section I). The next section (Section II) addresses conceptually the politics of the governed, with reflections on Jawlani-Palestinian solidarity and the political impacts in the Jawlan of the 2011 Syrian uprising. Substantive aspects of Jawlani political identity are covered in the remaining three sections – the politics of Jawlani art (Section III), the politics of Jawlani youth and education (Section IV) and Jawlani political ecology (Section V). While we make no claim to comprehensive coverage of Jawlani life under occupation, we argue in the Conclusion that the perspectives expressed throughout the book project the Jawlan as a counter-geography of an alternative, justice-centred future.

Section I offers a theoretical framing of everyday colonization and anti-colonial politics in the Jawlan. Chapter 2 covers the first conceptual focus of the book – processes of *everyday colonization* in the occupied Golan since the early 1980s. Michael Mason draws on an influential variant of critical social theory to examine how settler colonialism is bound up with wider processes of state and capitalist development. Through the concept of 'lifeworld colonization' – the harmful encroachment on everyday life of political and economic power – the chapter offers observations on how Israeli settler colonialism in the occupied Golan is shaped by, and harnesses, bureaucratic and market logics, as well as the types of political responses that may be expected from those suffering the pathologies of lifeworld colonization. At the same time, Mason also raises necessary questions about the limits of Western critical theory in grasping the violent political-economic and ecological dynamics of settler colonial regimes.

Section I ends with a reflection by Bassel Rizqallah on the 1982 Great Strike – the six-month general strike enacted by Jawlanis in opposition to Israel's unilateral decision to annex the occupied Golan. Through personal recollections from leading figures involved, this reflection presents the strike as a case of collective political action affirming the

1981 National Document by the Syrian citizens in the occupied Golan Heights, issued in response to the Golan Height Law. The reflection also emphasizes how the Jawlanis, placed under siege and isolated from the outside world, used creative tactics to maintain unity among themselves in the face of efforts to impose Israeli citizenship. While the reflection focuses on an historical event, it argues that this was a formative part of a collective identity that has shaped community politics to this day. The first English translation of the National Document is included after this reflection.

Section II investigates the politics of resistance and solidarity. In Chapter 3, Munir Fakher Eldin addresses the second conceptual focus of the book – *the politics of the governed* among the Jawlanis. The chapter charts a semiotic social-political world in which Jawlani identity maintains itself over time by evolving and adapting across multiple fronts and situations. This treats the relationship between the ruler (occupier) and the ruled (occupied), the governing and the governed, not simply as an exercise of coercive or disciplinary authority but as a dynamic set of relations across multiple fields of political and cultural power. The power of Jawlanis to resist hegemony is seen to be intricately tied to their capacities for political association and communication while being deeply caught in hegemonic relations. These semiotic aspects of politics exist beyond the confines of official spaces and channels of power production, such as collective activities focused on the expression of a Syrian national identity and the community-based institutionalization of social and cultural activities outside Israeli organizational forms, including solidarity exchanges with Palestinians. However, as Fakher Eldin notes, the witnessing by Jawlanis of authoritarianism and conflict in Syria has, in recent years, presented increasing challenges which the Jawlanis are yet to fully confront and overcome.

The two reflections in Section II investigate further the politics of Palestinian-Jawlani solidarity and the political narrative of Jawlani youth. Diaaeddin Horoub narrates, in Reflection 2, the story of Palestinian solidarity and mobilization with the Jawlani community after 1967. The epitome of this solidarity was in 1982, during the Jawlani general strike and demonstrations against forced citizenship and annexation. Multiple Palestinian groups and initiatives mobilized to support the Jawlanis, whose villages were blockaded and placed under curfew. Horoub focuses on the solidarity activities in the Jawlan organized from Birzeit University, notably the student volunteer camps of the

1980s, which mainly helped on the land, including with fruit harvesting. The 1980s was a watershed decade for Palestinians as well, as the First Intifada sparked a succession of events, community mobilizations and political protests, which Jawlanis expressed support for, although Israeli blockades and closures (including of Birzeit University for extended periods) undermined physical interaction between the Palestinians and Jawlanis struggles. While it can be argued that joint political action has declined since the high watermark of the mid-1980s, cultural linkages remain strong. The rekindling of relations among younger Palestinians and Jawlanis, energized by social media, offers avenues for rebuilding solidarity.

Adding to this counter-narrative, Aram Abu Saleh focuses, in Reflection 3, on whether a crisis of political identity for the Jawlani has been created in light of the 2011 Syrian revolution and its aftermath. The Syrian uprising has triggered social divisions within Jawlani communities, with the younger generation generally more critical of the regime of Bashar al-Assad. Jawlani youth have been at the forefront of recent transformations in the meaning of national (Syrian) identity, the social hold of religion and forms of collective mobilization. Their reaction to the perceived silence of local social-religious leaders on the massacres and the bloodshed inside Syria has, Abu Saleh argues, seen inter-generational differences become political ones, allowing openings for Israeli to seek greater social control over the Jawlan as younger members of the community take Israeli citizenship.

Section III addresses the politics of Jawlani art. In Chapter 4, Wael Tarabieh and Munir Fakher Eldin consider the politics of sculptures since the mid-1980s, notably the conditions under which they are created and the community's engagement with them after installation. Sculptures and monuments are important objects of analysis as they are installed in prominent sites in the built environment of communities, reflecting and documenting key events and dates in the collective memory and identity of groups. Tarabieh and Fakher Eldin argue that such artefacts reflect complex processes of power and control over the utilization of public space by state and community actors. In this chapter, sculptures are seen as living objects, performing rites of self-determination and identity expression under settler colonial rule in the occupied Syrian Golan. When publicly displayed, communities react to them either by restoring and changing their messages or by vandalism and sometimes destruction. Therefore, sculptures in the occupied Syrian Golan are symbolic and powerful artefacts to understand societal dynamics and shifting political and cultural realities.

In Reflection 4, Abdel Qader Thweib comments on the relationship of Jawlani art and identity. He focuses on four prominent Jawlani artists – Hassan Khater, Wael Tarabieh, Randa Maddah and Fahad Al-Halabi – examining their understanding of how questions of identity, belonging and politics are entangled with their work. Each has responded with great creativity to exceptional circumstances. Drawing on interviews with these artists, he discusses the development of their artistic identity within the highly charged context of the Israeli occupation.

Still within the cultural domain, Nadine Musallam comments in Reflection 5 on the development of Jawlani literature and music. She notes the fragmentation in pan-Arab sentiment marked by the setbacks in 1948 and 1967, the brief expression of a more confident fiction and poetry after the October 1973 war, then the emergence of a literature that defined itself against the long occupation of the Jawlan. Similarly, Jawlani music became a major artistic form for expressing the realities of Israeli occupation and, through the creative mixing of musical forms, articulating a new energy of collective resistance.

Section IV examines the politics of Jawlani youth and education. In Chapter 6, Amal Aun provides an important investigation of 'minorities education' in Israel, showing how the state employs tactics of 'minoritization' and ethnic manipulation against the Arab Druze communities in the occupied Syrian Golan and Israel in order to maintain its ethnocratic regime. Institutionalized efforts of manipulation include the separation of Druze from the Arab school system, the construction of separate Druze holidays and, for Israeli Druze, mandatory conscription to the Israeli army. Within the education system, this manipulation has created a Druze community that is uninformed about its history, disconnected from its culture and confused about its identity. While Syrian Druze in the Golan do not serve in the Israeli army, these intensive and intentional attempts at manipulating identity have been magnified by the protracted Syrian civil war, with complete closure of the border with Syria. This closure has caused the Jawlani Druze to increase cultural and religious links with the Druze in Israel. Aun relates that Israel is obliged, under human rights law, to provide an education to the Jawlani Druze that is culturally acceptable and factually correct. This includes an accurate representation of the borders of the state, inclusion of notable Arab

Druze historical figures in the curriculum and education about Arab culture and heritage.

For Reflection 6, Jumanah Abbas responds to the representation of Jawlani lands in Israeli official maps, which erase the names of destroyed Syrian villages and redraw boundaries. She asks whether it is possible to conduct a *counter-cartography* to subvert this colonial gaze. Can a visualization mobilize, deploy and influence tools for learning about those under-represented communities in the occupied Jawlan? Taking the form of a visual essay, the reflection counters the Israeli spatial narrative by showing different ways of mapping the Jawlan, highlighting issues, resistance and memories pertaining to the Jawlani community.

Reflection 7 by Ali Aweidat focuses on current youth mobilization in the occupied Jawlan and reflects how 'youth' as a concept has been appropriated and configured by settler colonial policies on one hand and societal structures and norms on the other hand, leading to a weakening of youth activism and political mobilization. The youth group 'Youth Popular Mobilization in the Occupied Syrian Jawlan', established in 2018, is seen as a means of resistance to coercive settler colonial policies which aim to depoliticize Jawlani youth and incorporate them into Israel's institutions. He shows how resistance to the occupation since 1967 has culminated in the growing discontent and mobilization of Jawlani youth. Moreover, this mobilization is also breaking away from conservative social norms and traditional decision-making, with young people gaining influence over local social and political realities.

Section V considers what we call Jawlani political ecologies – the co-production of environmental change in the Jawlan, as shaped by the power-laden interplay of human and ecological relations. Chapter 6 anchors this section with an innovative agroecological study of the Jawlan as a highland plateau (*haḍaba*) by Omar Tesdell, Muna Dajani and Alaa Iktash. Precipitation and snowmelt in the Jawlan highlands are significant for downstream freshwater flows in the Jordan River Basin, and secure access to these upper catchment sources (including the Banias River) remains, for Israel, a key hydropolitical justification for its occupation of the Syrian Golan. Human communities are at the centre of the agroecological history of the Jawlan, yet they play a supporting role to the high biodiversity made possible by the elevation, rains and other beings in the highlands. Tesdell, Dajani and Iktash adopt the critical geographical concept of *makaneyyah* to show how the highland landscape has supported many generations of communities and has been a driving factor for colonization of the area for strategic purposes. The chapter considers the key role of apple-growing in shaping Jawlani political identity and also how Israeli nature reserves serve as an instrument of settler colonial control.

In Reflection 8, Alaa Iktash considers the development of Mount Hermon ski resort and the associated Jewish settlement of Neve Ativ on the southern slopes of the mountain cluster known by the Syrians and Lebanese as Jabal al-Shaykh. Through an extended conversation with a senior and long-time resident of Majdal Shams, he recovers from the erased landscape some recollections, some fragments of the history of the Syrian village of Jubbatha Ez-Zeit, which was depopulated and demolished to make way for Neve Ativ. The creation of Mount Hermon ski resort on communal village lands seized from Majdal Shams, only 2 kilometres to the east, bears witness to a coercive and discriminatory model of settler colonization that bulldozes through other histories and cultures.

In the Conclusion, we revisit the central themes of the book – everyday colonization and the politics of the governed – to consider the idea of the Jawlan as a *counter-geography*; that is, the material and imaginative construction of an ethno-geographic community that contests the spatial Judaization of the Israeli occupation. What does it mean to represent such a counter-geography – both to depict the lived experiences and aspirations of the Jawlanis, and to imagine the social, political and ecological conditions of possibility for a just future? Informed by the contributions to the book, we offer preliminary comments that are properly part of a much wider political conversation about Jawlani (and Palestinian) futures for those living under settler colonialism.

SECTION I

EVERYDAY COLONIZATION

FIGURE 2.1 Israeli police disperse protestors opposing municipal elections, Majdal Shams, 30 October 2018. Courtesy of Fares Al Welly archive.

2 THE POLITICS OF LIFEWORLD COLONIZATION IN THE OCCUPIED GOLAN

MICHAEL MASON

Introduction

Israel's occupation of the Golan Heights deploys multiple techniques of sovereign power. As in other settler colonial contexts, the control of land – over territory, resources and bodies – was secured first by the large-scale displacement of a native population then followed by the marginalization of remaining, mostly Druze, communities. The contributions to this volume reveal the scope of settler colonial practices in the occupied Syrian Golan Heights, focusing on the period of de facto annexation, that is, the application of Israeli law, jurisdiction and administration to the territory mandated by the 1981 Golan Heights Law. Annexation is an act that violates international legal norms prohibiting the acquisition of territory by force. Indeed, it was in these terms that the UN Security Council declared the Israeli Golan Heights Law 'null and void and without international legal effect' (UN Security Council Resolution 497). However, annexation was enacted in practice through Israeli domestic law, switching the occupation regime from military to civil government. Despite Israeli efforts at normalization, a key argument running through the chapters of this book is that this annexation has intensified settler colonization in the Golan Heights, which is experienced by the Jawlani people as institutionalized injustice.

Settler colonialism is a political-economic formation featuring the appropriation of land and resources through territorial conquest and settlement: across centuries, settler colonial enterprises have displaced and devastated indigenous populations (Choi 2016; Veracini 2010). Settler colonial logic is shot through with violence, with the physical uprooting and material dispossession of indigenous peoples matched by an erasure of their cultures (Bourdieu and Sayad 1964; Mbembe 2003: 25–30). The symbolic violence of settler colonial uprooting can intensify social pathologies tied to more general processes of state development and capitalist accumulation. While scholarship on contemporary settler colonialism, covering subaltern/indigenous studies and other critical perspectives, is aware of its diverse forms of domination, the links to these wider political-economic processes are arguably less well understood. They point to a need to treat Israeli settler colonialism in the occupied Syrian Golan not simply as a state of exception, reducible to a Zionist project of ethnic cleansing, but conjoined with other state and market processes which have transformative consequences for the Jawlani people and their land.

Within critical social theory there is a broader idea of colonization to denote certain pathological tendencies within advanced capitalist societies, most notably, the *lifeworld colonization thesis* of the German philosopher and sociologist, Jürgen Habermas (1987). Expressed simply, lifeworld colonization describes the harmful encroachment by political power and market-led exchange on the integrity of ordinary human life – those areas of culture, society and personality which generate shared values and meaning. To what extent is lifeworld colonization, elaborated on below, relevant to understanding the effects of settler colonization in the occupied Golan Heights? More specifically:

1. How are settler colonial processes affected by market and bureaucratic logics?

2. How do settler colonial processes contribute to lifeworld colonization?

3. What are the political implications for those communities resisting settler colonialism?

These three research questions are not simply abstract enquiries, for the goal of critical social theory is to explain and evaluate processes which impact on everyday lives and livelihoods, uncovering new possibilities for self-determination. In this chapter, I argue that the lifeworld colonization thesis offers a useful starting point for examining how settler colonial practices interact with, and intensify, processes of political and economic domination for occupied peoples, though this framing must reckon with the material and symbolic violence of settler colonialism.

The lifeworld colonization thesis

For Habermas the lifeworld is the taken-for-granted stock of background knowledge which facilitates everyday social interaction. Reproduction of the lifeworld takes place through shared processes of interpretation which shape cultural knowledge, social integration and the socialization of individuals. Modern life, Habermas argues, involves a rationalization of the lifeworld, such that its structural components (culture, society, personality) become differentiated and more reflexive: cultural traditions are openly questioned, societies are integrated by more abstract norms (e.g. law) and individual personalities draw on more diverse identities (Habermas 1987: 140–8). However, to function as practical knowledge, the lifeworld still provides a largely taken-for-granted horizon for communication. Think, for example, about how many individuals keep dogs as pets without reflecting on the cultural traditions and social values that mark dogs as companion animals, or without questioning the instrumental breeding of dogs for desired traits, such as appearance, docility or aggression. To question the idea of the dog as pet makes little sense for those whom this is part of the natural order of things. In many societies dogs are treated as akin to family or community members: for people under occupation, dogs and other companion animals may indeed support precarious human lives and highlight wider relationships of injury and care (Johnson 2019).

Separate from the rationalization of the lifeworld is the core argument, put forward by Habermas, that its communicative reproduction is systemically degraded under advanced capitalism; that is, under a state-regulated market economy. The thesis of lifeworld colonization is that runaway systems of market-led exchange and governmental decision-making disrupt social integration, creating a 'pathological deformation of the communicative infrastructure of the lifeworld' (Habermas 1987: 375) – that is to say, unrestrained market exchange (driven by profit maximization) and administrative interventions overwhelm people.

Rather than relating to each other in more or less autonomous terms as workers and active citizens, individuals increasingly assume the passive roles of consumers and bureaucratic clients. Political and economic systems are experienced as holding overbearing and unchecked power over the lives of ordinary people. This generates, he argues, three major social pathologies (Habermas 1987: 140–3):

1. Loss of meaning: commodification and bureaucratization suppress the lifeworld reproduction of culture, overwhelming the capacity of actors to make sense of new situations. This may lead to the unsettling of collective identities as cultural knowledge loses its continuity and coherence for everyday life.

2. Anomie: commodification and bureaucratization displace lifeworld-enabled forms of social integration, such that individuals experience a fragmentation of collective identities and a loss of solidarity with other community members.

3. Psychopathologies: individuals face serious threats to their mental well-being from disturbances to their sense of self. A reduced ability to cope with the proliferating, exacting demands issuing from market and bureaucratic systems results in experiences of alienation and other forms of psychological harm.

These are complex cultural, social and psychological processes which open up various avenues for research across multiple disciplines. However, several methodological implications are clear for applying the thesis of lifeworld colonization to situations in which market exchanges or bureaucratic measures are experienced by individuals as unsettling and harmful. Examining damaged lifeworlds invites a substantive focus on *specific pathologies and the sociopolitical reactions to them*: for example, political alienation, contested educational settings, economic exploitation and the degradation of valued environments. Empirical access to the meaning-rich structure of lifeworlds typically requires *qualitative methodologies* (e.g. narrative interviews, participant observation, oral histories and hybrid archives) that can capture the cultural texture of everyday lives. At the same time, as demonstrated in this book, these empirical investigations are best based on a *co-investigation model* in which diverse representatives from the communities studied take a major role in shaping the scope and practices of research.

In settler colonial contexts, the idea of lifeworld colonization may be analytically useful insofar as it helps us identify, and explain, the extent to which settler colonial processes harness market and bureaucratic logics. Settler colonialism as a governance structure features sharp asymmetries of material and ideological power, so we would expect lifeworld colonization to be intensified for indigenous inhabitants, creating antagonistic conditions for political exchange between those communities and the settler state. And this politics is likely to feature protracted struggles over the collective identities of subordinated groups, invoking such markers as place, nationality and faith. However, there is a theoretical question as to whether the lifeworld colonization thesis fully captures the structural effects of Israeli settler colonialism. For a self-professed critical intellectual prominent in public debates, Habermas untenably refused to comment on Israeli politics (Limone 2012), while the relevance of the theory has been questioned in non-Western cultural contexts (Bailey 2013: 3). Although it shares many institutional properties with European democracies, Israel's 'illiberal democracy' or 'ethnocracy' is not the Western model of welfare capitalism analysed by Habermas: its military expansion and settlement of occupied territories rests on an ethnic particularism at odds with constitutional commitments to democracy and other universal values (Harel-Shalev and Peleg 2014; Yiftachel 2006).

Similarly, it is also justified to query whether the account of lifeworld colonization given by Habermas can grasp the systemic damage to lived experiences from forms of domination which may not simply arise from money and bureaucratic power but also reside already in the lifeworld, such as subordination based on gender, sexuality and race (Fraser 1985; Simpson 2019). In the occupied Golan Heights, there are also complex relationships over the reproduction of the Druze religion in Jawlani society – for example, the erosion of the authority of religious leaders over social and cultural norms, and how this impacts political leadership (see Chapter 3). To be sure, the lifeworld colonization thesis does not claim to register all forms of symbolic change to persons and communities, nor does it assume that lifeworlds are 'innocent' of internal forms of domination. It claims to identify specific vectors of harm damaging everyday subjectivities through overbearing processes of market and political power. The central question here is whether settler colonial rule aggravates these pathologies of lifeworld colonization.

A convergence of settler colonialism and lifeworld colonization in the occupied Golan Heights?

The theoretical reservations previously discussed counsel against an uncritical application of the lifeworld colonization thesis in the Golan Heights, yet there remains a genuine analytical need to establish how wider circuits of commodification and state control impact on a Jawlani population marginalized by annexation. Responding to the research questions listed in the introduction to this chapter, I present three broad findings that suggest a significant convergence of settler colonialism and lifeworld colonization in the occupied Golan Heights: (i) the settler colonial skewing of market and bureaucratic logics, (ii) the intensification of lifeworld colonization under settler colonialism and (iii) a major political role for identity-based resistance.

Settler colonial skewing of market and bureaucratic logics

In the lifeworld colonization model, money and state power regulate social relations instrumentally, which become more detached from lifeworld processes of linguistic communication and mutual understanding (Habermas 1987: 154). Colonization occurs through the encroachment in everyday lives of capitalist economic and bureaucratic systems. In advanced capitalist societies, these market and state logics acquire a growing hold over individuals, although neoliberal capitalism features a turbocharged commodification throwing off regulatory constraints. The evolution of the Israeli economy mirrors neoliberal changes in the global political economy, with a major drive towards market liberalization from the mid-1980s. While influenced by these ideological shifts within Israeli capitalism, settler colonization in the Golan Heights has followed a more primitive model of capital accumulation. Its *skewed institutionalization of market and state governance* is founded on the state-orchestrated appropriation of land and other resources, allied with settlement subsidies and commercial incentives for those moving into the Golan Heights from Israel. In contrast, the remaining Jawlani population, prevented from travel to Syria, was pushed into wage labour within the settler economy or otherwise forced to seek alternative livelihoods within a constricted local economy.

In economic terms, therefore, the Israeli occupation of the Golan enacted a form of primitive accumulation, in which capitalist market expansion is realized by seizing land and assets from populations treated as economically unproductive (Bin 2018; Harvey 2003). To be sure, geostrategic defence served as the immediate justification for the conquest of the Golan Heights, and the first Israeli settlements were defensively dispersed across captured Syrian territory. Settlement activity accelerated in the period following the 1973 Arab-Israeli War, including the planning and construction of Katzrin as an urban centre (Kipnis 2013: 157–60). Primitive accumulation in the Golan Heights involved the state-sanctioned appropriation of natural resources and other assets by parastatal agencies (Jewish National Fund, the Settlement Department of the World Zionist Federation). In July 1967 Military Orders No. 20 and No. 21 authorized, respectively, the unhindered acquisition of 'abandoned' private property and government property. Military rule (1967–81) facilitated early colonization, with state support for Jewish settlements and infrastructure development, although the number of Jewish settlers fell short of settlement planning targets (Kipnis 2013: 144). De facto annexation marked a significant change in the regime of primitive accumulation towards greater freedom for Israeli market actors to invest in and steer economic development in the Golan. Economic activity increased after the collapse of peace negotiations between Israel and Syria (1993–2000), which removed uncertainty over possible withdrawal by Israel of at least some occupied Syrian territory. For the Golan, the Israeli turn to export-oriented neoliberalism in the 2000s saw expansion of agriculture, tourism, high-tech industry (Katzrin Industrial Park) and oil exploration.

However, Israeli neoliberalism is still heavily steered by state preferences, notably a national security paradigm that views colonization of occupied territories as critical to the sovereign realization of a Greater Israel (Kampf 2018; Mandelkern and Shalev 2021). Thus, the protracted conflict in Syria prompted Israel to boost settlement activity and economic investment in the Golan Heights. The 2014–19 regional development plan featured the creation of 750 farming estates for settlers on 30,000 dunums (3,000 hectares) of annexed land, supported by state investment in agricultural training and water infrastructure (Al-Marsad 2014). In summer 2018 the Syrian government regained full control of the eastern Golan Heights and the border with Israel, but the Israeli government remained concerned about the presence of pro-Iranian militias and Hezbollah within or alongside Syrian military forces deployed in the region. Addressing the United Nations Security Council in April 2020, Syria's representative to the UN reasserted the right of the Syrian Arab Republic to reclaim sovereignty over the full Golan Heights.

US recognition in March 2019 of the occupied Golan Heights as Israeli sovereign territory emboldened plans to deepen its domestic economic integration consistent with national industrial policy. The territory is at the heart of a renewable energy drive tied to Israeli support for investment in green technologies. In January 2020 the Israeli government announced NIS 250 million of state investment to develop northern wind turbine farms consistent with the operational needs of the military (Halon 2020): objections from the Israel Defense Forces had previously stalled the construction of wind turbines. The largest planned wind turbine development is in the Golan Heights, with a number of public and private Israeli companies developing wind farms which will feed electricity to Israeli settlements and to the national grid. One major wind farm project, planned since 2013 by the Israeli company Energix with support from the Israeli Committee for National Infrastructures, is due to be located on Jawlani agricultural land and the site of the former Syrian village of Sahita. According to Al-Marsad – an Arab human rights NGO in the Golan Heights – Energix had, by 2018, persuaded about forty Jawlani landowners to sign lease agreements (Southlea and Brik 2019: 17–20). Broader consequences of the wind farm development are projected to be restriction of the expansion of adjacent Jawlani villages and the destruction of agricultural land, which will further undermine Jawlani economic self-determination in the Golan (Southlea and Brik 2019: 47–9).

The bureaucratic logic of political integration in the occupied Golan Heights is also skewed towards settler colonial interests because the Israeli state – including its defence and security apparatus – is invested in consolidating its annexation of the territory and exercising greater control over communal structures of Jawlani authority. Political autonomy continues to be denied to the large majority of Jawlanis who have refused Israeli citizenship since 1981, excluding them from meaningful participation in regional and local decision-making. Indeed, the Israeli annexation of the Golan Heights has produced a distinct political formation of 'statelessness' in which those most of the remaining Jawlanis, who were previously Syrian citizens, are categorized by Israel as having 'undefined nationality' on their identity cards. The statelessness of the Jawlanis in the Golan Heights is an indicator of the symbolic violence of the occupying power, enacting differential rights to settlers and the colonized, while at the same time seeking to legitimate and normalize its presence through the civil administration of annexation (Mbembe 2003: 25–6; Ram 2015). The extensive bureaucratic apparatus of 'Israelification' within the territory creates multiple 'client' roles for those consuming Israeli public services in areas such as education, drinking water, emergency services and culture. At the same time, though, the ongoing production of 'statelessness' by Israel is a source of political instability insofar as those Jawlanis refusing citizenship regard other national (Syrian) or religious (Druze) categories as oppositional to the Israeli state (Kastrinou et al. 2021).

This is evident in the politics of Israeli-controlled municipal government. Since 1974, Israel has directly appointed the heads of local councils in the Jawlani villages. An attempt at bureaucratic normalization took place in October 2018 when the four Jawlani villages were included in the round of municipal elections taking place across Israel. While the Israeli authorities represented this to the Jawlani residents as an opportunity to register their political concerns (they were all afforded the right to vote), they roundly rejected the elections. The skewed political logic of annexation was evident in the fact that only Israeli citizens could stand for election as village mayors. Jawlani candidates with Israeli citizenship withdrew from the mayoral elections in Buq'atha and Mas'ada, while voter turnout was only 1.3 per cent in Ein Qiniya and 3.3 per cent in Majdal Shams. In Buq'atha the Israeli authorities reappointed by fiat the existing unelected mayor (Delforno 2019: 36–7). For the Jawlanis, rejecting the municipal elections was also a political affirmation of their own community structures, notably the long-established village *khalwat*, the Druze congregation houses, which have assumed increased political significance since annexation by serving as a vehicle for popular mobilization (Fakher Eldin 2019: 81–3).

The settler colonial skewing of market and political logics in the Golan Heights may suggest conditions more severe, and therefore far removed, from the economic and bureaucratic processes claimed by Habermas to drive lifeworld colonization in European capitalist states. As with other instances of Israeli military conquest (Cohen and Gordon 2018), the seizure of resources and ethno-racial classification of land seem to bear little if any resemblance to the liberal market systems governed by Western democracies. However, Israeli settler colonialism is a major historical variant of what Ince (2018) calls the constitutive violence of capitalist market relations – a structural property not captured by the lifeworld colonization model, which analyses a late stage of European capitalism detached from its bloody genesis in colonial expansion and racial domination. The occupation then annexation of the Golan Heights by Israel lays bare the 'capital-positing violence' of primitive accumulation (Ince 2018: 900) – the use of military-political coercion at the frontier to enact the capitalization of social relations through resource dispossession and the economic subordination of the Arab population. Thus, while there were arguably higher levels of 'unregulated' state violence enacting primitive accumulation during the first years of military occupation (e.g. population displacement, direct seizure of resources and destruction of civilian objects), the later shift to civil rule and market-led investment in the annexed Golan Heights represents a *consolidation* rather than reversal of primitive accumulation. Under annexation the state-driven project of settler colonization has intensified, bolstered more recently by the fragmentation of Syria and US recognition of Israeli sovereignty over the Golan.

The intensification of lifeworld colonization under settler colonialism

The Israeli military invasion in June 1967 marked a violent rupture in the lives and livelihoods of the rural communities in the Syrian Golan. In the 1960s, there was already heavy militarization, with frequent Syrian-Israeli border clashes prior to the June 1967 war. The massive devastation caused by that war, including the displacement of the majority Sunni Muslim population, is carefully documented elsewhere (Murphy and Gannon 2008). While settlement in the Golan was not a motivation for the military capture of the area and some Israeli political leaders were willing to consider territorial concessions for a peace agreement with Syria, settlement planning began in October 1967 (Kipnis 2013: 82) and the state-led promotion of permanent settlement proceeded apace in the 1970s with a focus on agricultural enterprises. The settler colonial regime of primitive accumulation in the occupied Golan Heights overturned a system of property relations nominally governed by state socialism (under variants of Ba'athist ideology), although the rural economy was mostly subsistence-based agriculture. Over time, both communal and often private land was seized as Syrian property law was extinguished.

The 1981 Golan Heights Law marked a further step-change in natural resource exploitation, as the move to Israeli civil law and administration created conditions more open to private economic investment. Visible landscape-level changes – oil drilling, viticulture, cattle ranching and the development of Mount Hermon ski resort (on land taken from Majdal Shams village: see Reflection 8) – attest to the growing capitalization of the settler rural economy since annexation.

My claim that *lifeworld colonization is intensified under settler colonialism* refers to the cumulative social-cultural impact, in the Golan Heights, of these three phases of colonizing power. First, there was the abrupt, external shock on the Syrian population of an Israeli military invasion that destroyed civilian infrastructure, displaced people and seized land. Second, there was the systemic harm to the remaining Druze communities caused by the first round of primitive accumulation under military occupation (1967–81). For Israel, economic 'modernization' in the Golan meant investment and employment opportunities in early settlement enterprises, but this was experienced as brutal dispossession by the Syrian Druze in the north, as the bulk of their lands were seized and zoned for exclusive Jewish use. Lastly, the annexation in 1981, the shift from military rule to Israeli civil administration, created social conditions open to the type of lifeworld colonization attributed by Habermas to advanced capitalism, as growing commodification and bureaucratization penetrated everyday lives. However, only to associate lifeworld pathologies with the normalization logic of annexation would be to miss the deep, enduring legacy of lifeworld damage in Jawlani communities – the cultural, social and personal harm produced by the sharp economic and political asymmetries of settler colonial rule.

Arguably the principal *symbolic damage* unleashed by settler colonialism in the occupied Golan is the wholesale devaluation by Israel of the cultural and social standing of a non-Jewish population no longer regarded as 'native' (Mamdani 2020: 254). The efforts of the displaced Syrian population to maintain family and other cultural ties with those still living in the Golan Heights have long been frustrated by restrictions placed by Israel on cross-border movements, while there are also unresolved restitution and compensation claims for lost and destroyed property (Internal Displacement Monitoring Centre 2007; Russell 2018). At the same time, the remaining Druze communities clustered in the north have faced a *systemic misrecognition* of their place-based Jawlani identities, which are erased by a state-led Zionist ideology celebrating the 'return' of the Golan Heights to the land of Israel. This injustice of misrecognition is distinct from, but inextricably fused to, the distributive losses of resource dispossession and political disenfranchisement (Mason and Dajani 2019).

The material legacy of material destruction from the occupation also underwrites the social and cultural devaluation by Israel of the Jawlani people. Within months of the start of the Israeli occupation in June 1967, the army had systematically demolished hundreds of Syrian villages and farms, ostensibly for security reasons. In the village of Kushniyah, the mosque remained as the only standing structure (Figure 2.2), used by the Israeli military for training exercises. In 1974, as Israel withdrew from further gains made in the Golan Heights during the 1973 Arab-Israeli War, Jewish National Fund tractors bulldozed the Syrian city of Quneitra, a regional centre for Circassians since the late nineteenth century (Kipnis 2013: 160–1). These actions violated international humanitarian law prohibitions against extensive damage to, and material destruction, of civilian objects, including cultural heritage (Hague Convention for the Protection of Cultural Property in the Event of Armed Conflict 1954, ratified by Israel in October 1957). In dissolving a Syrian territorial space,

FIGURE 2.2 Ruined Al-Kushniyah Mosque, April 2019. Photo by author.

the selection of place names for Israeli settlements, parks and forests in the Golan Heights also serves as an important instrument for Zionist landscape transformation, with the new names reflecting various Jewish ideologies and settlement types. Jawlani geographic markers face both cultural appropriation, as when the Arabic names of destroyed Syrian villages are subsumed into Hebrew versions, and cultural erasure, when ancient names invoke biblical and Talmudic authority to signal historic Jewish presence on the land (Cohen and Kliot 1992).

The intangible properties of cultural reproduction structuring lifeworlds are particularly vulnerable to debilitation by an occupying power. Empirical evidence that settler colonial practices intensify lifeworld colonization in the Golan Heights would encompass the full range of crises encountered when there are disturbances in cultural reproduction, social integration and socialization (Habermas 1987: 143). Some pathologies in Jawlani life experiences may simply reflect stresses from wider impacts of 'cultural globalization', though these are often inflected by settler colonial policies and practices. Under occupation/annexation, there can simultaneously be processes of cultural homogenization (the use of Hebrew by younger Jawlanis in social media) and politically motivated cultural division (the co-opting by Israeli-appointed municipal councils of local artists). There are also internal social tensions between religious leaders and the wider community over, for example, loyalty to the Syrian government or conservative positions on gender equality. Moreover, the idea of Jawlani indigeneity, as a vehicle for social integration, is both defined against and made unstable by settler colonization. Systemic misrecognition of the Syrian and Arab faces of Jawlani culture is consistent with Israel's essentialist 'othering' of them as Druze: for example, the Israeli-imposed 'Druze curriculum' in local schools, which represents the Jawlani population as a Druze minority separate from regional Arab communities and identities (Chapter 5: see also Abbas 2020; Aun 2018).

Finally, lifeworld colonization in the Golan Heights is intensified by the particular *ecologies of violence* generated by settler colonialism. A major lacuna in the notion of lifeworld formulated by Habermas is its anthropocentric disregard of underlying ecological conditions – the fact that culture, society and personality are entangled with, and sustained by, metabolic interactions with more-than-human entities and processes. Military conflict and occupation produce transformative ecologies, in which the production of harm is often a complex bio-psycho-social wounding (Abu Sitta et al. 2016; Mason 2011). Through its occupation and effacement of Syrian territory, Israel opened up Mediterranean grassland landscapes to capitalization and commodification. Not only did this feature the dispossession of Jawlani land and water resources but also the production of settler ecologies – for example, the planting of non-native forests by Keren Kayemet LeYisrael/Jewish National Fund (e.g. Mevo Hama Forest), the extensive creation of nature reserves (a zoning applied also to the Banias River and Lake Ram) and attempts to reintroduce to the Golan Heights such 'biblical animals' as the Nubian ibex and the Jacob sheep (Kastrinou et al. 2021: 11–13). The recreational commodification by Israel of the Golan Heights – as a popular holiday destination – makes great play of the green open spaces which are an ecological palimpsest over an erased agrarian landscape. Israeli settler colonialism in the Golan Heights thus adopts 'environmental protection' as a technology of occupation, with conservation and other investments in ecological assets naturalizing domination. These transformative settler ecologies are an inherent part of lifeworld colonization in the occupied Golan Heights.

A major political role for identity-based resistance

In its original formulation, the thesis of lifeworld colonization addresses 'new' potentials for political protest emerging in late capitalist societies since the 1960s, such as feminism, environmentalism, the peace movement, religious fundamentalism, anti-regulatory campaigns and movements for autonomy. Habermas claims that these protest tendencies, which encompass both reactionary and progressive forms, are driven less by distributional conflicts than the defence of conditions of life threatened by the growth and reach of economic-administrative systems. Resistance to experiences of lifeworld colonization can therefore be expected to feature a major role for political mobilizations by those fighting social-cultural marginalization (Habermas 1987: 391–6). More generally, this type of reaction can motivate the formation of a *resistance identity* that challenges a hegemonic logic of cultural devaluation and stigmatization (Castells 1997: 6–12). To what extent is the identity-based resistance in the Golan Heights motivated by lifeworld colonization? In the occupied Syrian Golan, the round of primitive accumulation unleashed by Israel in 1967 had major distributional consequences –

notably resource dispossession and population displacement – which have yet to be peacefully resolved. However, the continuation of older distributional grievances is not necessarily inconsistent with, and may feed into, an identity-based politics of Jawlani resistance. The question is what types of protest mobilization would likely be motivated by the oppressive economic and political control over Jawlani lives exercised by Israel in the Golan Heights?

If settler colonial practices are indeed intensifying lifeworld colonization, we would expect to see forms of protest consistent with the claim that political resistance would feature prominently the defence of the Jawlanis as a distinct ethno-geographic community. This seems particularly to be the case since the de facto annexation at the end of 1981, which triggered six months of strikes and mass demonstrations by Jawlanis, then saw the longer-term emergence of a collective strategy of non-violent resistance informed by the idea of *sumud* (steadfastness). Rootedness to the land is at the heart of Jawlani strategies of political mobilization in the Golan, which have also forged solidarity with those Palestinians invoking sumud as strategy of resistance. It motivates those cooperative organizations supporting agriculture – notably the reclamation of common land and cultivation of fruit trees – and the development of alternative water infrastructure (Dajani and Mason 2019; Kastrinou et al. 2021), alongside initiatives favouring sociocultural autonomy, such as community health care delivery and alternative educational and youth events. In the wake of annexation, various civil society groupings emerged to provide social alternatives to the Israeli colonization of Jawlani social and cultural space – the Golan Academic Association (now the Arab Association for Development), the Women's Committee in the Golan and, more recently, the human rights organization Al-Marsad (since 2003).

This collective strategy of non-violent resistance, which draws on religious beliefs as well as secular political ideas, informed the overwhelming rejection by the Jawlanis of the October 2018 municipal elections administered by Israel. The public announcement of the elections by the Israeli government actually forged new political unity among a population divided over the conflict in Syria. This created a broad-based coalition which issued a statement reaffirming the Syrian identity of the Jawlan and rejected the proposed election as the illegitimate act of an occupying power (Alaawar 2018). What followed was a series of political statements, demonstrations and a one-day strike (Delforno 2019: 31).

On election day (30 October), after gathering early in Sultan Al-Atrash Square in the centre of Majdal Shams, about 500 demonstrators marched to the polling station to protest peacefully outside, attracting another 500–1,000 supporters. Shortly after midday, Israeli police forcefully dispersed them with tear gas, stun grenades and rubber bullets, injuring thirty-six protestors (Figure 2.1). This use of violence provoked further protests and a further collective statement condemning the elections (Delforno 2019: 34). Fakher Eldin observes an identity-based politics motivating what may seem a paradoxical rejection of an opportunity to vote: 'the Jawlanis decided not to play the occupying power's game; they chose to fight for whatever autonomy they had managed to carve out and to continue having a say in determining their political outlook as well as the symbols and sentiments that govern their private and public lives' (2019: 88).

The Jawlani Youth Movement, which had been instrumental in the campaign against the municipal elections, also organized protests against the development of wind energy in the northern Golan Heights, including a major demonstration in January 2020 of thousands of Jawlanis in Sultan Al-Atrash Square. In 2018, Al-Marsad had undertaken a comprehensive investigation of the wind farm plan, then convened a committee of community activists to organize public meetings to discuss the project: the overwhelming response was to oppose the placing of wind turbines on Jawlani land (Southlea and Brik 2019: 4–5). Dajani (2020a) draws attention, among those opposing the wind energy project, to the young educated Jawlanis who mostly live outside the Golan Heights in Israeli and Palestinian cities. In their representation of the wind farm proposals as 'green energy colonialism', they sustain – from their scattered locations – a resistance narrative that the protection of Jawlani land is a defence, and affirmation, of collective identity against an occupying power. The landscape-shaping power of the wind turbines, promoted by their developers as a benign, low-carbon technology, is seen as a threat to Jawlani ways of life.

Jawlani political mobilization is not free of internal divisions, for resistance to annexation coexists with the everyday pressures of normalization, which provide practical conveniences and tangible benefits to those accepting, or resigning to, their fate as residents of Israel. Normalization has seen several Druze religious leaders ('uqqal) co-opted by Israeli state actors. In this context, it is remarkable that, in the face of Israel's considerable material and symbolic power over their land and resources, the Jawlanis continue to be able to contest and sometimes override Israel's local domination. Fakher Eldin (2019) attributes this in large part to the continuing influence of the congregation houses in the boycotts of the Israeli municipal elections and opposition to Israeli wind turbine development adjacent to Druze villages. The khalwat represent a focus of moral-political authority, outside Israeli state structures, validating Jawlani life experiences and collective identity. As such, they are not raising policy-oriented demands of a state but articulating *anti-colonial* claims against a state in defence of communal norms of autonomy (Fakher Eldin 2019: 82). The long history of anti-colonial resistance in the Golan Heights reaches back over a century to liberation struggles against the French Mandate and the Ottoman Empire (Neep 2012). It is no surprise, therefore, that the recent demonstrations against the Israeli municipal elections and wind energy development both converged in Sultan Al-Atrash Square, around a monument to the Druze military leader who had fought both the Ottomans and the French. This monument and its setting serve as a lifeworld resource for the Jawlanis – a public space facilitating collective anger as a legitimate form of political expression against oppression (Srinivasan 2018).

Conclusion

The thesis of lifeworld colonization was developed to account for systemic tendencies in advanced capitalism which, it is claimed, fracture the semantic coherence and continuity of everyday life. Colonization describes the damage to cultural reproduction, social integration and socialization caused by the growing intrusion into the lifeworld of processes of commodification and bureaucratization. In this chapter, I consider the relevance of the theory of lifeworld colonization to the settler colonial context of the occupied Golan Heights. Israel's occupation of the Syrian territory displaced most of the native population and marginalized those that remained, while facilitating Jewish settlements and enterprises. However, while there was both material and symbolic colonization, the market and state logics employed – primitive accumulation and military rule – enacted less an encroachment than a shock treatment skewed towards colonial domination. The transition to Israeli civil administration in 1981 did not temper this coercive assault on Jawlani lifeworlds. As shown by the chapters in this volume, lifeworld colonization was intensified by annexation: we can observe a wholesale, ongoing devaluation by Israel of a diverse range of Jawlani social-cultural and ecological practices.

There is a conceptual reckoning here for a critical theory of the lifeworld that is silent on settler colonial violence, although it is instructive to explore whether its critique of advanced capitalism helps us to understand at least some of the power dynamics of a settler colonial state accorded a privileged position within the global economy. Israel was accepted into the OECD in 2010 without any interrogation of its economic exploitation of occupied territories or other forms of institutionalized discrimination against Palestinians and Jawlanis. The lifeworld of these peoples, their 'common-sense reality', is articulated amid the political, economic and cultural colonization of the occupying power. Wrenched politically from their Syrian citizenship, the remnant Jawlanis have largely defined themselves in opposition to the Israeli occupation of their land: the 'Jawlani' identity is a dynamic hybrid of place-making, Syrian nationality, the Druze faith and secular political ideas. The major role for identity-based protests expected by the lifeworld colonization thesis seems borne out by Jawlani political mobilization in the Golan Heights. As noted earlier, there are a wide variety of efforts to defend and promote Jawlani ways of life. At the same time, Jawlani 'statelessness' means that their grievances are not equivalent to those raised by Israeli citizens *as citizens* about harmful policies of a state otherwise treated as legitimate; instead, they are the more basic articulation of anti-colonial resistance against an occupying power. This antagonistic political subjectivity has been energized by the Israeli state using the US recognition of Israeli sovereignty over the Golan Heights to justify further settlement-building and economic development in the territory. Jawlani resistance is also energized by right-wing Israeli governments doubling down on domestic policies that marginalize non-Jewish groups, such as the 2018 Nation-State Law (which provoked opposition from the Israeli Druze community, including serving and retired members of the Israeli military). In these circumstances, the Jawlanis have identified an existential threat to their lifeworlds.

Finally, we can recall that, as a theoretical claim, lifeworld colonization invites the collection and assessment of relevant evidence, above all from the first-person perspective of those Jawlanis living under conditions of political, economic and cultural domination. Critical social scientific research must be open to inclusive methodological strategies for capturing the textures and traumas of everyday life within the Golan Heights – the impaired, but also robust, processes of cultural reproduction, social integration and socialization which shape Jawlani lifeworlds. This is a reflexive task for the researcher and one that informs the contributions to this book, notably those Jawlani voices under-represented in Anglophone literature on the region. The extent to which the idea of lifeworld colonization helps to explain the power dynamics of settler colonialism requires an empirical interrogation that is receptive to the social and cultural forms of expression of those marginalized. To be valid in the setting of the occupied Syrian Golan, it should explain how processes of commodification and bureaucratization under Israeli state capitalism manifest as settler colonial policies and practices experienced as harmful by Jawlanis. And to understand how, in the face of such an over-determined colonization, Jawlani communities somehow remain able to realize alternative ways of living and undertake collective resistance.

THE 1982 GREAT STRIKE: CEMENTING JAWLANI NATIONAL IDENTITY THROUGH CONFRONTATION

Bassel Rizqallah
Translated by Carol Khoury

Introduction

The Israeli occupation of the Syrian Jawlan was unceasing in its efforts at erasing the national (Syrian) identity of the Jawlanis while also imposing policies to entrench the Israelification of both the territory and the population, separating remaining communities from Syria. This colonization process was implemented on two levels.

The first was through *cultural measures* aimed at bringing up a generation of young Jawlanis who would identify with Israeli national symbols and customs. After the occupation in 1967, Israeli curricula were imposed on schools in the occupied Syrian Jawlan: pupils were forced to celebrate Israel's Independence Day and to raise the Israeli flag in schools. Across the remnant Arab villages in the Jawlan, expressions of Syrian patriotism were banned, and residents were pressured to apply for Israeli citizenship (Al-Batheesh 1987: 23). Over time, Hebrew names were applied to regions and places, including the installation of Hebrew and English road signs in place of Arabic ones (Al-Batheesh 1987: 21).

The second involved *political-administrative measures* – the diverse laws, regulations and elections that were imposed on the Jawlani people. At the start of the occupation, a military ruler was appointed, and several military orders were passed to secure Israeli control of land (Al-Batheesh 1987: 57–63). Various coercive practices were also employed to suppress political resistance to the occupation: these included backfilling water ponds used for irrigation and as drinking water for animals, house demolitions, denying construction permits and closing shops (Al-Batheesh 1987: 39–40). Restrictions on livelihoods and heavy taxes attempted crudely to integrate the Jawlanis in the Israeli economy as a cheap labour force (Abu Jabal and Ayoub 2009: 27; Qassem 1984: 39). The Israeli military administration directly appointed local councils in 1974 to replace the local Jawlani leadership, but these failed to gain any significant support from the population (Qassem 1984: 33).

In August 1980, as Israeli politicians discussed annexation, it was decided to give the Jawlanis Israeli identity cards (Qassem 1984: 88). Opposing this move, in March 1981 the residents of the Jawlan issued a National Document that affirmed the national identity of the Jawlan as part of Syria, the identity of its Syrian Arab population and the non-recognition of Israeli measures in the Jawlan (people in the occupied Syrian Golan 1981). Israel effectively annexed the Jawlan in December 1981 through the enactment of a legislation in the Israeli Knesset (the Golan Heights Law) and commenced arrangements for granting identity cards to the residents of the Jawlan (Abu Sharar 1982). This triggered a wave of protests by the Jawlanis (Figure R1), culminating in the Great Strike (aldrāb alkabir), which began on 14 February 1982 and lasted almost six months. A broad-based popular mobilization challenging the occupation, this general strike was a formative event in the history of the Jawlan. It is continuously evoked by the Jawlanis to affirm Syrian national identity and has informed the ongoing political struggle against occupation, although no subsequent act of resistance has matched its size and duration.

The 'milk of patriotism'

In March 1982, at the height of the Great Strike, Ayman, a seven-year-old Jawlani boy, declares: 'even if they deprive us of drinking milk, the milk that we have drunk is sufficient for us – it's the milk of patriotism (hālīb hubb alwatanī)' (Natour 1982). Ayman's words reveal that the principal Israeli tactic to break the strike was the physical and economic isolation of the Druze villages, with a curfew imposed and the grazing of dairy cattle prohibited. These words are also the expression of a popular consciousness of national resistance acquired by children and adults in equal measure – one that contributed to the strike and was strengthened by it. This would not have been possible without the people themselves participating so actively in the popular resistance to annexation.

FIGURE R1 Jawlanis discard Israeli ID cards, Ein Qiniya, 5 April 1982. Courtesy Dan Hadani Collection, National Library of Israel.

The strike was not the first instance of rebellion and defence of the Jawlani national identity but acted as a decisive event in its favour. In 1969, during the early years of the occupation, teachers in the Jawlan refused to participate in the Histadrut elections (Israel's General Federation of Labour),[1] rejecting integration into an institution that would have annulled their Syrian identity and integrated them into an element of the occupying state. Defined against an occupation, the Jawlanis' awareness of their Arab and Syrian identity began to strengthen.[2] It manifested itself in the rejection of all control and Israelification measures imposed on the Jawlan, culminating in the 1981 National Document that defined the Jawlanis as 'inherently' Arabs and Syrians against efforts to impose Israeli nationality on them. The National Document has become *the* text of collective political expression for Jawlanis whenever an event threatens their national identity, playing such a role during the Great Strike. Acceptance of Israeli sovereignty and nationality would have erased this oppositional solidarity: 'We shall be annulled when we abolish our identity – we shall no more be existent.'[3]

A demonstration at any moment

With the community-wide mobilization of the Jawlanis, the ability and willingness to demonstrate was high. As Hala Fakher Eldin recalls: 'We were ready to start a demonstration at any moment . . . at times, a young boy would say there's a demonstration and people would take to the streets immediately.'[4] Under the febrile atmosphere, the residents of the Jawlan were prepared for confrontation and an uprising, which contributed to strong feelings of danger: 'The minute there's a sound of a bullet, people start to gather.'[5] However, the collective resistance was driven by a realization that a Syrian national identity was being effaced: 'The residents of Jawlan would not accept the occupation imposing itself as a fait accompli. People were brimming with reasons to protest against this new Israeli approach.'[6] This shared sense of an existential threat, as well as the inclusive decision for a general strike, played a key role in motivating participation in the strike and in making it last for six months.

The political meaning of the Great Strike of 1982 was also informed by an understanding that as a long and comprehensive action, the Jawlani were creating a new front for struggle across all the Arab territories occupied in 1967. It was preceded by popular protests, like the Palestinian Land Day mobilizations, commemorating the general strike and march in March 1976 in the Galilee, and other acts of popular resistance against Israeli land expropriation and other forms of oppression. Before the Great Strike started in the Jawlan, there was a warning strike for three days in which the first popular meeting was held in Majdal Shams to coordinate the protests.[7] It was then that the collective struggle against the occupation in the Jawlan gathered a powerful popular momentum.

Syrian national events also played a role in increasing the intensity of the marches during the Great Strike, such as the march of 17 April 1982 in Majdal Shams on the anniversary of France's withdrawal from Syria, which was the largest demonstration of the strike, with 6,000 people taking part.[8] This march further affirmed the Syrian national identity of the Jawlanis. Another example was the 3,000-strong demonstration held in May 1982 in response to the trial of those arrested for refusing Israeli identity cards.[9] Such demonstrations were certainly not futile – they were sometimes able to achieve quick successes, such as lifting the Israeli curfew on Majdal Shams in March 1982.[10]

The Jawlan commune

The residents of the Jawlan agreed that should the harvest day arrive with the strike still going on, the harvest of the season would be distributed to all people.[11] Furthermore, a scheme of providing services for free for the people was also agreed, in which everyone with a profession (from barbers to doctors) would provide his or her services without charge.[12] This created a high level of social solidarity that intersected with national and political solidarity, strengthening the steadfastness of the Jawlani resistance and prolonging the strike. It effectively turned the Druze villages of the occupied Syrian Jawlan into a commune rebelling over the economic as well as political control of the occupation. One expression of this was the refusal to pay taxes and take part in Israeli land surveys, which led to the arrest of four people from Ein Qiniya, who were later released due to popular pressure.[13] The strike-era economy was therefore based on sufficiency and on the provision of free services, which became ever more important with the tightening of the Israeli siege on the Jawlan. In an attempt to break the strike, curfews were imposed and each of the Druze villages was blockaded, preventing essential supplies (such as food and milk for babies) reaching residents and banning the grazing of dairy cattle, which increased shortages of milk.[14] The occupation authorities also cut water and electricity to Ein Qiniya, and threatened the same to Majdal Shams.[15] Nevertheless, these attempts to subjugate the residents of the Jawlan served only to increase their social solidarity: 'You feel that you are part of a collective spirit.'[16]

This solidarity worked to undermine the Israeli moves to break the strike, even over the shortage of milk: 'The Israeli authorities tried to exploit the situation by providing milk through the local councils, but the people boycotted this move, and managed to distribute milk amongst themselves.'[17] The milk of patriotism was Jawlani milk. The rejection of Israeli identity cards and the Israeli-appointed local councils collaborating with the occupation were principled rejections with widespread support across the Jawlani people, thwarting attempts to breach the strike.

Feminizing the strike

In her testimony about the Great Strike, Hala Fakher Eldin, one of the organizers of the marches, talks about the participation of women in giving speeches during these protests. Thus, the strike played a major role in bringing women out into the public sphere as active political subjects.[18] Indeed, they were part of the decision-making in the meeting at the Majdal Shams khalwa which announced the strike.[19] On 16 March 1982, a statement was issued by the Women of the Jawlan, calling for an end to the siege, condemning the arrests that had taken place and stating that the lack of milk meant that they resort to feeding their children with water and sugar.[20] Women also participated in the reception of Palestinian delegations visiting in support of the Jawlani.[21] Women like Jamila Shams[22] were among those arrested during the marches, and many other women were arrested for attempting to graze their cattle in violation of the siege imposed on the Jawlan.[23] On 7 May 1982, nine residents of Buqʻatha village were injured, including two children and a woman, as a demonstration was broken up by Israeli soldiers.[24]

Therefore, the participation of Jawlani women in the Great Strike was not their traditional role of supporting or deferring to the men. Rather, it was an active involvement from the first day of action as they participated in the decision-making on political mobilization, despite conservative social conventions that, for example, separated women and men in meetings. The wide-ranging participation of Jawlani women gave the popular mobilization greater political effectiveness and momentum. In her recollection of the events, Hala Fakher Eldin talks about how she called for and organized demonstrations, explaining that the Great Strike created an opportunity to widen and strengthen feminist activism, which creates a more prominent place for women in the public sphere and subsequently allowed them to make a greater contribution in all aspects of Jawlani social and political life.[25]

Conclusion

The social solidarity among the Jawlani population – the revived national awareness, the organization of the demonstrations and the participation of all segments of society in the Great Strike – cemented their Syrian national identity. And the participation of women was not separate, pouring into the marches and building social solidarity. All this crystallized under the national identity of the Jawlanis, both men and women. It was not a historical coincidence but a conscious act, a result of political and national awareness of what was going on around them. In the end, the general strike achieved its immediate goal to reject the imposition of Israeli citizenship (in identity documents Jawlanis are 'residents' rather than 'citizens'). Although the occupation continued, it became a foundational event for affirming the national identity of the Jawlanis. It is an event that is recalled with every act of anti-colonial struggle in the Jawlan and that political memory influences these continuing acts of resistance.

We can see the impact of the Great Strike even after four decades. In October 2018, the Jawlanis adopted similar protest methods for opposing the elections for village and local councils imposed by Israel. A broad-based coalition was created, which issued a national statement reaffirming the Syrian identity of the Jawlan and rejecting the proposed elections as the illegitimate act of an occupying power. This statement was followed by a series of political statements, demonstrations and a one-day strike (Khanjar 2018).

Despite major socio-economic transformations that have taken place in the Jawlan, including the emergence of new generations not born at the time of the Great Strike, the national identity and the rejection of the occupation remain present in the Jawlani political imagination. The strike, even if in a limited way, continues to be a tool of the political struggle. The one-day strike adopted to oppose the 2018 municipal elections was repeated as a tactic for protests in 2020 against Israeli wind turbine development in the occupied Jawlan (Sharaf 2020). Times are different from those of 1982, but confrontation persists against ongoing attempts of Israelification of the land and the people, taking place – for the wind turbines project – under the pretext of economic development. If it seems difficult to recapture the scale of the Great Strike as a tool of resistance again, it remains a key part of the political imaginary. Its achievement in forging the national identity of the Jawlani people and the land of Jawlan is always present, serving as a catalyst for the continuing resistance to occupation.

THE NATIONAL DOCUMENT

BY THE SYRIAN CITIZENS IN THE OCCUPIED GOLAN HEIGHTS

We, the Syrian citizens in the occupied [Golan] Heights, see it as incumbent upon us to address the official and popular bodies in the world, the United Nations and its institutions, as well as public opinion in the world and in Israel. For the sake of truth and history, we seek to convey, in honest and clear words, the fact of our position regarding the Israeli occupation and its continuous efforts to obliterate our national personality – annexing the occupied land on the one hand, and imposing Israeli laws upon us, on the other.

Israel deploys various means to forcefully integrate us into its entity and 'melting pot'. It seeks to strip us of our Arab Syrian nationality, which we proudly and honourably belong to and seek no replacement for. We have inherited from our dignified ancestors our nationality, together with the Arabic language – which we proudly speak [and regard] as our only national language – and our land, which we cherish with our hearts. This land has gone from father to son since the beginning of the Arab person in this region thousands of years ago, mixed with our sweat and the blood of our forefathers. Throughout history, our fathers saved no effort to defend and liberate this land from every conqueror and forceful occupier.

We take an oath for life to remain loyal to our lands. We shall not forego any part of our lands, no matter how long the Israeli occupation remains, no matter how intensely the occupying authority tries to compel or seduce us to negate our nationality, and no matter how precious our sacrifices may be.

It is perfectly natural and only common sense that we take this stand – the stand of all people existing, partly or completely, under occupation. We have issued the following document out of our sense of historical responsibility towards ourselves, our sons, and our future generations:

- The Occupied Golan Heights is an indivisible part of Arab Syria.
- The Arab Syrian nationality is our true attribute, which passes from father to son.
- Our land is a sacred property of the Syrian members of our society under occupation. Any citizen who is tempted to sell, forfeit, or give up any inch of land to the Israeli occupiers, commits a grave crime against our society, and an unforgivable national treason.
- We do not recognize any Israeli decision to mould us into the Israeli entity. We absolutely reject the Israeli Government's decisions that aim to negate our Arab national personality.
- We do not recognize the legitimacy of the local and religious councils because these institutions were appointed by the [Israeli] military governor and receive orders from him. Under no circumstances shall the heads and members of these councils represent us.
- The persons who are known to actually reject the occupation, and who may be from any sector of our society, are the ones who are qualified to, and can, express the conscience and the inner feelings of their fellow members of society.
- Any citizen of the occupied Syrian Golan Heights who is tempted to give up his nationality for an Israeli nationality injures our collective dignity, our patriotic honour, our national belonging, as well as our religion and traditions, and is considered a traitor of our homeland.
- Our decision is final and cannot be retracted: Anyone who becomes an Israeli national, or violates this Document, shall be condemned and expelled from our religion and social matrix. Any exchange with such a person is banned. The ban shall be extended to participation in his merry and sorrow [family] events and to entering marital relations with him, until he admits guilt, retracts his fault, seeks forgiveness from his society, and [thus] retrieves his honour and real nationality.

In adopting this Document, we are empowered by our genuine spiritual, national, and human heritage, which obliges us to protect our brothers, to command good and forbid wrong, and to be deeply loyal to the homeland.

The people in the occupied Syrian Golan
25 March 1981
(Translated by Munir Fakher Eldin)

THE POLITICS OF THE GOVERNED

FIGURE 3.1 Protest march in Mas'ada, 14 March 2004. (The banner reads: 'Our land is Arab, our identity is Syrian.') Courtesy of Fares Al Welly.

3 MAPPING THE POLITICS OF THE GOVERNED AMONG THE JAWLANIS

A SEMIOTIC APPROACH

MUNIR FAKHER ELDIN

Introduction

In various occasions in their public life, the Jawlanis under Israeli occupation proudly and defiantly raise the Syrian flag. They have begun this assertive symbolic act precisely during their encounter with the Golan Law of 1981 and their rejection of Israeli citizenship. For a long decade henceforth, the Israelis fought the practice, chased those (mostly youth) who raised the flag and imprisoned them. But since the global geopolitical changes after the cold war, marked regionally by the Madrid Peace Conference of 1991 among other things, a noticeable shift in the everyday politics of occupation took place. The Syrian flag had since then flown in the public squares or private rooftops to pay due respect to the fall of a martyr from the community or to mark national anniversaries or express solidarity with national events unfolding in Syria or elsewhere in the Arab world, without police intervention. The flag may fly in specific occasions when the community feels danger to its political identity or land and again the Israeli police seem to have learned to ignore this symbolic negation of its presence. What I propose here, in a nutshell, is that the Israelis seem to be able to regard the Syrian flag as a message that existed beyond their radar, as a communicative means directed elsewhere. The Syrian flag thus marks a parallel semiotic territory of communication that does not always collide frontally – neither with the official or the hegemonic semiotic net nor with the objective or densely visible reality of laws, economic norms, and other symbols and artifacts of Israeli sovereignty. At the same time, this semiotic plain does not exist simply up in the air; it has had deep impact on the life of the Jawlanis. Mapping the semiotic networks of power and politics and territorial relations (their contradictions, overlapping, accommodative and differential spaces) helps us understand this paradox.

There are several critical studies of how Israeli rule managed to shape a new Druze identity for the Palestinian Druze communities inside Israel, creating a radical sense of them as Israeli Druze rather than Arab or Palestinian. These studies suggest a range of theoretical frameworks and methodologies, which included notions of hegemony and state ideological apparatuses (Khaizaran 2020), invention of traditions (Firro 1999) and disciplinary and normalizing power (Saba-Saʿdi and Saʿdi 2018). These studies can be useful to understand how Israel formed its policy towards the Jawlanis as well, that is, how it defines their Druzeness as an ethnic-religious identity rooted in particularistic minority cultural attributes, distinct from its wider historical and cultural geography.[1] The effects of disciplinary power, especially through education and other normalization structures, may indeed be observed in various aspects of the Jawlani culture and everyday life, especially after more than five decades of intensive colonial governmental work. The problem which I see in these approaches, however, is that they seem to restrict power to official locations and channels.

The flag symbolism I noted suggests a semiotic aspect of how politics works, which exists beyond the confines of official spaces and channels of power production. Whether speaking of laws, policies or political speech, people read messages and intents beyond the explicit text. They put to work interpretive frameworks through which to conceive power or break its message. A lot of what we call the politics of identity must be understood as an interpretive activity of what the state is seen to do or want and a communicative strategy that seeks to set itself free of the limits of hegemonic situations. Politics in that sense lends itself to Geertz's perception of culture as 'deep play' and requires 'thick description'

(Geertz 1973). But to grasp the message one needs to follow semiotic acts and try to understand how they form spatial networks of social and political agency.

Jawlani identity in the settler colonial semiotic field: An overview

Settler colonial domination works, among other things, through what Veracini has called narrative transfer (Veracini 2010). The native's 'I am from here' narrative becomes a marker not of originality but of non-belonging to the collective settler national story of arrival and its complementary version of the settler's 'I am from here' narrative. Although in other settler colonial regimes the geographic identity of belonging (the terms 'indigenous', 'first nations', etc.) may be used as part of the official classificatory logic, Zionist governmentality works through the imposition of anthropological (ethnic and/or religious) rather than geographic criteria. There is no category for 'natives', but rather of different minorities: 'Arabs', 'Muslims', 'Christians', 'Bedouins', 'Druze', 'Circassians' and so forth. Ethnic classification exists also for the settler group (marking the countries/cultures of origin of the various Jewish immigrants has been an old and well-established practice in the history of Zionism and Israeli governance), but it works differently; it is presented as a background for a national narrative of *kibbutz galuyot* (the gathering of the diaspora) and nation-building. For the natives, there is a fundamental denial of a binding native nationalism, or at least it is assumed that for some of the natives there is a nation elsewhere, outside the settler's claimed historical land. But not all the indigenous groups 'enjoy' even that exogenous national being – the Bedouins are regarded as fragmented tribes, without a binding national consciousness or territoriality; the Druze are seen as an ethno-religious group, an ethnic nation without sovereignty; the Circassians are obviously not Arabs and constitute only a minority diaspora from a remote nation/land. The Israel's official terminology refers to its 'ethnic mosaic' as a sign of Israel's multiculturalism, an Israeli virtue constructed by denying the agency of each of the fragments of the mosaic. But the point for us here is, how do these minoritized native subjects react to these colonial classifications?

Critical literature concerned with indigenous politics speaks about the right to identity as a fundamental right that ought to be recognized as indigenous groups fight the fragmentary policies of settler regimes. This of course refers to the politics of appropriating the straitjacketed categories of 'indigeneity', which had been invented as a tool of control and elimination of indigenous sovereignty. For indigenous activists what constitutes indigeneity is not any notion derived from past 'authenticity' but the changing conditions and the ongoing need to build solidarity in the face of continuous fragmentation, denial, and oppression (Maddison 2013; Barakat 2018). But the project of inventing notions of governed minority identities is far from a past issue. The regime of 'permanent minority' identities within the settler colonial project is an ongoing project (Mamdani 2020).

One way this project has worked and continues to work is by imposing population classifications as semiotic frameworks of reference not only in standardized but also in dynamic communication with the community. By standardized, I mean the ways in which faceless governmental power works through population classifications. The education system is the most salient example, as it divides the population into sectors (the 'Druze and Circassian sectors', the 'Bedouin sector', 'the Arab sector', etc.) and devotes to each special policy. The life domains in which governmental population classifications provide interpretive frameworks for governmental work are numerous. Personal status issues are governed by special sectarian courts. Municipal budgetary policies may also be drawn according to population classifications, where the 'Druze' municipalities, for example, may receive certain treatment. Basic human rights issues such as family reunifications, naturalization and residency rights are of course major arenas governed by the settler/native dichotomy, but also within that dichotomy residents in the occupied Golan may get special treatment which their counterparts in Jerusalem (who have the same legal status as residents) may not. The land regime, of course, is governed by a thick ethnocratic regime (Yiftachel 2006), and so on. By active communication, I refer to the kind of public/private discourse in which government employees, officials, media personnel, and so forth, may engage in direct or indirect discourse with subject groups, the kind of sensibilities they may project or anticipate. This domain of communication or semiotic exchanges in everyday life is crucial for the reproduction of the colonial situation. In dealing with all pressing issues, the Jawlanis find themselves compelled to perform a subjectivity that is already set for them. They find themselves obliged to perform a semiotic structure which is impossible for them to master. While they do perform a lot of what James Scott has mapped of the 'weapons of the weak', of concealed acts of defiance or resistance (Scott 1985). In many ways, their Syrian identity developed to counterbalance the grave asymmetry they felt. It allows them to pull the locus of their sense of self away from the hegemonic centre, while still being deeply entangled in its power relations.

In their major 'battle of identity' (*maʻrakat al-huwiyya*) of 1981–2, the Jawlanis interpreted Israeli citizenship as acceptance of the same political predicament of the Palestinian Druze who were, unlike the rest of the Palestinian communities in Israel, mandated to serve in the Israeli military. This subjugation came with a whole mythology of an imagined historical 'blood pact' between the Druze and the Jews (Firro 1999). The Jawlanis saw this rhetoric as reprehensible. By rejecting Israeli citizenship, they sent a clear message that they belonged to a wider national time and space, and that their fate will not be tied to a passing foreign domination (see the most expressive text in this regard, the National Declaration of 25 March 1981, included in this volume). Implicitly, the Israelis were not seen as any more permanent than the Romans or the Ottomans who dominated the region for long periods of time. But of course, social life and the flows of power and resistance never stop at dramatic moments of radicalization and can never be captured by the semiotic reversal of meta-narratives alone.

The communicative scope of Jawlani identity: Two critical fronts

Perceptual schemes of course are generative of possibilities of symbolic and tangible actions and exchanges. The Jawlani rejection of Israeli citizenship was a powerful gesture in more than one direction. The Jawlani voice made headings in the world and in the region, and very significantly also among the Palestinians inside Israel and in the 1967-occupied territories. On the Syrian front, it pushed the Syrian regime to recognize that it had a genuine community of Syrian citizens still under occupation. As we are told by several Syrian friends – opposition intellectuals and artists who came of age politically in Syria in the 1970s – the official propaganda of the Assad regime had convinced Syrians that the Golan Heights had been already liberated in the 'heroic'

1973 war.[2] In 1981–2, the Jawlani call was suddenly heard and broke the official silence, challenging the regime to revise its narrative, to embrace its forgotten people. While breaking the regime's silence, the Jawlanis also broke the political siege imposed upon them by the Israeli occupation.

It is important here to present these two fronts of communication and interaction – the Palestinian and the Syrian, respectively – as both semiotic and material at the same time. One of the most tangible connections which the Jawlanis forged in opposition to Israeli rule was with the progressive Palestinians and Jewish activists and leaders in the Israeli Communist Party.[3] The communist party's newspaper *Al-Ittihad* provided a unique platform for the Jawlanis to talk about their predicament under occupation. Regular letters were sent by activists who broke the silence and disrupted official propaganda. Through these connections, Jawlani activists were able to extend the higher education scholarship programme in ex-Soviet bloc (which the ex-Soviet Union extended to allied communist parties and third world governments) to the Jawlanis. This created a true material reward for resistance, turning Jawlani identity into a real asset in the world, outside Israeli control.

The Jawlani-Palestinian connections also expanded to the West Bank and Gaza through prisoners and university students' networks.[4] When the Jawlanis were cut off after the 1967 war from Syria's markets, especially in Damascus, they quickly reached to Palestinian markets in the West Bank. They took their excess apple produce to be sold in Jenin, Nablus, Jerusalem, Hebron and Gaza. And in return they imported cheaper merchandise than the ones offered in the Israeli market, received healthcare services, dental care and so forth. The trade between the two regions has gone through a lot of changes over the years and is beyond the scope of this chapter. But the significant point is that gradually the relationship between the two regions developed into new domains: political solidarity, influence in the domain of institution building and later art, music and cinematic production networks. In the early 1990s, Jawlani activists took advantage of the 'NGO-ization' process among the Palestinians and managed to conduct a sociological survey for developmental purposes in cooperation with Palestinian sociologists and the Norwegian Fafo Research Foundation that invested heavily in the Palestinian civil society on the eve of the Oslo Accords (Abu Libdeh et al. 1994). Concurrently, a group of Jawlani activists established the first registered NGO called the Arab Association for Development (AAD, later the Golan Association for the Development of Arab Villages) with the primary focus on improving the neglected domains of health care, education and cultural activities. The success of this association in the health services was most remarkable, but it also had a noticeable role in developing an independent Jawlani art and cultural scene.

The very registration of the AAD in the Israeli Ministry of Interior, however, raised heated debates about how a registered NGO can represent the national position or speak in the name of the community while being officially recognized by the Israeli authorities. And this is an excellent point to turn to the Syrian front. The activists who objected to registration split off and took the issue to the Syrian regime. Some of them had leanings to the ruling Baath Party's ideology and developed direct contacts with the Syrian intelligence.[5] The Syrian regime played the role of a wise arbitrator who sought to reconcile the differences and protect internal Jawlani solidarity. The story ended by changing the name of the association, but its significance is echoed in more than one way still today. The key question behind the debate, that is, how to defend the Jawlani Syrian identity while engaging in improving life and struggling through means available through Israeli rule, still presses the community today in powerful ways; one example where this is felt is in the ongoing struggle against a wind turbine project which an Israeli private company backed by the government is planning to execute on Jawlani land (Fakher Eldin 2019). The political tension between the parties was rooted in ideological differences and only grew since then poisoning personal relationships and the possibilities of cooperation between the two factions, leading to the bitter confrontation around the Syrian uprising against the Assad regime in 2011. But this was not the only dimension of contact with Syria. The larger picture is needed.

The Israeli Golan Law of 1981 had ended all previous special arrangements and contacts which were based on Israel's tacit recognition of the international status of the region as an occupied territory. This included several arrangements mediated by the International Red Cross, especially after the ceasefire agreement between Syria and Israel in 1974. Most importantly, these included periodic meetings of separated families in UN field camps across the ceasefire line and student movement to Damascus University. In response to the tightened separation after 1981, the Jawlanis invented a new space of communication – the Valley of Tears adjacent to Majdal Shams, which became a major site for political rituals and actual family communications through personal megaphones and binoculars. This situation lasted until the early 1990s. In the context of the indirect diplomacy between Syria and Israel around and in the wake of the Madrid Peace Conference (1991), a noticeable gap emerged between Israeli assertion of sovereignty over the territory and the special policies it was willing to recognize regarding the community. Students' movement to Damascus was renewed in much larger numbers than before. Instead of organizing family meetings in temporary tent camps (as it was arranged by the Red Cross in the late 1970s), people were allowed on several occasions to cross through the UN-controlled Quneitra crossing point to Syria to visit separated family members. Religious men were also allowed to go on annual pilgrimages to holy sites in Syria and in one of those meetings they met with President Hafez al-Assad and the incident was televised by the Syrian broadcast authority. Funds were transferred from the Syrian government to a long list of men and women who claimed retirement fees for losing their employment (even temporary and short-term employment) in schools under Israeli occupation. Later, the Jawlani apple produce was sold to the Syrian government to alleviate the economic burden on the farmers. And yet, as the Jawlanis went on shaping what it meant for them to be a people under occupation, transgressing the occupation's material and symbolic fields, the contradiction of their entanglement in the occupation's power relations steadily increased.

While Syria provided hundreds of Jawlani students with free education and easy admission policy in popular professions such as medicine, dentistry and civil engineering, the Israeli market absorbed them. While experiencing the dark side of totalitarianism and hidden sectarianism in Syria, settler colonial discrimination seemed to many a lesser problem; it came with a liberal atmosphere that put the Jawlani narrative of the occupation as sheer oppression under serious doubt. These contradictions were confusing. For many students who graduated from Damascus and retuned to progress in their careers in the occupied Golan or in Israel, the real Syria they had experienced under authoritarian rule and social disintegration, killed for them the idealistic image of the homeland. One of them once conveyed to me a general sense among many of his peers, claiming in retrospect that Israel has consciously allowed the Jawlani students to go to Syria precisely with the intent to generate this effect – to undo their national spirit. It seems to me very doubtful that such an intention can explain Israeli policy, but even if it was true, the significant fact remains that such effects can never be measured with accuracy. Political emotions, as one insightful anthropologist noted, are not about who we are but who we want to be (Hage 2009). The Syrian uprising of 2011 has split the community, generated intense feelings of animosity between the pro-regime and the anti-regime forces. It was thus a tragic proof that the community was intensely Syrian in its political divisions and passions, despite the growing and infiltrating normalization process under Israeli occupation. Ironically, the pro-regime stand was explicitly sectarian, and that induced people who were never interested in the Syrian national spirit of the 1980s and 1990s (who many would label pro-Israeli) to come together with the Baathists and the religious sector in defense of the Assad regime. And in this ironic process of becoming as Syrian as ever when the world observed Syria being shattered and destroyed, the old ban on Israeli citizenship began to appear in a new light to a growing number of people. The old specter of permanent co-optation in a 'blood pact' which called for sacrificing the self for another nation (Israel, the Jews) became thinner than ever. Young and middle-aged men and women are being caught in a social imaginary of a life less burdened by the imperative to communicate sharp political affiliations, to flow with the here and now. But countering this new culture, again, there is a growing sense of urgency to redraw the boundaries of a distinct Jawlani Syrian identity vis-à-vis the Israeli occupation, benefiting from new networks and interactions with new Palestinian forces and internationally.[6]

Identity and agency: Community-bounded exchanges

Identities as communicative actions and interpretive frameworks require agents to perform them, and they pertain not only to situating the communal subject vis-à-vis the external world but also and primarily to the micro dynamics of everyday life. The most important 'monumental' declaration of identity by the Jawlanis – the National Declaration of 1981 – is a perfect, but far from being the lone, example. Although the declaration is regarded by many as an authentic symbol of Jawlani identity and resistance, there is a no less significant story behind it. It was a group of five young nationalists and leftist-leaning activists who decided on 25 March 1981 to sit down and pen the document with the aim of collecting the signatures of as many activists and family heads as possible on it. This was a bold gesture of taking matters to hand. The essence of the document reflected a consensus reached through intensive contacts between religious and family leaders and the young activists in response to the Israeli policy of allowing the Jawlanis to apply for citizenship already in 1979 (which had foreshadowed the Israeli Golan Law). The community rejected this policy and eventually the religious leaders issued a social and religious ban (*hirm*) against citizenship, excommunicating those who were promoted or benefited from the new policy. The application of the *hirm* strongly deterred people from breaking the communal consensus, creating the necessary solidarity to face the impending annexation. The religious leaders have unprecedently politicized a key communal instrument of enforcing moral conformity and social authority. In an innovative move they turned national identity into a marker of personal morality and admission to religious life and normal social exchanges.[7] But this by itself was not sufficient for the nationalists who wished to make the language of communal authority coherent with the larger national imaginary, to communicate beyond the boundary of the local and parochial. But first and foremost, their message was internal.

This was a message about the need for change in the very structure of status and power in the community. Those who possessed the real quality to represent the community, by virtue of their national faith, dedication, education and right mindedness, have the right to speak and lead. Ultimately, the older logic of status-based social hierarchy and hereditary leadership ought to give way to the newer logic of social role based on merit. The *hirm* politicized existing social norms and boundaries, but what was now needed was a change in the meanings of those norms and boundaries. The National Declaration signified the rise of a new political culture of identity representations, a new domain of *'amal watani* (national work). The Jawlanis had quickly developed a culture of street demonstrations and learned how to deal with police violence and criminalization through myriad of popular and legal tactics. They organized political festivals and began to commemorate all Syrian national events. They organized press conferences, forged political relations and exchanged solidarity visits with like-minded Palestinians. Very few of these activities had a specific demand at their core; they were not issue-based protests and had no concrete demands except the end of occupation and assertion of identity. At their core they were expressionist or representational activities; their *symbolism* was the goal itself. Sociologically, however, this new culture reshaped the qualitative aspect of communal identity. Engaging in popular politics granted people status and impact, a new source of legitimacy and validation, which cannot be found in that older religious leadership and family structures. From a Bordieuan perspective, it is possible to claim that national identity became a new arena of distinction which people competed for, as a symbolic and social capital, which could be translated from one field to another.

This new logic of social validation coexisted and contributed to the emergence of a wave of popular institutionalization of social activities, such as sports clubs, academic, women, professional organizations and cultural initiatives. These activities marked the symbolic boundaries of the community, as they were autonomous and distinct from the dominant colonial fields. The Jawlani football teams bore the names of Syrian football clubs, took no money from the Israeli football association and organized exclusive Jawlani competitions, often exchanging friendly games with Palestinian teams. While marking the community's external boundaries, these activists created new internal spaces for participation and confronted inner boundaries. For much of the 1980s, the religious leaders fought social change and the spread of secular culture, symbolized by the Academic Association and its progressive activities that transgressed traditional gender perceptions and promoted anti-patriarchal and anti-religious sensibilities. The religious leaders had banned girls from attending high school education, exercising the power of the religious *hirm* on their parents. But in the 1980s this ban fell apart; people simply disregarded it. Later, the *hirm* was used to prevent young women from attending higher education institutions in the Soviet Union and later in Damascus, but again the religious leaders failed to impede these developments. The list of similar failures can go on, but the point is that these failures reflect not the diminishing of religious life but the sharpened polarization in the attitudes towards religiosity and the limits that emerged on religious social authority. This cultural polarization and the retreat of religious authority is one of the most observable aspects of Jawlani life nowadays. But while it was deeply rooted in the politics of identity resistance in 1980s (when the 'national spirit' had been a major catalyser of social change, and social change was seen as going hand in hand with a national struggle leading to a better future of social justice and liberation), nowadays, an individualistic spirit of liberty and self-accomplishment has taken over.

Powered by a globalized consumerist culture and social imaginaries, increasing integration into Israeli professional labour market, tourism and commerce, a hybrid new middle class has emerged, with segments of it seeking to assert secular culture in a non-nationalist fashion. But this transformation is far from being a one-sided process. The cultural encounters within the community have become multisided, marking more than one (or no particular) political tendency or well-defined group agency, far from being a zero-end game.

The message we send out to people: A case of mourning, *hirm* power and religious authority

In March 2021, a relative of mine from Majdal Shams died from a Covid-19 infection. He was sixty-one years old, a simple man, a caring father and grandfather. Like millions of victims of the pandemic worldwide, his sudden death was particularly sad. In exceptional circumstances like these, of global emergency and suffering, one could expect that some personal and social considerations would be altered; that society may relax some of its rules, put politics away and let people bond and heal. Indeed, so believed his sons. But the dilemma and the social pressure they felt proved them wrong. The incident proved that the community can be occupied less with the virus, as with an old fear of symbolic infiltration by excommunicated people.

Only two years ago, the deceased had disinvited his young brother from his son's wedding because the latter had broken the four-decade old *hirm* against Israeli citizenship. Had this excommunication happened in the 1980s or even the 1990s, things would have been clearer to the family. Back then, communal solidarity was much stronger, and rules were much less negotiated. But now, a growing sense of a shift in the community's political and social traditions made the decision much harder. Why politicize basic humane events, one of the deceased's sons poignantly exclaimed! Why a man that has done no tangible harm to others, never stolen to assault anyone, is denied the right to respectfully mourn his brother? Others expressed bitterness about how 'simple people' are treated harshly in the community, while 'the strong' get away with both material and symbolic harms they commit against others.

I was caught off guard when someone approached me to intervene, as being a close member of the family. I had to make a quick decision. At first, I sided with the son's position out of a human consideration and refused to intervene, but then the dilemma got harder. Under the growing pressure from the religious side of the family, I had to rationalize the incident to minimize the expected harm. I recognized the basic unfairness in the social distribution of status and 'worth'; those who possess a special status or social capital and conduct themselves in certain ways that project power, and so forth, may indeed at times pass with a special treatment. Their social capital in one domain can suddenly cover up their deficit in another. The rules of acceptance and esteem seemed to be ritualistic and formal more than real; a person who had no misconducts except that of receiving Israeli citizenship was seen as bad or impure, but another who has encroached on communal land or cooperated with the Israeli authorities behind the scenes without breaking the formal rule of the *hirm* passes for normal. The feeling that the family perceived of itself as having to prove its correctness and treat one of its members harshly was indeed bitter. For some it reflected questionable self-esteem, a sense of deficit in symbolic power and so on. But I had to put all this aside. I had to reduce my ethical question to one: what would the deceased have wanted? What kind of message and reward he would have liked people to engage in? Would he have been a conformist once again or a challenger of the power structure in the community? The answer was clear to me. I simply had to inform the brother about the 'gossip' behind the scenes. He immediately nodded and left, assuring me that he is not hurt, but that he holds no respect for and does not care about 'this society'. Once he left, a quick cellphone call was made by someone, and the pious and highly esteemed religious man entered from the other side of the hall. All went well, the deceased received 'a good funeral' and the social order was reaffirmed.

It is widely common in speaking about communal identities to forget the question of social identities; while the first indicates a common relationship, equal in quality and nature, between all members of the community, the latter reveals the high differential nature of personal or group power relations to others within the community. To ignore social identities is indeed to miss the essence of political and social experiences. But to account for social identities does not mean that class or cultural differences mean the disintegration of community. The differentiation between social identities, in as much as it relates to the variable access to the common symbolic and material power of a community, reasserts the boundary of the community. And I think this is true not only in the case of 'communal' nations (or settler colonial splits within the national community) but also in so-called 'civil society' nations. It seems that the state's genesis as 'the holder of a sort of meta-capital granting power over other species of capital and over their holders', to quote from Bourdieu, remains caught in transition, open to conflicts, struggles and fragmentations (Bourdieu 1994: 4). The fact that the Jawlanis created their own symbolic capital reveals their complex entanglement with the dominant settler colonial field; while they interact and are deeply shaped by it, they seem always to have ways to connect beyond its limits as well, both through politicizing their everyday life and by reaching to other networks and power fields.

Concluding remarks on communal politics

The semiotic approach I adopted here can shed new light on key questions about popular politics, communalism, sectarianism and social contract theory. Although there is a neo-orientalist interest in this topic since the first Western invasion of Iraq in the post–Cold War era, Arab scholars have long written about the problem from a variety of modernist, liberal and Marxist perspectives.[8] By and large, there has been a wide consensus against sectarianism and communalism as obstacles to the emergence of civil society and citizenship sensibilities, healthy public spheres and political systems, national development and social progress. These representations, however, are derived from a theoretical tradition that has largely ignored colonial and post-colonial subjects, and an agent-based or everyday approaches to political and cultural encounters around social spaces and the 'public sphere'.

As discussions in post-colonial theory and critical settler colonial studies show, there is a need to revise normative conception of the social contract theory. Scholars dealing with the politics of Israeli citizenship among the 1948 Palestinians have in recent years adopted the settler colonial framework (Rouhana and Sabbagh-Khoury 2016). This framework allows us to see the bifurcation of settler colonial citizenship and its exclusionary structure, and thus to make sense of how 'native nationalism' makes use of settler colonial citizenship and challenges the limits of the hegemonic public discourse of citizenship rights. Rather than limiting discourse to the question of social and economic equality and the official rhetoric of narrowing of gaps (which is ultimately easily linked to the discourse of rights and obligations of equal citizens), radical indigenous Palestinian politics insists on raising the tough question about historical elimination, settler violence and destruction, and national reconstruction. But again, this seems to relate to official channels of confrontation and not the semiotics of everyday power relations.

Part of the title of this chapter is borrowed from Chatterjee's book *The Politics of the Governed: Reflections on Popular Politics in Most of the World* (Chatterjee 2004). In his book Chatterjee argued for a widening of our understanding of democratic politics to include forms of communal imagination and practices that do not align with bourgeoise culture and norms of property and virtuous citizenship. Chatterjee asserted that this kind of politics is specific to the post-colonial democracies, of which India is the biggest example. In that context, popular politics depends on the electoral system which allows for demands and entitlements to be raised based on community-specific social or cultural needs, which would otherwise be completely ignored by programmatic national plans or agendas. The politics of 'the governed' for Chatterjee calls for the widening of our perspective on what constitutes democracy. Although Chatterjee specifically speaks of the post-colonial democracies, which is not our case here, his argument is still very relevant, especially in its underlying assumption that hegemonic citizenship norms form only a *part* of modern political life of interaction between the people and the state.

By adopting a semiotic approach, we can better explore these forms, without reducing them to electoral politics. Chatterjee's discussion relied on analysing the ad hoc battles which communities wage to raise their moral entitlements to livelihood. Here I tried to chart a semiotic social-political world which produces identity meanings and maintains itself over time by evolving and adapting, across multiple fronts and ad hoc situations. This brings us to offer a new line of research or theorization of how the ruling and the ruled, the governing and the governed, relate to each other through distinct semiotic fields. The power to resist hegemony is intricately tied not to the capacity of speaking truth to power per se, or to making yourself heard in the hegemonic public sphere, but to make possibilities for the capacity *not* to converse with your hegemon, to converse to yourself and to others with whom you forge solidarities while being deeply caught in hegemonic relations.

THE OCCUPIED SYRIAN JAWLAN AND BIRZEIT UNIVERSITY: A STORY OF SOLIDARITY

Diaaeddin Horoub
Translated by Luay Hasan

It became one of the beautiful seasons that expressed the brotherhood and unity of the two issues, the issue of the occupied Syrian Jawlan and occupied Palestine, from this door and from this angle we used to go the Golan Heights.[1]

Since its occupation in 1967, the Syrian Jawlan has not been alone under occupation but has been in contact with occupied Palestine, which I discovered through discussions with a number of Jawlani prisoners inside and outside prison, specifically those who began their activities and national work in the mid and late 1970s and early 1980s, where there was a communication between the national movement in the occupied Golan and the Palestinians in the West Bank and the occupied interior and the Palestine Liberation Organization (PLO). The volunteer work camps set up from the 1970s by Birzeit University in the Golan Heights were the culmination of this relationship and an affirmation of political and social unity to confront the Israeli enemy.

Today, approximately 26,000 people live in the Syrian Jawlan, spread over the remaining five villages: Majdal Shams, Buq'atha, Mas'ada, Ein Qiniya and Al-Ghajar. As in the Syrian Jawlan, in the West Bank people were displaced and the territories occupied, and those who remained live under the military occupation and the decisions of the officers of the occupying army. Nearly 850,000 Palestinians lived in the West Bank before the 1967 war, about 599,000 remained after the war, while about 250,000 Palestinians or 30 per cent of the West Bank population were forced to leave their homes, villages and lands (Gordon and Ram 2016). The Palestinians were not far from everything happening, as they were facing the same policies as Israel attempted to control over all aspects of their lives. Outside, the Palestinian revolution was in the countdown to the military confrontation with the PLO that followed the Israeli invasion of Lebanon in 1982. The atmosphere of resistance to the 1981 annexation in the Golan Heights reflected itself on the street in the occupied West Bank and Gaza Strip, so people went out in demonstrations and confrontations and clashed with Israeli soldiers in Jerusalem, Dheisheh camp, Nablus, Balata camp, Jenin, Gaza and Hebron.

Although the moment of the Great Strike waged by the Jawlani people in 1982 was an influential moment at all levels, specifically in raising the voice of the Golan Heights and its situation, and manifesting the relationship between Palestine and the occupied Golan Heights, this relationship did not start at this moment, passing several stages and witnessing many forms. In the 1970s, it took the form of economic cooperation over the marketing of agricultural products as well as, within the framework of the Palestinian revolution and the PLO, through participation in the guerrilla action, specifically in the 1970s. Israeli prisons were an important meeting place and the central link in the history of this relationship. Salman Fakhr Eldin from Majdal Shams, a political activist and prisoner, who was one of the most important people to make a significant contribution to this relationship, says:

> The relationship between the Golan Heights and Palestine is twofold, a normal daily human part, born with trade and mainly the markets of Nablus, as well as Jerusalem, Hebron and Jenin, but the political aspect was born in prison, between Golan prisoners and Palestinians, in the early 1970s, in the sense of a broad and collective relationship. If there were individual relations before, I do not deny them but I am not a witness to them, perhaps one of our martyrs, Ezzat Abu Jabal, who was martyred in 1972 as he crossed the border with occupied Palestine, had been organized within the ranks of Palestine Liberation Organization.[2]

Likewise, the Palestinian uprising in 1987 was a witness to the strength and durability of this relationship, and during the days of the First Intifada, a delegation from the occupied Golan Heights through a joint group with the Druze Initiative Committee in the Palestinian Galilee – led by Sheikh Jamal Maadi and in coordination with the Council of Birzeit University Students' Union – visited Balata refugee camp in Nablus and the Women's Union Hospital, which hospitalized the first wounded of the intifada from Balata camp. After visiting the hospital, members of the delegation went to the camp, breaking the Israeli curfew imposed on the camp, and there was a hand-to-hand clash with the border guards at that time.[3]

Volunteering as a tool of resistance and resilience

Birzeit University and its student movement at that stage constituted a pioneering struggle that caught the attention of the Palestinian masses. Its students and staff were creative in devising methods of struggle and confrontation, focused on mass action in which the largest possible number of students participated, beginning with marches and demonstrations calling for an end to the occupation and the establishment of an independent Palestinian state, and then the formation of campaigns against the occupation and its policies to target the university and its staff. An example for that is the right to education campaign which began its work in the years of 1970s, when the university began providing legal assistance to its students and staff who faced imprisonment and detention by the Israeli occupation forces. It documented Israeli violations and launched a global campaign to support the academic rights and freedom of Palestinian students, professors and teachers and educational institutes, addressing the military closure orders imposed on the university: the longest closure lasted for four and a half years (1988–92) during the First Intifada.[4] As a collective response to the occupation, volunteerism became a key and important part of the university's identity in particular and the Palestinian National Movement in general. The national action groups relied on voluntary work as the main and basic method to reach the Palestinian masses, and the unified national leadership of the First Intifada used voluntary work as a way to mitigate many economic and social problems that the Palestinian masses were suffering from due to the occupation and its policies. The most important form was volunteering to educate people and create relations of economic solidarity (Al-Batsh 2013).

Since 1972, Birzeit has adopted a volunteer programme that obliges every student to finish 120 hours of collaborative work during his/her study years at the university, and has established a specialized department to accomplish this task with the students, who in turn formed a volunteer work committee in the Student Council to promote the public contributions by students in public (Jahshan and Yahya 2014: 20), strengthening the social fabric in the face of occupation projects. In this sense, and in the context that the procedures and policies of the occupation target Arab land, and that Birzeit University, with its students and staff, was not far from the occupied Syrian Jawlan, the area became a regular location for volunteer work. As one of the leaders of the student movement at the university, Ali Hassouna, recalls:

> In 1979, there were international camps [with volunteers] from 25 countries from Europe and America. There were three camps per year and each camp was for two weeks, and the aim of these camps was to see and tour several areas, such as the Gaza Strip, the occupied interior, Hebron and the Golan Heights, and to participate in volunteer work in these areas, where approximately 100 Birzeit University and foreign students participated in the camps.[5]

The Golan Heights and Birzeit University

'The relationship with Birzeit University came in the shortest and strangest way',[6] states Salman Fakhr Eldin, talking about how connections developed with the Jawlani people. He continues:

> The relationship came through the Jewish Solidarity Committee with Birzeit University where there was a solidarity committee with Birzeit comprising Jews and Arabs, but it was made up mainly of communist Jews, and was headed by a professor of physics at the Hebrew University, Danny Amet, who I expect lives today in London, because he decided to leave the country. This relationship came through Felicia Langer, Lea Tsemel and her husband Mikado, who had a strong relationship with the Public Front for the Liberation of Palestine and the relationship with Birzeit began from the early days of being prosecuted, and there was a group, including Jewish and Arab university professors, where I met the Jews, specifically the Jerusalem Group, and hence the story of Birzeit began for me.[7]

Birzeit's name was not far from what was happening in the Golan Heights, generating a politics of solidarity in the 1980s, which was manifest during the Great Strike in 1982. Fakhr Eldin was in charge of the media committee for the strike and at that time he started a public mobilization tour in occupied Palestine. On this tour, the left-wing anti-Zionist Jewish activist, Michel Warschawski, nicknamed Mikado, invited him to attend a meeting of the Solidarity Committee with Birzeit University and told him that he could join this meeting in one of the houses in occupied Jerusalem. Fakhr Eldin attended the meeting and explained to the audience the goal of the strike, and during this media campaign, during the first week of the strike [February 1982], the Israeli Communist Party announced its support, arranging a press conference and then launching a public mobilization campaign in all the cities and villages of occupied Palestine.[8] The relationship between the university and the people in the villages of the occupied Golan became stronger, with well-attended volunteer camps taking place between 1985 and 1987. In 1985, the Council of the Student Union and the Cooperative Department of Labour in the Deanship of Student Affairs at Birzeit University organized voluntary work trips to the occupied Golan Heights in coordination with local councils and political activists. The labour camps in the Golan Heights were concentrated in the fruit-harvesting season, picking apples, cherries and peaches for which the Golan region is famous, with the participation of 150–250 male and female students per season.

Students were arriving in the Golan in mass buses and welcomed by Jawlani people and stayed in the farmers' homes in Mas'ada, Majdal Shams and other villages, with Birzeit University coordinating with them on numbers and their ability to accommodate. By repeating the camps from 1985, local people became more able to accommodate larger numbers and the volunteer season became vital and highly welcomed by Jawlani people (see Figure R2). Jamal Al-Salqan, head of the Birzeit Student Council at that time, recalls the way in which people of the occupied Golan welcomed the university students, saying: 'We felt it through cheers and flowers on the balconies and rice sprinkling, a tradition known to people of the Golan Heights, southern Lebanon and northern Palestine.'[9] The volunteer work camps were political par excellence, specifically in the Golan Heights. Their goal was to confirm that the cause of the Palestinian and Syrian people is one, and that they have a common concern, as well as an affirmation of the pan-Arab dimension of the liberation project. The camps also built solidarity with the people in the Golan Heights, so that they were not besieged and isolated by the policies and practices of the occupation, as confirmed by Al-Selqan: 'The season became one of the beautiful seasons that expressed the brotherhood and unity of the two issues, the occupied Syrian Jawlan and occupied Palestine, and from this door and from this angle we used to go to the Golan Heights' (Figure R2).[10]

It was an opportunity to get to know each other, according to Hassouna:

> since the Golan Heights is faraway and whoever goes to it only goes to Jabal al-Shaykh as a tourist area and does not visit the villages in the Golan Heights. Also, these visits allowed the creation of a relationship between Palestinians and Syrians from the occupied Golan outside the prison walls, whereas the beginning of acquaintance and the relationship between them was in Israeli prisons. Because the relationship arose in the detention centres, we did not feel that there was a difference between us as Syrians and Palestinian; and when we went there, we didn't feel that we were going to areas that are foreign to us or non-Palestinian, and to learn from the people about the special and distinct experiences in the Golan Heights and the destroyed villages there. Because of the steadfastness of the people of the Golan Heights and their resistance to occupation, we had a thirst to meet them, as there is a common experience of struggle between us, and we had a feeling that it was a distinct and special experience in life, and we felt that they exchanged these feelings with us.[11]

When Ali Hassouna was asked about a picture or a souvenir from those days, he said:

> We could not take pictures for security reasons because there were liberated prisoners among us as well as among people of the Golan Heights and a number of them were constantly subjected to administrative detention, like the freed prisoner Salman Fakhr Eldin, and therefore we did not want to put them at risk and endanger ourselves, as we were aware that the occupiers only viewed this activity as a political act that must be fought.[12]

People of the Jawlan teach Birzeit University students

The volunteer students were participating with farmers in harvesting, packing, collecting and cleaning, putting fruits in boxes and processing

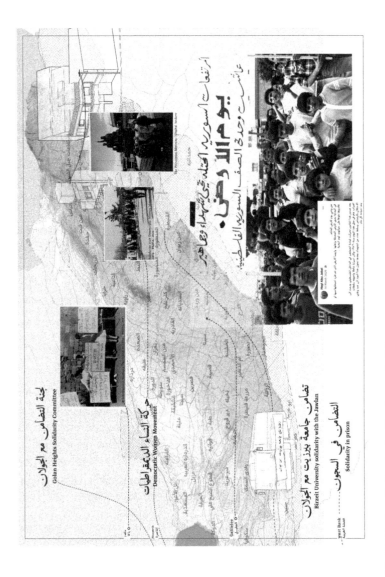

FIGURE R2 'Solidarity with the Jawlan' by Jumanah Abbas.

them, and sometimes the volunteer activity was interspersed with agricultural field work, such as helping to dig horticultural ponds and helping with some rubble, chains and tilling, and the work of weeding and cleaning land. The work took on a serious character, as the goal was to help farmers, support and stabilize them on their land.[13] The participation did not stop there: students were learning a lot from local people and gaining new experiences in managing lands and crops, including how to be self-reliant. This is among the most memorable things for Ali Hassouna, who recalls:

> It was an important opportunity to learn about distinctive experiences, for example: how the land is rehabilitated, how to move soil from the valley to the mountain on their own to grow apples, to build water tanks for farmers, cooler cooperatives, where every five to seven farmers were building a cooler to store crops in them, and experience in building water tanks, where each group of farmers was building a 500-cup water tank. . . . In the Golan Heights there is a constant need for heating, so people were making the fireplaces themselves, and sometimes we saw that, and there were no bakeries or ovens to make bread, because people were the ones who made bread, and they were not buying milk and yogurt, but they produced it in their homes, so for us it was an inspiring experience of self-sufficiency.[14]

The learning for the Palestinian volunteers was, therefore, not limited to agricultural techniques, but gained inspiration and influence through a mutual human experience of respect and resilience, which remains engraved in their memory of the students to this day. Hassouna adds:

> We did not have the feeling of subjectivity and selfishness among the people in the Golan Heights. We experienced them as one group and this is what made us feel a special love for them. At the meal, they invited us to eat at the Abu Zar al-Ghafari shrine as a symbol of austerity, and each one came with a quantity of food and what remained was left there for others to eat, so none of them would take the food back to his house.[15]

The relationship, which was in the form of solidarity visits and voluntary work camps, remained until the First Intifada, and a delegation from the Golan Heights used to visit Birzeit University periodically in

'Palestine Week'.[16] After the outbreak of the First Intifada, visits were almost suspended, due to the Israeli closure of the university for four years, resulting in the dispersal of students and undermining of student political activities. The imposition of barriers between villages, cities and regions made it very difficult for students to reach the occupied Golan. The return of some authority to the PLO in the West Bank and Gaza Strip through the Oslo Accords undermined the popular communal work as the PLO transformed from a liberation struggle to a state-building project. This impacted voluntary work efforts, since the Palestinian political parties steered away from it and this negatively impacted the political Palestinian-Jawlani relationship. However, interaction has remained in other forms, perhaps more cultural, through literary and cultural figures, cultural institutions, artistic groups and some youth groups.

THE OCCUPIED SYRIAN JAWLAN AFTER 2011: THE CONSTANT AND VARIABLE

Aram Abu Saleh
Translated by Luay Hasan

The Arab Spring in general, and the Syrian revolution in particular, has significantly changed the societies that rebelled against the old republican military regimes and significantly transformed the power dynamics within them. The impact of the Arab Spring on the Arab region can be decisively divided into two types: a direct type in which republics have radically changed the country's conditions and resulted in changing the existing governance, such as in Tunisia and Egypt and later on in Sudan or failed to change the existing governance and turned into a genocide, as in Syria (or were unsuccessful as in Lebanon and Iraq). The second type of impact is indirect, where countries or peoples have not made direct revolutions, and there were no attempts to 'overthrow the regime' such as Palestine and Mauritania.

The occupied Syrian Golan Heights, and its remaining community after the occupation of 1967, is effectively located between the direct impacts that characterize Syria and its people and the indirect impacts that characterize its restricted and possible geographical extension under Israeli occupation (extension to the occupied Palestinian territories). Taking into account the 'queer theory' of identity in the Jawlan as performative – meaning a relational (non-essentialist) understanding of national identity as a diverse set of social and cultural practices defined *against* 'normal' categories of the 'nation', society' and so on (Ibraheem 2015) – this contribution presents the impacts of the 2011 Syrian revolution on social power structures, political dynamics, and individual and collective identity in the occupied Syrian Golan Heights. The Golan Heights before 2011 has been transformed after 2011, and this is a fact that every Jawlani knows. Here, I argue that at the heart of this radical transformation, the Syrian revolution exists as both a revolutionary and a catastrophic event on a humanitarian front as experienced by the Syrian Jawlani population undergoing Israeli colonialism since 1967.

2011–13: The revolution and the societal rift

Since the early beginnings of the Syrian revolution, the Jawlani public opinion was actively engaged with ongoing events. Ten days after the popular uprising in Syria, which started on 15 March 2011,[1] a statement entitled 'You are the voice and we are its echo' was published, stating the following:[2]

> Our great Syrian people,
>
> (. . .) As we are an integral part of our Syrian homeland and its social fabric, we stand shoulder to shoulder with our Syrian people, and firmly believe (. . .) that whoever attacks them by, killing, brutalizing, arresting, torturing, displacing or looting is an enemy, no different at all from the Israeli occupation, whoever that perpetuator might be!
>
> Our existence under Israeli occupation does not in any way mean that we stand neutral. In any case, we are a natural and inevitable extension of our Syrian people, and for large segments of it, and we consider that the continuation of the status quo and its consolidation as a fait accompli had all the impact of reaching the bottom of who we are, and that Israel has been the greatest beneficiary of all of this.

Taking this position, it is nothing but a sincere expression of our commitment to the concerns of our Syrian people and their legitimate aspirations towards restoring their freedom, and a commitment to the spirit of our 'National Document'. The National Document is a constitution or a founding sociopolitical contract, written by the Jawlani people during the general strike in 1982 (see Reflection 1). The statement provides a collective allegiance to Syrian identity and resistance to Israeli occupation, including rejection of enforced Israeli nationality. The National Document is of great symbolism in the history of the Jawlani struggle and linking it with the support of the Syrian people in their revolution against the regime of Bashar al-Assad is an important moral and symbolic act. The popular mobilization (*Hirak*) in the occupied Golan Heights has accompanied the popular Hirak in the rest of Syria, with weekly demonstrations organized on Fridays, liaising with weekly demonstrations in the rest of Syria in the Martyrs' Square in the village of Majdal Shams, calling for freedom and the overthrow of the Assad regime. These demonstrations carried the thought and spirit of the beginnings of the Syrian revolution in 2011, represented by the values of democracy, civil rights, peace and pluralism (Figure R3).

Soon, the Hirak clashed with violent opposition and repression from supporters of the Assad regime in the Golan Heights, sometimes resulting in violent physical clashes and confrontation between the two sides.[3] As the situation in the Syrian homeland worsened with the conflict between the regime and peaceful demonstrators intensifying, and with the horrific massacres committed by the regime against the Syrian people and the number of martyrs increasing, the rift between the pro-revolution party and the anti-revolution party in the occupied Golan Heights intensified. This rift became an existential one that could only be overcome if the regime in Damascus changed, and this has not happened at the date of writing of this paper.[4]

FIGURE R3 One of the first Jawlani demonstrations in support of the Syrian revolution, Majdal Shams, March 2011. Courtesy of Atef Al-Safadi (from left to right the placards read: 'Shame on them!', 'One, one, one, the Syrian people are one' and 'The Syrian people will not be humiliated').

After 2011, everything in the so-called Syrian National Movement[5] became a subject of debate and disagreement, causing paralysis in national and popular mobilization. My main claim in this paper is that it is impossible to comprehend possibilities of rectifying the Jawlani condition without addressing the Syrian revolution and its consequences. Syria became two 'Syrias' after 2011: the first Syria is inevitably linked to its ruler and his regime, and this is what its supporters mean when they call it 'Assad's Syria'; and the second Syria is linked to the values of the Syrian people's uprising in its beginnings (2011–13) against the ruler himself and his regime. The two Syrias have distinct flags and anthems, contradictory symbols, contradictory values and, most importantly, collective political-historical narratives which fully contradict each other. It is therefore a grave fallacy to describe such a rift between the two Syrians as a 'difference of opinions', because these two Syrias, in the occupied Golan Heights in particular, and Syria in general, have nothing in common except the category 'Syrian'.

The most important consequence of this clash between the supporters and opponents of the Syrian revolution has been this rift between the components of the national movement, which led to nearly a complete paralysis of its activity, resulting in the cessation of many cultural activities and spaces in the Golan Heights. This resulted in a large political and cultural vacuum which the Israeli establishment tried to exploit and fill (Karkabi and Ibraheem 2020). This contradiction between the two Syrias put the new generation of the Golan Heights, which grew up with awareness of the events after 2011, in a state of loss, between the triad of forces that might contribute to an identity formation at the individual level: the Assad regime, the Syrian revolution against it, and the Israeli occupation. This type of identity loss alerts us to the collapse of collective political possibilities as affirmed in the Great Strike of 1982. In addition to other factors such as globalization and the rise of global neoliberalism, the rift contributed to a sense of individual liberties that didn't exist prior to 2011.

After 2013: The collapse of the national framing of the Syrian conflict

With the confinement of the peaceful popular movement inside Syria, and the increase in violence and repression by anti-revolutionary groups in the occupied Golan Heights coupled with the collapse of the national framework of the Syrian conflict, the Syrian revolutionary movement in the occupied Golan Heights disappeared – or was concealed – from the public sphere.[6] This gave supporters of the Assad regime the opportunity to monopolize the political position in the Golan Heights until 2018 and to a lesser extent afterwards. The conformity to the ruler of the state[7] that characterizes the pro-regime party in the Golan Heights altered the significance of Syrian 'national' events from 2013 to the present day. While the Jawlani people used to commemorate events, such as the Evacuation Day and Martyrs' Day, as confirmation of their Syrian identity, such events have become marches in support of the leadership and the army in Damascus. This has caused a great aversion to all that is 'Syrian' among the younger generation, compounded by the separation in the public discourse between Syrian nationalism and Assad's rule. The Israeli establishment clearly exploited this aversion and employed it in its official discourse, such that Assad regime supporters in the Golan Heights have contributed, intentionally or unintentionally, to empowering those that accept the occupation.

However, the physical absence of the revolutionary movement from the Jawlani public space does not negate its impact on political consciousness and practices in the Golan Heights, as the Syrian revolution also represented an idea of national liberation in the Golan Heights prevented by the Israeli occupation. This consciousness be observed in individuals who are not necessarily activists, and even among those who are anti-revolution. Jawlanis have experienced the revolution from afar – detached from the killing, destruction, torture and displacement – but they have fully engaged with its radical core and its potential for transformation. Prior to the clash and then the rift described above, essential and existential debates ensued regarding the individual and collective issues facing the Syrian citizen, such as women's rights, sexual rights, democracy and pluralism. These discussions did not preoccupy us Jawlanis in the same way and with the same depth before 2011.

These deep-rooted sociopolitical effects of the revolution in the Jawlan are enduring. They have led to social division and fragmented local identities. However, the support shown by clerics and traditional leaders of the Assad regime – their monopolization of public discourse and space in the occupied Syrian Golan Heights – have contributed to the weakening of their legitimacy as local leaders outside of the narrow circles of their supporters in the Jawlani community. Their silence on the paralysis of traditional [Syrian] national institutions and the nihilistic monstrosity of the massacres and the bloodshed inside Syria have all become factors in accelerating the radical weakening of the traditional social-religious structures that have been followed for hundreds of years in the Golan Heights.[8]

Conclusion

Everything became possible in the occupied Syrian Golan after the 2011 Syrian revolution – traditional religious, social or political rules became less binding. Even the national identity, which had been a firm and binding concept of social loyalty, became a subject of debate and deliberation among a generation that gained its political awareness in the context of post-2011 Syria.

Seeing the most important Syrian event in 2011 as a cumulative starting point, in addition to other factors related to the nature and characteristics of the Jawlani community, may answer the question as to the causes of the sudden and rapid 'openness' shown in the villages of the Golan Heights, so that the collapse of social rules and prohibitions and various attempts to redefine them, and the political openness that followed, cannot be separated in the Golan context from the events of the Syrian revolution. This is all taking place while the Israeli settler state continues its efforts to implement its hegemonic projects and cultural and political assimilation of the Syrian community that remains in the Golan, while continuing unabated its settler colonial practices of the historic and geographic transformation of the Syrian lands and villages depopulated in 1967.

Complementarity

It's not halfway
I have one foot with which to jump from stumble to stumble,
And you have an amputated foot,
Whose weight has not ragged the shoe,
If you are waiting to arrive
Take what's left from my body and put it in your shoe
For I would be happy that part of me got what we desire.

تكامل

لا يَنتَصفُ الطريقُ
ولي قدمٌ واحدةٌ أقفزُ بها مِن عثرةٍ إلى عثرةٍ،
ولكَ قدمٌ مبتورةٌ لم يهترئ مِن ثقلها الحذاءُ،
فإن كُنتَ تنتظرُ الوصولَ
خُذ ما تبقّى مِن جسدي
وأدخلهُ في نعلِكَ
سيُفرِحُني وصولُ بعضي إلى ما نشتهي.

YASSER KHANJAR
Translated into English by Ghareeb Iksander. Original Arabic poem (2019) published with the kind permission of Al Mutawassit.

SECTION III

THE POLITICS OF JAWLANI ART

FIGURE 4.1 *A Quote* (2012), pencil on paper, by Randa Maddah. ('This work is a visual interpretation of a text written by the wife of a martyr.') Courtesy of Randa Maddah (see Reflection 4).

4 SCULPTURES IN JAWLANI PUBLIC SPACES

REFLECTIONS ON THE WORK OF IDENTITY

WAEL TARABIEH AND MUNIR FAKHER ELDIN

Introduction

The 1982 popular mobilization against Israeli colonial annexation of the Golan Heights left enduring impact on public spaces in the Jawlani villages. In the subsequent two decades, the main squares of Majdal Shams and Buqʻatha won several sculptures that asserted the Jawlanis' connection to the land and their national identity. Indirectly expressing the popular sentiment against the Israeli claim of sovereignty over the Golan, all these sculptures returned to the Syrian national memory of anti-colonial fight, martyrdom and quest for liberation from French colonial rule. Sculptures enabled physical and symbolic reclamation of the identity of the place, reaffirming faith in the temporal and spatial continuity of the Syrian nation. The first was installed in 1987, called *al-Masirah* ('The March') in Arabic. We will take it here to represent the whole genre, without entering the variations that followed. We shall then contrast *al-Masirah* with a recent failed attempt to install an unnamed 'post-modern' sculpture, in the form of a hollow head or a mask, that projected a different kind of contemplation of identity. Before the content-representation of the new work caught any attention, it quickly won the wrath of an angry man, who tried to destroy it. The artist never reinstalled the damaged work, but the debate around its destruction gave it a meaningful place in public debate. Forty years after the 1982 mobilization, under a prolonged and deepening Israeli settler colonial rule, the Jawlani identity exists nowadays between the pulls and pushes of these two extremes: the hallow memory of anti-colonial fighting and martyrdom, the entrenched sense of identifying with the land and the ancestors, on the one hand, and the fragmented sense of the individual who experiences the social world through a deep sense of alienation in time and space, on the other.

Public monuments are often rich scripts of artistic traditions, private and collective experiences, social and political visions, and searches for identity, cohesion and emotional-political inspiration and energy. We will try to offer here a decoding of the two sculptures through narrating their stories of emergence and analysing their contents, receptions and political meanings as representational spaces. Through this methodology we aim to reach deeper to a level through which we see how indigenous identity works in the context of settler colonial modernization.

In his classic book on modernity, *All That Is Solid Melts into Air* (1983), Marshall Berman distinguishes between modernity and modernization, to capture what he calls the 'contradictions of modernity'. The process of modernization radically changes and transforms the social world through huge networks of financial and bureaucratic forces and ideas, and in doing so it demolishes and builds, using people as its tools. However, there is always the possibility of people employing the process to protect themselves, to resist destruction and to struggle to own their destiny. Thus, modernity is not totally spiritless, as it contains this dialectic of control and liberation. This critical reading, however, is typical in that it misses the lived cultures of 'most of the world', to borrow from Partha Chatterjee (2004). As Chatterjee among many others observed, popular politics in the global South, and we shall also add indigenous contexts facing settler colonial erasure, requires rethinking of the norms and categories of analysis born in the Western modernization process.

Israeli modernization is not simply a universal modernity process of destruction and construction but a process of cultural and political differentiation, subjugation and resistance. As noted recently by Mahmood Mamdani (2020), settler colonial contexts produce 'permanent minorities' as subordinate political subjects (see the Introduction to this book). The expansion of settler colonial citizenship does not mean overcoming the settler colonial difference. In this regard, it is important to see how the colonized capitalize on this difference to protect themselves from settler state hegemony. While submitting to civil rule, indigenous nationalism disrupts the performance of the colonial state as what Bourdieu called 'the holder of a sort of meta-capital granting power over other species of capital and over their holders' (Bourdieu 1994: 4). Indigenous identity infuses the social world with values that enable both accommodation and resistance within colonized social fields. The outcome is a heightened tension between the imposed subjectivity and inner subjectivity through which the complex world is experienced. Deciphering and decoding the Jawlani sculptures will further allow us to see how identity works in this context.

The first statue: *Al-Masirah*

General background

Israeli conquest and military occupation in 1967 meant isolation of the small remaining Syrian community (after massive expulsion) and its physical severance from its homeland and national space. Unlike the 'open bridges' policy that existed with Jordan and Egypt in the case of the West Bank and Gaza, no crossing was allowed to Syria. But the Jawlanis did not give up. They repeatedly sought ways of reconnecting with their nation. Pressed by the shortage of higher education in the community, the Jawlani activists and leaders demanded through the International Red Cross for their sons to be allowed to study in Damascus. Their demand seemed to have borne fruit in the consequence of the 1974 ceasefire agreement. During the next few years, dozens of high school graduates crossed to Damascus to acquire education in engineering, medicine, dentistry, as well as arts professions, such as geography, history, language and literature. But this conditional retrieval of the basic right to education and national normalcy was stopped on 15 February 1982. The Jawlanis had declared their famous open general strike on 14 February. The next morning a group of students was supposed to cross through the UNDOF base in Quneitra, but the Israelis closed the crossing gate and forced the students to return. Conditional crossing to Damascus was restored only a decade later as a consequence of the 1991 Madrid Peace

Conference but was again disrupted in the wake of the 2011 uprising against the Assad regime and the Syrian civil war that followed.

Israel's annexation policy and the timing of the 1981 Golan Law reflected both deep political changes within the Israeli ruling elites and geopolitical assessments following the Camp David Peace Accords with Egypt. They had very little if anything to do with concerns about the Jawlani response, but the way the Israelis tried to impose their rule reflected determination to receive a sort of native recognition, a message which would have aided them in arguing against the international condemnation of their illegal annexation. During the first decade of military rule, the Israeli government advanced a discourse of native collaboration and secured allegiance from some of the traditional leaders of the community. Concurrently, they launched aggressive cultural Israelification through the education system and its extracurricular activities (enforcing the Israeli curriculum designed for the 'Druze sector', discussed more in Chapter 5). Along with using education as a colonial measure, the Israeli labour market was also opened to Jawlani labourers, and some state welfare services were extended. At the same time, after the 1973 war, Israel uncovered underground groups of young Jawlani activists engaged in secret communication with the Syrian army intelligence: the activists were subjected to harsh trials in the hope of deterring others from following the same path. All these measures contributed to the emergence of an everyday routine that depoliticized Jawlani public expressions. Indeed, the Israelis may have had good reasons to rely on what they perceived as political passivity or docility of a small minority that cannot dare to face the state's fist. In preparation for the idea of the annexation, the Israelis issued in 1979 a special amendment to the Israeli Citizenship Law to allow residents of the occupied Golan to apply for Israeli citizenship. Rumours circulated that without citizenship people cannot secure jobs or a valued livelihood. But these measures had exactly the opposite outcome. In response, Jawlani resistance surfaced from the underground into the open as an everyday struggle. The community refused Israeli citizenship and stepped-up public expressions of Syrian identity. The strongest of these expressions, reflected in the 'National Document' of 25 March 1981, was the social and religious boycott issued by the religious leaders of the community against anyone who accepted Israeli citizenship (see translation in this volume). Yet while managing to reject colonial enfranchisement, the Jawlanis were forced to accept the status of 'residency' in Israel. Despite international moral support and UN Security Council Resolution 497 (1981) declaring the Golan Law as having invalid, they had no option but to submit to Israeli civil rule. In this context, identity politics became a critical resource for the Jawlanis to influence and shape the consequences of their new political condition. They rejected the idea of political participation in any form of Israeli governance, including local municipal councils. They built instead their own political rituals and forms of representation that defied the legitimacy of the colonial state as a patron and agent of their identity and culture. Since then, their refusal to cooperate forced the Israeli authorities to appoint local council heads who lacked legitimacy as community leaders. A recent attempt by the Israelis to carry out municipal elections was massively boycotted (Fakher Eldin 2019: 87–8; see also Chapter 2). This civil resistance, especially in the 1980s, helped the Jawlanis to preserve their sense of moral autonomy as a political community. This meant a spirit of popular initiative and action that rejected the value system of the colonial state while having to engage with its laws and formalities.

Underneath this communal political unity, however, laid contradictory social processes. Already in the 1950s and 1960s, the Jawlanis witnessed the spread of both proletarianization and education. But the radical disturbance of agrarian life under settler colonial economic, bureaucratic and spatial rule greatly intensified the pace of these changes after 1967. These dynamics of change provided fertile ground for the spread of new cultural attitudes and convictions about the meaning of life, social relations, justice and power, which imagined not only the disappearance of colonial rule but also the toppling down of the community's patriarchal norms and social life. These new attitudes were not purely idealistic in nature; they found material translations in actual social practices, fuelled by the new national energy and symbolism.

A new subculture had indeed emerged in a range of spheres and had a transformative impact on the whole community: from mass action on the streets to attempts to institutionalize cultural work and form popular organs with the high hopes of leading society and transforming its lived conditions. The 'Golan Academics Association' (*Rabitat al-Jami'iyyin*, henceforth shortened as al-Rabita), born in 1983, the year after the Great Strike (Reflection 1), was one of the best manifestations of this new culture. Its membership and vision went beyond its name. In a progressive measure it opened membership to all men and women wavering the 'elitist' or guild-like requirement of formal university education. Al-Rabita's vision had little to do with serving the community of Jawlani university students or graduates per se. It was rather perceived as a democratic popular institution capable of utilizing volunteer work to educate and spread knowledge, and to offer other community services. Regardless of the volume and scope of its activities, al-Rabita turned quickly into a platform for popular mobilization, capable of influencing decision-making and popular opinion in the community. Its successful competition with the religious and conservative circles led the latter to voice criticism and express objections to some of its activities. But still, for much of the 1980s, these internal tensions and dynamics of social change added strength and energy to Jawlani political unity, rather than the opposite.

FIGURE 4.2 'The March' (1987) statue by Hassan Khater, April 1987. Photo courtesy of Fares Al Welly archive.

The statue

In this general context, and in the context of al-Rabita's activities, the first artwork emerged, as the landmark symbol of the political identity of the place and its people (Figure 4.2). Hassan Khater, the sculptor of *al-Masirah*, was the first Jawlani professional artist to graduate from the Faculty of Modern Fine Arts at the University of Damascus. When he returned to the Golan in 1984, he joined al-Rabita. There, he found the best environment for translating his vision about art into action. His belief in the need for art to express popular sentiment and be accessible to all led him to think of a permanent public sculpture that will be part of the daily experience of people in the community. Hence *al-Masirah* was conceived. Its parts were moulded in the artist's home and al-Rabita's rented hall. At the centre of the statue stands two main figures, symbolizing the 'two pillars of the nation', according to Khater: the pen and the sword.[1] Sultan Basha al-Atrash, the leader of the Great Syrian Revolution against the French (1925–27) in his traditional dress, pointing his sword forward in the face of the colonizer. On his right side stood a young gentleman, wearing urban (Western) clothes with books in his hand. Education not only brought men and women to the fold of the nation but made its new leaders. The figuration of the statue was completed with other figures that represented the participation of all in the national struggle and becoming: a local religious man with a rifle symbolizing the Jawlanis active engagement in the 1925 revolt; a mother shedding tears and screaming, with the body of a young martyr who fell in battle laying on her lap; and on the back of the sculpture three children, one carrying a school briefcase, and two – a boy and a girl – holding together a small pile of wheat straws to symbolize education, prosperity and the coming of gender equality.

Al-Masirah quickly acquired a popular name, the 'Statue of Sultan al-Atrash'. Popular naming, to our mind, conjured a subaltern consciousness of the revolt, which plotted it not on the scale of a progressive time-space of the nation but rather in a circular time of survival and divine intervention. In this consciousness, Sultan al-Atrash had won the battles of glory and honour against the French, despite his military defeat. His victories carried the signs of divine guidance, against which the loss of the war was meaningless. The French were gone at the end: this happened two decades later, but nonetheless proved the will of a force that laid beyond this seen world.[2] This subaltern consciousness never sat very well with the imagination of the post-colonial Syrian nation state, but Khater's work successfully converses with it.

The community at large venerated the work and saw it an authentic part of a continuous culture of resistance, past and present. *Al-Masirah* was borne in confrontation with the occupation. Khater narrates that when he and his friends from al-Rabita began to prepare for installing *al-Masirah* from late February 1987 they were repeatedly harassed by the Israeli police, who regarded it as a hostile symbol. Knowing the precise date set for the installation work to begin, the Israeli police and intelligence services raided the artist's neighbourhood, chased and harshly arrested him in the street causing a deep cut in his lip. Khater narrated how long hours of delay of treatment, interrogation and intimidation aimed to 'convince' him to refrain from installing the sculpture or otherwise seek the approval of the chairman of the Israeli-appointed local council, only strengthened his conviction to install it. People waited for him all day long in the main square. Moved and inspired by the popular sentiment, he decided to improvise the installation on the spot, lest the Israeli authorities do something unexpected to disturb his plan. People were enthusiastic and rushed to help in all ways possible. 'One man rushed to work the cement with his bare hands', Khater recalled. By midnight, the different parts of the structure were assembled, leaving the refining touches to the following days (see Figure R4). An inauguration ceremony was organized a few weeks later, on 4 April 1987, to celebrate the statue. Palestinian solidarity activists were invited. Everything was organized and went as planned. But one week later, on 10 April 1987, a loud explosion was heard in the early morning hours. People rushed to the central square to learn that two witnesses, who had spotted an Israeli military vehicle leaving the main square, were arrested by the Israeli police. The men were known as respected and *watani* members of the community. All knew that this was a ploy by the occupation authorities. The crowd remained many hours in the square to chant against the occupation and to send a message of unity and perseverance. One old man, probably a veteran of the 1925 revolt, came close to the statue amid the crowd to salute and speak words of consolation to the venerated leader. The distinction between the old memory and the new representation seemed indeed thin. Luckily the explosion did not destroy the statue. The structure weighed 15 tons of reinforced concrete. During the installation, Khater recalled, he went against the advice of his friends who studied civil engineering and refused to use fixed attachments to the elevating base. *Al-Masirah* slid backward a few centimetres, without absorbing all the pressure into its mass of concrete. The expulsion left a cavity in the size of a football in the belly of the martyr, and Khater decided to keep it as a permanent fixture, adding another layer of signification to an already rich sculpture.

Not all public sculptures in the Jawlani villages had the same popular significance as *al-Masirah*, in both its symbolic content and its story and reception. It became a symbol of a deep existential experience of political identity and the reincarnation of collective memory. After thirty-five years, it still maintains its originality and uniqueness, despite deep transformations in political emotions, lifestyles and senses of social identity. We would also venture to say that its significance goes beyond that of an authentic expression of identity, changing social perception of art and marking the birth of a new cultural or art scene/'field'.

To speak about a local art scene or 'field' we mean the minimal existence of collective experiences and initiatives of co-learning, conversing, sharing and competing between cultural actors who vie for the institutionalization and specialization of what they do. In the 1990s, several organized initiatives emerged in various domains of culture and art lasting varying periods of time. Bayt al-Fann (The Art House) was established in 1996 followed by the Music Center, the Cultural Forum, Fateh Al-Moudarres Center for Arts and Culture, 'Uyoun Theatre, the Dhikra Troupe, and Tawasoul Cultural Center, Mas'ada Cultural Forum, the Arabic Language House, Hanna Mina Cultural Library, Alwan Center, Toot Ard band, Hawa Dafi band and more recently a growing number of cinematic works. Within this 'field' we may also include publications in poetry, stories, children's literature and journalism, as well as cultural festivals, workshops in art, music and theatre; exhibitions; sculpture festivals; and countless musical and theatrical performances. It is beyond the scope of this chapter to go into details about these initiatives, but nonetheless we can draw some general observations about them.

What is interesting about these initiatives was that they were conceived not only to address the cultural needs of a growing and modernizing community but also as actions deeply rooted in the Jawlani culture of political identity. They took from al-Rabita its 1980s' spirit of volunteer work and defiance of the institutions of the colonial state. Registration as recognized civil society institutions in the Israeli Interior Ministry may have opened to them ways of receiving foreign or even Israeli state funding, but they saw this as a political and cultural taboo. Except for Bayt al-Fann and 'Uyoun Theatre, who were supported partially by a local NGO – the Arab Association for Development (AAD), established in 1991 with European civil society funding and to be discussed further – almost all of them depended on volunteering or self-funding. Not all were sustainable, even the ones who received support from AAD. Some of the musical bands were more successful than others, both in external exposure and reception and in financial durability. The cinematic field is also tied to complex networks of production and funding, and only a few individuals could make it. In the art scene, some of the successful artists had to leave for work and/or study in Europe or in Palestinian cities (Karkabi and Ibraheem 2020). In general, it might be said that individual professionals did not outgrow their local collective experiences, as much as they took it with them to new and wider networks and relevant themes. Some looked for professional opportunities within the Israeli colonial cultural field, but the focal point of the Jawlani cultural identity remained insolent and antithetical to the domination of the cultural capital of the colonial centre and its minoritized domains.

The second statue: A controversial artwork

General background

The development of the Jawlani art field coincided and was influenced by changes within the field of political identity. Sensing the limitation of volunteer work, by the late 1980s and early 1990s al-Rabita's leading activists began to think of establishing a professional body – a registered NGO – capable of raising funds and developing community services in education, culture, agriculture and health. In 1991 the Arab Association for Development was registered in the Israeli Interior Ministry with support from European civil society donors – especially the Dutch Church-based Interchurch Organization for Development and Cooperation (ICCO). This measure had two main consequences, which left an enduring impact on Jawlani politics. First, the professionalization of community was a sign of tremendous weakness in al-Rabita's vision of volunteer work and openness as a popular democratic initiative, leading to its quick dissolution into the organs of AAD. Only a few of its influential activists remained involved as either employees or members of the board of directors of AAD. The new organization played a role in supporting some of the cultural initiatives that emerged since the 1990s, but its major success was limited to developing local health services. By and large, the art and cultural scene had to grow on its own. Second, the registration of AAD as an Israeli NGO led to strong opposition by segments of the Jawlani activists, who had strong loyalty to the Baath regime. Their attitude tacitly echoed the Assad regime's ideological and hostility to civil society and Western funding. They spoke against registration as a recognition of Israeli sovereignty and viewed European funding as a form of Western imperialist influence and hegemony. This debate had a deep impact on the Jawlani political culture, leading to strong polarization and lack of unity. This polarization meant at depth that the Jawlani political culture became increasingly influenced by agendas emerging in Syria – by both the regime and the opposition – which paradoxically reaffirmed the Jawlani Syrian identity, but left its debates increasingly distant from the emerging, everyday life and structural challenges facing the community under occupation. This polarization reached breaking points with the eruption of the Syrian uprising in March 2011. The Jawlani 'national movement' split into two antagonistic camps, leaving a political void through which the Israelification project gained a significant momentum.

While the Jawlani activists were preoccupied with debate about the legitimacy of activism through registration of NGOs, and later passionately divided in their attitudes around the political identity and future of Syria, the professionalization process went on apace. Beyond politics, a professional class of doctors, dentists, engineers, teachers and tech workers had emerged, thanks largely to the acquisition of free high education in Damascus. In many ways, the quest for higher education was motivated by ideals and aspirations that had a strong mark of the Jawlani passion for political distinction and identity vis-à-vis the colonial state. But it was the Israeli market that provided the Jawlanis means of materializing their newly acquired cultural capital in higher education. Professionalization had to go through the colonial fields, necessarily impacting cultural, social and political attitudes. While education was seen as part of building an autonomous field of social life and perception, life careers blurred the boundaries of this field. It has become clear in recent years that the Israeli media is conscious about this blurring of Jawlani identity. Media coverage of stories of success of Jawlani doctors during the Covid-19 pandemic offer good example of these changes. These stories are framed as Israeli stories of success in absorbing 'minorities', or developing the 'Israeli periphery'.[3] The Syrian part of the story – these doctors studied in Syria and so forth – becomes a bundle of minor details.

Sharing these Israeli media reports on the social media, the Jawlanis most often render them proofs of the Jawlanis' pride, detaching them from politics. But the politics of such everyday life experiences is far more complex. Since 2014, Israeli-sponsored civil service projects and youth programmes began to be active, such as the 'Druze Scouts',[4] the labour Zionist 'General Federation of Working and Studying Youth',[5] and other Zionist initiatives such as the 'Benjamin de Rothschild (BR) Ambassadors Programme'[6] targeting schools in the occupied Golan in a focused manner. In their efforts to recruit the younger generation, these programmes use culture, art and sports to influence the preferences and convictions of the younger generation, to ingrain what we call the discourse of cultural minoritization. They even appropriate parts of the late poems by the Palestinian icon poet Mahmoud Darwish to make life under settler hegemony seem normal and open to the universal. This project is far from a natural reflection of changes taking place normally in people's lives. It comes in the context of an official effort by the Interior Ministry and the Defense Ministry, felt strongly in the 2010s, to pull the Palestinian youth in Israeli to national civil service, formerly regarded part of the mandatory army service, from which most of the Palestinian citizens in Israel are historically exempt (Shihadeh 2014). The Jawlani school children and youth were targeted by the same project, and it required intensive mobilization and consciousness-raising on the part of activists in various parents' committees to fight back. People involved in this struggle testify to the difficulty of following up on the plethora of ideas and projects promoted by officials to subside the rise of a clear-cut popular consensus against these projects. This reflects change not only in state policy but also in people's readiness to divert energy and time to a renewed, open political confrontation with the colonial state. It seems that the Jawlanis are now experiencing a period of subjugated life routines reminiscent of the first decade of occupation.

The statue

In June 2020, in the midst of these circumstances and complications, the unnamed artwork (a sculpture in the form of a hollow head or a mask) by Ayman Al-Halabi, who is also a graduate of the Faculty of Arts at Damascus University and one of the prominent artists in the art scene in the Golan, was installed in one of the squares of Majdal Shams (Figure 4.3). Some

FIGURE 4.3 Unnamed (2020) statue by Ayman Al-Halabi, June 2020. Courtesy of Nabih Aweidat archive.

points of comparisons with *al-Masirah* are due here, especially given that public discussion around this recent work seemed to deliberately avoid the comparison. First and foremost, in stark contrast to *al-Masirah*, this work was commissioned by the local municipal authority, thus breaking part of the Jawlani political culture. But it is also remarkable that this act seems to have been intentionally downplayed by the artist, as no inauguration ceremony was prepared and no public statement about the commission was made. Perhaps this projected some minimal sensitivity about popular sentiment, one that regarded the municipal authority as a branch of state bureaucracy responsible for basic life services, but not an agent of Jawlani identity and culture. Regardless of this hypothesis, the fate of the sculpture was decided upon by one angry young man who came at night and smashed the face's ear and nose, leaving the hammer in the place to be seen by all. Rumours about the identity of the attacker circulated, but his real intention remained vague. Sensing that his act/ message did not really pass, the attacker returned few days later, this time driving his tractor in broad daylight. Quickly, he tied the sculpture with an iron chain to the tractor and pulled it to the ground, before smashing it further with his hammer. Passers-by and security cameras in the vicinity recorded the incident. The man is known to many. One man accidently driving his car nearby stopped to intervene, but the attacker punched him in the face. The footage went viral on the local social media groups, arousing an uproar of condemnation.

The attack on the work of art, regardless of the reason, earned it legitimacy and strengthened its symbolic capital. But opinions varied. Many commentators sympathized fully with the artist, regarding the attacker as a sick man. Many interpreted his action as stemming from a backward mind and a hatred of art and civility. Some concurred that the assailant partakes of the dark ideology of ISIS (of course, no direct or remote connection to actual ISIS organization is to be assumed), calling for the involvement of the Israeli police and legal prosecution in the defence of law and order. Some went for a more vulgar rhetoric of defence of Enlightenment, suggesting in bitter sarcasm that the best punishment for such a man is to be 'mounted in place of the destroyed sculpture until the artist made a sculpture of his exact face, so to be an example that would deter others in the future'.[7] Amid these responses, the question about the real motives for the attack never found a satisfactory answer in public discussions. Perhaps, unlike what Geertz famously suggested in interpreting the semiotics of human action, intentions are not always the essential part (Geertz 1973). In contemplating social phenomena commentators perform a sort of discursive analysis in which signs can be dismantled and reassociated within fields of signification beyond the question of the apparent winks and gestures.

Aside from condemning the barbaric act, several *analytical* responses that made tacit comparisons with *al-Masirah* are worth noting here. They can be divided into two groups, one dealing with the question of how the new sculpture reflects the question of Jawlani identity and the other dealing with the legitimacy of action and appropriation of public spaces – especially representational public spaces – by the Israeli municipal authority.

The local news and advertisement website *Jawlani.com* indicated that the work expressed a 'confusion of identity'.[8] Another local website, *Ashtarr.net*, wrote that 'the work depicts the Jawlani case and expresses its painful details . . . the absence of the loved ones, the absence of the homeland, the confusion of identity.'[9] Commenting on their Facebook pages, others objected to the symbolism of the work and even cheered its destruction. They went on to say that it was a bad omen (the 'Jinx statue'), 'ugly and inexpressive of the people of the Golan', suggesting that a statue of our saint al-Khadir[10] is needed in its place.[11] One commentator condemned those who 'attacked the man who removed the depressed face statue, which lacked taste or manners', calling them 'the arrogant group' that said nothing when the statue was 'dictatorially imposed on the people'.[12] But all these comments take identity to stand for a content rather than a complex social and psychological act, which further comparison with *al-Masirah*, as we suggest in the Conclusion, may indicate.

The second set of comments occupied the least space on the social media, but nonetheless reflected deep sentiments that many Jawlanis still feel and contemplate. One of the commentators was subtle in saying: 'It is necessary to consider public opinion before erecting any statue in a public place. . . . Art is beautiful and has its place, of course, but there are many people who preferred the presence of the fountain [which was installed a few years ago by the municipal authority] over the presence of the statue.' He added: 'In the end, the town is not registered in the name of anyone, and no one can alone decide what to do with it.'[13] Another comment, more overtly critical, came from a well-known activist, Majeed Qadamani, who wrote:

> The squares in Majdal Shams and in the rest of our villages are public spaces owned by the community, and the decision about the erection of statues there or giving names to these spaces [. . .] is the legitimate right of the people themselves. The local council does not have the right to decide on this [. . .]. This point should be clear and unambiguous. Belittling people and disregarding their pride, bullying and excluding them in such public issues by the Israeli-appointed council or any authoritarian body is something that should not be tolerated.[14]

Conclusion: Two sculptures and the politics of public space

In indigenous contexts, identity is inherently about territory. *Al-Masirah* in that sense appears in a prominent public space not as a superficial fixture, not as a representation of an interesting idea or story, but rather as a symbolic mirror of the untold story of the Jawlanis and their attachment to their land. It is primarily a representation of an indigenous revolt to defend life and honour in a particular place, a representation of sovereignty of a community and its nation on its land. In that sense, *al-Masirah* functions as a representation of a higher ideal self, of the capacity and need of self-association with heroes who stood for the greatest virtues of defence of land, honour and life. Take *al-Masirah* to a square in another place, it loses completely its function in the local process of social, political and psychological identity construction. Take it to a Palestinian town it may connote resemblance to a local story, but it would not be understood the same. Take it to a settlement, it becomes a mockery of the native will to fight, a symbol of the native's defeat and plunder from the settlers' war. In other words, it functions as an organic part of the connection between the people and their land, a reflection of the story of the place and its people. Essential in this sense is not its appearance in space per se, but also its defiance of the colonial authority which regulates the lived space. It had to emerge in defiance of the local authority in order to express what it does. This has to do with a basic fact about how modern public law in general and the settler colonial notion of the public in particular work. The notion of 'public' assumes a corporate political community in the Weberian sense, that is, a social organization that extends its power and law over a given territory (Weber 1978: 910). Political community in that sense negates communities in the subaltern or indigenous sense, as a local association of moral and social power that perceives of itself in opposition to the foreign political community that occupies its territory. This community is a political community primarily in a moral sense and in a host of counter-spatial and social practices that relate to the colonial law as an exterior formality, an objective condition that reflects no direct symbolic value on the inner world of self-identification. The symbolic function of public law in that sense is to erase the local connection to the place and to install a sense of settler ownership of its meaning, past and future.

Now contrast this to the second sculpture. The 'hollow head' may, in fact, be taken to a nearby settlement or to a square in Tel Aviv, be installed there, without making a huge fuss, unless the identity of its creator is made into an issue. Public space in these locations can function as an empty homogeneous space that is owned by 'no one', given of course that this 'no one' is the other side of the settler corporate body. When abstract art is portrayed in homogenous public spaces, it reflects the quality of public space as a gallery, as a space that can be used to portray or showcase trends of art. The only mirror relation between the artwork shown in a gallery and the gallery itself has to do with the capacity of the artwork to reflect the field of aesthetics as a distinct, specialized field. This may allow us to think further about the disputed sculpture in Majdal Shams and its *political* relation to space. Interpreting the work within the context of the artistic project of the sculptor leads us to this conclusion. The mask is a theme that is repeated in the artists' previous works, both in sculpture and in painting. It seems that from an artistic point of view, when he accepted the municipality commission he had consciously or unconsciously saw an opportunity to use the gallery-quality of public space, to let his project out from his private studio to an external 'public gallery'. But this is of course a source of immense confusion given the fact that the patron of the artwork is the same authority that imposes the settler colonial notion of the public, which fundamentally eliminates the local indigenous identity of the place. Again, we must assert that symbolic actions escape the intention of their agents. Complicity with the colonial order here is not necessarily intentional but rather structural and that is what matters.

This brings us again to question of reception. Why was this structural complicity with the colonial law hard to expose expect by a few? Is this because people have indeed lost their holistic identity and acquired a fragmented or a 'Janus-like' one? Or is it because they do not see, or cannot really respond to, the inherently disputed notion of 'the public'? Some, it seems, is indeed conflated, whether intentionally or not, between modernity and colonial modernity, between abstract public space and the settler colonial appropriation of the symbolic content of the place. But if we judge from the political outlook of most Jawlani artists, we see high sensitivity and critical awareness regarding this conflation or myopia. Our assessment is also supported by the community's struggle against a wind turbine project planned to be on nearly a quarter of the agrarian land of the Jawlani community. The community is highly aware of the direct conflict between the notion of public interest and the discourse of national planning behind this project and its sense of communal good, communal well-being and right to the land (Fakher Eldin 2019). Perceptions of agrarian land and of public squares are not different in this regard. If so, why did not people made a loud outcry about the sculpture? How does identity work?

It seems to us that the answer to this question lies in the separation or absence of direct linking between the two sculptures, not simply as competing contents but as occupying different functions in identity work. This separation seems to us to reflect a distinction in the work of identity between the function of *self-association* with high ideal notions of the self (reflected by *al-Masirah*) and the function of *disassociation* from the mundane mirror-images, those fragmentations of the self in the context of the 'colonization of lifeworlds' (a thesis discussed in Chapter 2). 'Identities' of this second sense, which seems to be the reflection projected by the unnamed statue, are objectifications that need to be devalued for a sense of mastery and self-hood to emerge. Both psychologically and sociologically, not all acts have the same meaning or value in terms of identity. The fact that you may work in a settlement as a seasonal agricultural worker, for example, does not automatically determine how you perceive yourself or your social value within the community. Your worth is measured by a different symbolic order of values and virtues. The high ideal self provides the rod against which a value system is built; they are not meant to reflect everything we do, but rather allow us to put different values on acts and to contain a lot of what we do in the plane of the mundane which receives neutral if not negative value and hence is disassociated from the self. Both acts of association and disassociation are inherent to our social and psychological being, they are simultaneous rather than replacements of each other. In the context of defeat, there is always the possibility of conflating the two functions. When so radically contrasted to each other, when we stop to do things that reaffirm our ideal self, we began to be lured by possibilities of self-renewal through elevating of the mundane to the ideal. But the mundane is so imbued with reflections of power and subordination, with emptiness and lack, with angular and fragmented self-images, that it requires radical filtering. Can this radical filtering be a unifying activity again? This is the question that Jawlanis will be forced to face more openly and incisively as occupation continues unabated.

THE IDENTITY QUESTION FOR JAWLANI ARTISTS

Abdel Qader Thweib
Translated by Luay Hasan

This reflection seeks to engage with identity questions reflected in Jawlani fine art. As Nathalie Heinich contends, the sociology of art is where historical, social and political approaches intersect (Heinich 2011; Inglis and Hughson 2005). Such intersections of arts help us reflect on identity questions arising in the work of artists and allow us to deeply investigate and make sense of the art itself. What were the conditions that preceded its creation? Was it welcomed by the public? And many other essential questions to help us connect between the artist, their artistic productions and society as a whole.

Since the mid-1980s, fine art has been a new horizon for the Jawlani people, not only as a tool for resisting colonialism but also as a form of self-expression about questions of society, religion and identity. It began in 1987, when the 'Al-Masirah' ('The March') statue by Hassan Khater was installed in the centre of Majdal Shams, where it faced various Israeli obstructions and barriers to try to prevent Jawlani people from erecting it. Despite all these attempts, which included an attempt to blow it up by Israeli forces just four days after its installation,[1] the statue remains. This incident seems to have made Jawlani people aware of the great impact that art can have on the street and on the occupier.

Today, when we say 'Jawlani Art', it means a wide range of fine arts, expressive schools and styles. This reflection aims to document part of the rich Jawlani experience in fine art by explaining the way Jawlani artists have engaged with the question of identity, which is an important and complex question for the Jawlani artists who often find themselves obliged to pay attention to those Israeli cultural, academic and media institutions which seek to 'accommodate' them. Informed by interviews with four Jawlani artists – Hassan Khater,[2] Wael Tarabieh,[3] Randa

Maddah[4] and Fahad Al-Halabi,[5] – this commentary will focus on three aspects of great importance in this regard: the relationship of art itself with identity and whether there is a link between the form and content of artistic expression, while the second aspect focuses on the artist's relationship with the Israeli institution and how they see it, and the third side is a personal aspect about where the artist studies and the most important stages in their artistic life.

Hassan Khater

Hassan Khater studied at the Faculty of Fine Arts at Damascus University and graduated in 1982. He returned in 1984 to Majdal Shams and, since then, sees art as a message that he must deliver to the greatest large audience: perhaps that is why he turned to sculpture as an art seen on the streets, although his specialty was originally painting. He has participated in more than fifty sculptural exhibitions and festivals, and many of his sculptures are distributed in the squares and streets of the occupied Jawlan.

Khater's residence in the occupied Jawlan has limited his artistic options both during work and studying at Damascus University. Despite his desire to study sculpture, he decided to study painting for movement restrictions imposed by the Israeli occupation. These prevented him from bringing into the occupied Golan any art material more than two mm thick: even the paintings or photographs he completed during his studies had to have their wooden frames cut down to be allowed across the border. However, when he returned to the Jawlan after his studies, these restrictions did not stop him choosing sculpture as his specialty, although he had no basic practical means or financial support. With the help of his family in collecting clay for working on statues, he was able to accomplish his most famous work, *Al-Masirah* ('The March'), which depicts Sultan Basha Al-Atrash, the leader of the Great Syrian Revolution (see Figure 4.2). This statue is considered one of his most important works, not only on a popular level but also on an artistic level.

For Hassan Khater, art is a means of resistance not only against Israel but also against the societal values that reject women as contributors to militant action or subjects of resistance to the conditions of Jawlani life under occupation. With *Al-Masirah*, he shows the historical role played by women on the battlefield, which has made him vulnerable to criticism from some clerics, and his response was, 'Women were not just struggling, but also martyred.' He has tried to reconcile his choice of topics so as not to anger society as a whole but also not to give up the topics he wishes to embody in his works; so he chooses subjects that interest people and also speak to the past, the present and the future, notably about resistance and cultural knowledge. Hasan's choice of sculpture as an art form stems from his desire to create an ever-influential theme which forms part of the visual life of the Jawlani individual who sees the sculpture every day when they go to work, unlike paintings whose influence may not go beyond an art exhibition (Figure R4).

As for his engagement with the question of Jawlani identity, it can be concluded from his career that he belongs to the working class in practice and in thought, who in turn have interacted with his works, helping him to install them, challenging and rejecting the Israeli presence through the everyday challenge of his sculptures. When he decided to choose a site for *Al-Masirah*, he removed a cement column on which a public clock had been was put by the Israeli Bank Hapoalim, bearing the bank's name and logo, which led to his arrest. Nevertheless, the statue was successfully installed by local people (Figure R4), and he continues in his artistic career seeking to incite people of the Jawlan against the Israeli and societal authorities.

FIGURE R4 *Al-Masirah* ('The March') statue under construction, Majdal Shams, March 1987. Courtesy of Fares Al Welly archive.

Wael Tarabieh

Wael Tarabieh was born in 1968, studied at the Academy of Fine Arts–Reben Institute of Photography, Sculpture and Architecture in St Petersburg, graduating in 1996, with a major in graphic arts/linoleum printing techniques. He works mainly in the teaching of the arts at the Fateh Al Mudarris Centre for Arts and Culture, Majdal Shams, and runs the Economic, Social and Cultural Rights Programme at Al-Marsad (Arab Centre for Human Rights in the Golan Heights). He has participated in several art exhibitions in the Jawlan, Palestine and Damascus, as well as in two sculpture festivals in the Jawlan.

Wael's study at the Academy of Fine Arts in Russia had an impact on his artistic identity, as the Academy focuses on the foundations of European classical realism, and the ability to draw and photograph and understand concepts of composition in this tradition, while the use of modern art is limited to its theoretical study within the history of art, from the beginning to the middle of the twentieth century. Therefore, it can be said that Wael belongs to the realistic style in terms of artistic language, though without a strict commitment to its compositional rules. He believes that identity is reflexive in its relationship with itself and the whole complex relationships surrounding it, adding:

> I will not add anything new in this context, but I adopt that vision that sees identity in its transformative dynamics and in its multiple layers . . . and in addition to the elements of language, culture, history, psychological and social formation, class dimension and general imagination . . . and if they are indeed under permanent composition, then the physical and living condition and manifestations of the buildings of power – physical and cognitive – and the transformative phases of conflict . . . all together constitute the substance of identity and the cause of its permanent generation.[6]

Wael believes that the artistic field is an area in and on which, the dynamics of transformation, formation, destruction and restructuring are reflected. There is a conscious part of the productions of the artistic field, regularized in technical concepts and sayings, and there are other levels of unconsciousness and intuition. This combination of consciousness and intuition is what makes artistic production different from purely intellectual production. He believes that the idea of political commitment in the artistic field, specifically as stated in our Arabic literature, has some of the tyranny of the 'political' over 'intellectual' or the harnessing of 'artist' to serve 'propagandist', and he sees no need for it at all, with its clear tendencies of coercion and propaganda.

From Wael's point of view, this discourse of art as propaganda can be replaced with something simpler and closer to the inherent nature of artistic production: 'Art is either art or it is not'. This simple formulation is based on the intuition, in his opinion, that art can only be 'moral' and 'humane' – biased to the values of truth and justice, faithful to the truth and seeking to explore the excluded, the neutralized, and that which is veiled in the margins of discourse. If these intuitions are true, then every work of art is necessarily committed, committed to itself, its cause and its purpose. This is necessarily related to the meaning and content.

As to artistic form, language or formula, for Wael they are the wide and varied tools of artistic work, open to personal and taste choices and their appropriateness to the meaning. They are options and possibilities for expression which must remain open for the artist to their extent: 'The only valid question in this context is about the extent of its [art's] elitism and its ability to communicate with the recipient or recede in narrow elite circles'. He continues:

All of the above is based on a view that art should have a meaning and message and the art field should be a field of knowledge as well. It is true that the options for the Jawlani artist are limited and the temptations to join the paths of the Israeli institution are available, but I think the decision to refuse that is fundamental to the work and not marginal, because the exhibit spaces or the financing of artistic production are part of the process of its formation.[7]

Wael believes that the alternative is still possible, and considering this complexity, the Jawlani artist can remain free, as they have the gate of Palestine and its institutions and halls which form the nearest and most similar spaces and carry intersections with the Jawlan:

As an artist from the Jawlan, when you produce your artwork, you reproduce your individual identity and influence the reproduction of the collective identity. This is a great responsibility no less, if not greater, than in other fields.[8]

Randa Maddah

Randa was born in the Jawlan in 1983 and studied Fine Arts first at the Department of Sculpture at Damascus University and then at the École Nationale Supérieure des Beaux-Arts in Paris. She works in several artistic fields: painting, sculpture, cinema, video techniques and writing, and is a founding member of Fateh Al Mudarris Center for Arts and Culture in Majdal Shams. In 2018, she won a Prize for Excellence and the International Grand Prize, awarded by the Japan Takifugi Foundation, for her video 'Light Horizon' (2012), which features an actress carefully tidying up the room of a ruined house in the village of 'Ayn Fit, occupied Syrian Jawlan, which was destroyed in 1967 by the Israeli military.[9]

Randa Maddah believes that her identity has absorbed several geographical stations in its formation: it has grown, crystallized and developed from her presence in the Jawlan and then her studies in Damascus and Paris. During these stages, Randa was studying art and working to employ it in her life, and this road represents the relationship between her personal background and artistic career. She believes that the interaction of these two key components – *space/geography* and *lifestyle/language* – constitutes identity.

Accordingly, Randa identifies herself as an 'artist from the occupied Syrian Jawlan', and this first component of Randa's identification is linked to the relationship of her vision as an artist to how to deal with *Israeli space* and the Israeli occupation of the Jawlan. As for dealing with this space, as an artist, she refuses to deal or consider this space as a market for her artwork, and even when she was contacted officially and directly by Israeli actors, she refused to communicate with or be part of this space. This position is related to her vision of the Israeli presence in the Jawlan as an occupation and that Israel is a hostile state. This vision intersects with the environments in which the artist has passed through and experienced: her travel from the Jawlan to Damascus to study art, during an important period of her life, had a direct impact on this vision.

From her time in Damascus, Randa learnt that the traditional teaching of art from an academic perspective kills art: she came to see art as a question that simulates and challenges reality. In her case as an artist from the Jawlan, art raises questions about the situation in the Jawlan, about the conditions which people are experiencing because of its occupation: these questions directly suggest the organic connection of art with politics (Figure 4.1). Art is a political expression of reality, and her perception of art intersects with her relationship with the Israeli space that she refuses to interact with or be a part of it. Considering that art is a political question that must produce, for those under occupation, the expression of an act of cultural and political resistance, how, she asks, can this insurgent genre of art be displayed in the art galleries of Tel Aviv? Here artistic production and the art market are two compositions that cannot correspond to Randa's conception of art.

This perception of art was informed by the stages that Randa went through in the crystallization and development of her political identity, and here comes the second component of identity which is *the way of life and language*. Randa's family background had no direct effect on her artistic development, but also did not constrain it. She did not grow up in a family with a religious orientation that limited her interest or passion for art. Similarly, she was not in contact with her community in terms of religious issues, which made her isolated from their conservative influences. Her political awareness began to crystallize when she left the Jawlan to study in Damascus, and where she began to see how politically oriented matters affected her identity and her perception of art. Upon her return, she began to look for an artistic space that will accommodate her work, as the Israeli cultural and political space was outside her professional and personal identity: she saw Israel as an occupying state, as a racist space, and one which had caused her and her community a grave political loss.

Fahad Al-Halabi

Born in 1970 in Majdal Shams, Fahad Al-Halabi began painting before studying Fine Arts at Tel-Hai College in the Upper Galilee and completed his master's degree at the Beit Berl College School of Arts (Hamidrasha) in Tel Aviv. His artistic career began with the realistic drawing of family and social life in the Jawlan, based on his personal experiences. We observe in Fahad's works a reflection of this place-based experience; for example, his interest in painting large traditional families in the Jawlan intersects with the fact that Fahad's family consists of fifteen individuals. He also touched on the life of the construction worker, because he worked in this field, so he painted many paintings linked with the life of the construction worker, including helmets, work shoes, materials and so on. Although he first adopted a realistic style even before studying artistic techniques, he also produced abstract works and has developed through multiple techniques the conceptual aspect of his work, whether through painting, sculpture or video techniques.

The Jawlan is considered as a subject that Fahad has given a lot of attention to in his works, addressing not only social issues, such as family and work, but also the built environment. He is one of the first artists to paint the streets of the Jawlan as he documented the old buildings of Majdal Shams through his paintings, especially Majdal Shams Square, and has also addressed sectarian and religious issues. Everything Fahad has done, in one way or another, is something like a diary in which he records his struggle and his adaptation to a place and its content. He is still doing so, but now other than the Jawlan, for since 2012, he has started a new life in Germany.

Fahad's identity is linked to art and the expressive form of this art through the family context and the environment in which he lived. Both contexts worked to bring about changes and developments in his identity, in addition to the practical effects on the artist's development from difficulties in publishing his works and finding someone to represent him.

Fahad believes that identity is divided into two elements: *inherited* and *intellectual*. The first element is difficult to control and change, and is linked to the individual, his family and his religion/sect. For Fahad's artistic identity, this first element was linked to the context of his family and sectarian surroundings in the occupied Syrian Jawlan, which affected him and influenced his educational career and artistic orientation. For example, it involved a traditional education reflecting the patriarchal composition of society, where the oppression of women and the influence of religion alienated him from the Druze religious orientation. He distanced these inherited elements from his life, and also worked to reflect this effect in his works of art.

According to Fahad, the second part of identity, which is the intellectual element, changes and develops according to each age/intellectual stage of the individual. For Fahad personally, this includes influences from the German mentality and its modus operandi, as well as remnants of the influence of the Israeli identity from his exposure to Israeli spaces of experience during his education and work. This intersection was represented by rejecting the practices of the Arab environment towards the artist by not absorbing him, as is happening in Syria, Lebanon and the Gulf states. Even at the internal Palestinian level (e.g. in Ramallah), he suffered from difficulties in publishing his works and finding gallery spaces, perhaps because of his relative disconnect from the Arab cultural environment due to his presence in the Jawlan and occupied Palestine (1948 lands) during his study in Israeli universities. This made his task as an artist more difficult as most artistic circles in Palestine and Arab states culturally boycott Israel, despite the artist revealing his Syrian Arab identity and his boycott of Israeli cultural circles in recent years. All these factors and circumstances ultimately affected the political aspects of his artistic identity.

THE ROLE OF LITERATURE AND FOLK MUSIC IN RESISTING ISRAELIFICATION OF THE JAWLAN

Nadine Musallam
Translated by Luay Hasan

As in the case of colonization of Palestine and the Palestinians, appropriation was 'never limited to the land but always extended to culture, art, and even food' (Massad 2007). Folklore dance, music and cultural artefacts have been the site of cultural appropriation (Rowe 2011; Karkabi 2018) The Jawlan case shows how Israel followed the same strategy of not only appropriating land and natural resources but also subjecting the Jawlanis who remained after the 1967 war to a process of 'Israelification' that impacted all aspects of their daily life. The daily acts of Israelification included inclusion in economic life through opening job markets and the imposition of a 'Druze' educational curriculum that replaced the Syrian one (see Chapter 5). Therefore, in this reflection, I shed light on the resistance process carried out by the Jawlani people to confront Israeli policies through literature and music, to defend and protect the land and its Arab heritage, which the occupation is constantly erasing.

This chapter has two axes of reflection: the first focuses on Jawlani literature by presenting a comparison between literature before and after the occupation and how it was influenced by the reality to which it was subjected. The second axis deals with some of the musical works in the Golan Heights to clarify the effect of the reality experienced by Jawlani people on the art they produce and how music is used to resist occupation.

Jawlani literature: An extension of Syrian and Arab sensibility

Prior to the Israeli occupation of the Golan Heights, Jawlani literature was interested in describing the beauty of the natural Golan Heights where the Golan Heights found room in the ancient and modern literary memory, and perhaps the oldest historical reference of the Golan Heights is the one made by al-Nābigha al-Dhubyānī, the Arabian poet of pre-Islamic times, praising Al-Nuʿmān ibn al-Mundhir, the last Lakhmid king of Al-Hirah (Mohammed 2014: 17), in his saying:

> He led the horses, different kinds and ages, in sultry weather from the Golan Heights.

The Jawlan was also a fancy of modern writers, particularly during the Palestinian *Nakba* period in 1948, and the period of *Naksa* (setback) in 1967, when Israel occupied the Syrian Golan. Modern Arabic literature at that time entered a period of fragmentation and frustration, due to the decline of nationalist ideas, and intellectuals and writers of that period engaged in a period of comprehensive and critical reflection over pan-Arabism (Mohammed 2014: 20). After 1948, poets and writers like Abdel Majid Al-Faouri, originally from the village of Kafr Hareb in Fiq region of Quneitra governorate, reflected on the dialectical relationship between Palestine and Syria, where his first standard poem was entitled 'Palestine', published in 1956 (Talfah 2010). After 1967, the Jawlanis shared similar experiences of military occupation and settler colonialism with Palestinians. The Jawlani poet Yasser Khanjar in a poem entitled 'It Is Not Midway' addresses the issue of displacement experienced by people of the Jawlan after the Israeli occupation in 1967, sharing familiar experiences of dispossession and uprooting with their Palestinian counterparts (Khanjar 2019).

Many novels observed the conditions of the displaced people of the Golan Heights, as in the novel *Beyond a Day: Al-Zaftiya Notebooks* by Ayman al-Hasan (2011), which addresses the suffering of Jawlani refugees in 'Al-Zaftiya neighbourhood'. Al-Hasan depicts the harsh realities faced by Jawlani refugees who were forced to flee al-Jawlan, becoming strangers in their own homeland Syria. *Jawlani Stories* and the *Jawlani Diaries* are also examples of short story collection by novelist Essam Wegokh, who evokes memory of the Jawlan by describing finely its unique geography and culture.

The Jawlani poets praised the victories of the 1973 October War, including Suleiman Samara, who issued a number of poetry books, including *Between Darkness and Light* in 1983, *The Colours of the Golan Heights* in 1994, *The Clusters of Majdal Shams* in 2000 and *Golan Heights: A Message and Belonging* in the same year (Mohammed 2014: 21). In his book *Golan Heights: A Message and Belonging* (1999), Samara continues the approach he took in previous collections, in terms of preserving the original linguistic forms and words in defiance of the creeping wave of hybrid words arising from the occupation. He also adheres to the classic form of the Arabic poem within the framework of ancient poetry and the musical rhythm of his poetry collection follows both Al-Farahidy's poetic standards and Zajal – one of the traditional forms of popular (colloquial) poetry. Samara expresses in his poetry the national message of the Jawlan, its relationship with the motherland/Syria and how its people cling passionately to their land, despite the Israeli occupation and the Zionist restrictions and laws imposed on them. He also stresses the steadfastness of the Jawlani people in their struggle and their pride of their Arabism throughout history. The 'Jawlani Apple' poem by Samara is a celebration of the crop as a signifier of belonging and identity.[1]

The poets of the Golan Heights are the painful voice of the homeland

There are also several publications of the poets of the Golan Heights, such as Abdel Majid Al-Faouri, Riad Darwish, Hasan Qans, Mahmoud Mufleh al-Bakr, Wajih Badr, Yasser Khanjar and Jaber Abu Hussein, which reflect the details of the painful reality that the people of the Golan Heights are living under Israeli occupation. The Golan Heights are ever present in Jaber Abu Hussein's poems, who himself is from the village of Hadar which is situated east of Majdal Shams on the Syrian side. Abu Hussein's poetry oscillates between direct references and rhetorical allusions: among these poems are 'The Scream', 'The Necklace' and 'Our First Love'. The poem entitled 'The Golan', by the poet Essam Kamal, summarizes the position of the Jawlani people against the Israeli occupation by emphasizing the Arab and Syrian character of the Golan Heights and its rejection of all forms of Judaization practiced by Israel, including the attempted imposition of Israeli nationality and identity on the residents as a result of the 1981 annexation decision of the Israeli Knesset.[2]

When comparing the interests of writers and poets in the periods before and after the occupation of the Golan Heights, it is clear they were affected by the environment and the situation in which they lived. We find that their interests in the period before the *Naksa* were typically in celebrating the beauty of the Golan Heights and its natural manifestations, considered as part of the Syrian Arab Republic, while their poems and writings after the setback reflected the spirit of resistance, affirming the Syrian Golan Heights and the right of the Jawlani people to their lands, rejecting the occupation and the Israelification of its inhabitants.

Jawlani musical bands: Pioneering historical consciousness and the presence of the Syrian motherland

In their lyrics, Jawlani singers and bands express the reality of the people of the Golan Heights and we notice that the Israeli occupation of the Golan Heights has affected the music and songs as well as the literature. Songs in the Golan Heights before the Israeli occupation were based on traditional improvisational singing that depends on reciting poetry in spoken language, which may be in the form of a dramatic exchange between a number of zajalists. After the setback in 1967, music became a major artistic form for expressing resistance to the Israeli occupation (Karkabi and Ibraheem 2020).

The Jawlani-born Syrian artist Samih Choukair sang for the Golan Heights and was best known for the revolutionary patriotic songs he wrote and composed, including the song 'Oh, Golan Heights, who will not be humiliated'.[3] In this song, Samih Choukair emphasizes that the Golan Heights will remain part of Syria and the Jawlani people will free themselves from Israeli occupation, even if it costs them their lives. He also sings for the Israeli-occupied places of the Golan Heights, including Majdal Shams, Mas'ada, Buq'atha, Wasit, Jabal al-Sheikh, Al-Hammah, Al-Qan'aba and Ein Qiniya, emphasizing their Syrian identity and rejecting the Israeli one imposed on their residents. As Mayson Shokair writes (2021), Choukair participated for twenty years in the celebration of the Syrian independence day by standing in 'Ain al-Tineh, on the Syrian side of the border fence cutting off the occupied Golan Heights, singing the resistance song *Zaher al-Rumman* ('Pomegranate Blossom') which was released in 1990 (see Reflection 8).

When dealing with contemporary music in the Golan Heights, we should mention Jawlani bands like Hawa Dafi (Warm Breeze) and Toot Ard (Strawberries) from Majdal Shams. The bands' style is characterized by a combination of Eastern and Western music genres, such as jazz, rock, classical music, Gypsy and Reggae music, with an aim of introducing the Jawlan to the outside world (Karkabi and Ibraheem 2020). One of Hawa Dafi's songs is entitled 'The Freedom Sun'.[4] Through the lyrics of the song, the youth of the Golan Heights are encouraged to liberate their country from Israeli occupation, even by singing as a way of resisting. The significance of such contemporary bands is in their role of countering Israelification efforts on Jawlani youth, especially given the absence of an affirmation of Jawlani identity in local (Israeli municipal) cultural institutions.

There is also Nus Tuffaha (Half an Apple), a band founded by the artist Madhaa al-Maghribi, from Buq'atha in the occupied Syrian Golan. As for the name of the band, Al-Maghriby explains that the name was inspired by apples, which over time became a symbol of land-based resistance in the occupied Syrian Golan, while the band's choice of the word 'half' captures that which is unfinished – the incomplete lives of the people of the occupied Golan which is politically separated from its native Syria. Al-Mughribi also expresses the main goal of the band's launch, 'We sing because my grandmother wants to go back to her family, my friend wants to go back to his girlfriend, and my friend should display her paintings at Atassi Gallery'.[5] One of the band's songs, *Mahal Zghayer we Msakker* ('A Small and Closed Shop'), refers to the issue of the political strike and how people had to support the strike during the recent Syrian revolution against Bashar al-Assad's rule.[6]

To conclude, literature and music being produced by Jawlanis and about the Jawlan illuminate important yet distinct features of the Jawlan as an occupied geography. Karkabi and Ibraheem clearly illustrate these variations by examining Yasser Khanjar's poetry and Toot Ard's music. For the authors, Khanjar's poetry exemplifies 'a steadfast refusal . . . one that delinks from but returns to its inescapable geographies of dispossessions' (Karkabi and Ibraheem 2021: 8). Similarly, Toot Ard's music is seen as forging 'a stateless Indigenous self into the outside world' (Karkabi and Ibraheem 2020: 1), where the borders of nation states are seen as suffocating and where a global identity is the only way for Jawlanis to exist today.

Tranquility

With the disappointment of soldiers returning from their defeats
Loaded with despair and fatigue.
With the despair of widows standing on the edge of their grief
At the graves of their husbands.
With the fatigue that feeds on the breath of a child
Who runs in the valleys after a ball
Which rolls a little faster than him.
And with his sadness as he loses it.
And with the loss from which the living does not return alive.
I continue to sow the seeds of questions
In the bowels of this despondency,
At the joints of the fractures, I plant them
And proceed to the dream that I was waiting for
Not as a survivor from the clutches of fear
Nor as an addict for the despair of the victim
But it is the tranquility that drives me to
The temptation of anxiety.
There, the door has opened
Here I pass.

طمأنينة

بخيبة الجنود العائدين من هزائمهم
محمّلين باليأس والتعب.
بيأس الأرامل الواقفات على أعتاب حزنهن
عند قبور أزواجهن.
بالتعب الذي يقتات من أنفاس طفلٍ
يركض في الوديان خلف كرةٍ
تتدحرج أسرع منه قليلًا،
بحزنه وهو يفقدها،
وبالفقد الذي لا يرجع منه الحيّ حيًّا.
أواصل غرس بذور الأسئلة

في أحشاء هذا اليباس،
عند مفاصل الانكسارات أغرسها،
وأمضي إلى الحلم الذي انتظرتُ
لا ناجيًا من براثن الخوف
ولا مدمنًا يأس الضحية
لكنها الطمأنينة التي تقودني إليها
فتنة القلق.
ها إنه الباب قد انفتح
ها إنني أعبر.

YASSER KHANJAR

Translated into English by Ghareeb Iksander (2021) from Arabic poem (2020).

THE POLITICS OF JAWLANI YOUTH AND EDUCATION

FIGURE 5.1 Protest march of Jawlani school students, Majdal Shams, March 1987. (The banner reads: 'Overthrow the unfair occupation! Overthrow the traitors! Our fight in the Jawlan will continue until the occupation has finished!') Courtesy of Fares Al Welly archive.

5 ISRAELI EDUCATION POLICIES AS A TOOL FOR THE ETHNIC MANIPULATION OF THE ARAB DRUZE

AMAL AUN

Introduction

This chapter focuses on the institutionalized efforts of the Israeli government, through education policy, to create and then win over the Druze community as a 'non-Arab' ethno-religious 'minority' in support of a state defined by a Jewish national identity. I refer to *minoritization* as the tactic of separating and isolating a group to weaken them. The government's minoritization efforts in relation to the Druze, as a whole in both Israel and the Jawlan, include the labelling of their sect as a separate national entity in the State of Israel, something that is unheard of in Druze localities in Lebanon or Syria. They also included the mandatory army conscription in 1956 for Druze youth in Israel, and a separate Druze curriculum officially introduced in 1975 (Kaufman 2004).

The Israeli government has not kept its minoritization efforts of the Druze a secret. In a government reply, in June 1950, to a 'complaint letter' that included Druze signatories, the Government Office for Arab Relations explains:

The last people with a reason to complain against the state of Israel should be the Druze. Not only were they not oppressed, but they were given extraordinary rights. This was not done randomly, but with a plan and intention, which was to deepen and expand the distance between them and the Arabs among whom they live.[1]

Israel has used the school curriculum to deepen the divide between Druze identity and Arab identity. Indeed, Israel's efforts to create a separate Druze identity are part of a larger scheme to isolate each ethnic minority within the state. In 2015, for example, the Israeli Minister of Education at the time, Naftali Bennett, rejected a proposal to include a story depicting a romance between an Arab and a Jew in the state curriculum. The ministry's statement explained that there is a need to maintain 'the identity and the heritage of students in every sector', and such an intimate relationship 'threatens that separation'.[2] Alongside minoritization, I also examine such *ethnic manipulation*: how a group's collective identity is reconstructed by an external power to serve its interests. The importance of maintaining separation between minority ethnic groups and the controlling ethnic group is characteristic of Israel as an *ethnocratic* regime – a regime structured to serve the interests of a dominant ethnic group.

The Syrian Druze in the occupied Golan have had slightly different experiences and sources of influence affecting their collective identity. They have experienced over fifty years of continued militarization and occupation of their land, and many have lost their homes in the process (Halabi 1992). Their more direct and antagonistic relationship with Israel has resulted in lower degrees of assimilation with the Israeli society compared to the Druze in Israel proper. Additionally, according to Aamer Ibraheem, a Syrian activist from occupied Majdal Shams, the Syrian civil war has 'impacted every aspect of [the lives of people in the Golan]'.[3] With the eruption of war in 2011, the native inhabitants' already limited freedom to travel to Syria has been completely severed due to security concerns. Additional local resources that once provided cultural and political education, like summer camps and afterschool programmes, have also been terminated (Al-Marsad 2017). These regional political shifts, together with the imposed school curriculum and the reality of occupation, have all contributed to the unique identity changes for the Syrian Druze. In this chapter, I show how the Israeli state has replicated its approach of dealing with the Druze of

Palestine to Syrian Druze in the Jawlan, employing the same processes of minoritization and ethnic manipulation. I focus on education policy as a key instrument for this politics of minoritization of the Druze, including practices of cultural separation, historical erasure and 'de-Arabization'. Through school curricula, Israel is reconstructing a Druze identity that is ethnic in nature, and Israeli in geography and politics. Students in the occupied Syrian Golan who grow up in homes that identify as Syrian Arab go to schools learning how the borders of Israel include their ethnically 'Druze' towns and face conflicting processes of identity formation. Israel's education system does not differentiate between the Jawlan's Druze and Palestinian Druze as this would go against its intentional ethno-based divisions. They face an educational system that sees them as one unit, brought together through a newly reconstructed Druze identity.

A theory of minoritization and ethnic manipulation

Minoritization and ethnic manipulation are both characteristic of political governance in an ethnocracy. Oren Yiftachel, who has researched ethnocratic laws both in Israel and abroad, argues that an ethnocratic political system is built on two main principles: the allocation of state resources mainly according to ethnicity rather than citizenship; and the domination of public policy making according to the interests of the dominant group (Yiftachel 1997). The regime is motivated, therefore, by the moral obligation of securing the homeland for its people – for the State of Israel according to its Zionist identity, this means the 'Jewish nation'. What Yiftachel labels 'open-ethnocracies' usually face a recurring challenge to balance the dominant 'ethnos', the ethnic community in power, with the 'demos', the democratic rule of the community residing within its borders (Yiftachel and Ghanem 2004). However, according to the ideological premise of ethnocratic regimes, the 'ethnos' holds clear legal and institutional prominence as the main criterion for distributing power and resources (Kedar 2003).

Ethnocratic regimes maintain the exclusivity of religion, especially when it is reflected in cultural and linguistic boundaries. Israel, like its British predecessors, maintained the Millet system, an Ottoman heritage that allowed for religious communities to be organized and represented in front of the ruling powers according to their specific community (Karayanni 2016). The Israeli government uses this system as evidence of its pluralism and inclusiveness to this day, with Druze religious courts established in the early 1960s (Sezgin 2010). A deeper understanding of this 'tainted pluralism', as Karayanni (2016) describes it, reveals Israel's underlying objective in maintaining this system: namely, to reinforce the governing ethnocracy. Religious segregation is paramount in maintaining the hierarchy of power, especially when inter-related with ethnicity (Karayanni 2016). In Israel, it is a decision forced on the different religions by the state. Personal matters, like marriage and divorce, can only be conducted in religious, not civil, courts (Karayanni 2014). Just as the Millet system has historically been leveraged to categorize and separate colonial subjects, Israel maintains it as a tool to minoritize and segmentize the Palestinian-Arab community.

Minoritization

Minoritization can be defined as 'subordination processes and discrimination practices of particular people subjected to and excluded from dominant national entities, because of their language or [ethnic or national] origin' (Tsibiridou 2011: 295). In his book *The Emergence of Minorities in the Middle East*, referring to French Mandate Syria, Benjamin White (2011) shows how the development of 'minorities' is related to the development of nation states, facilitating the concentration of power for majority groups. Scholars have described processes of minoritization of indigenous populations in Mexico, Asians in the United States, Palestinian women and Bedouins in Israel, and Kurds in Iraq (Eqeiq 2013; Lee 2008; Shalhoub-Kevorkian 2012; Shields et al. 2005; White 2011). It is interesting to see how governments use different legal tools to implement these policies. Shields et al. (2005), for example, explain how schools in Israel and Mexico implement 'pathologization methods' as a means of minoritizing indigenous populations. Whether by demonizing local cultures, languages or habits, educational institutions aim to minoritize their indigenous populations by disconnecting them from their identity. As an extension, the Israeli government has been using both existing and new legal tools to maintain Jewish geographic, social and political control over Israel/Palestine. As I show further, the legal heritage from both the Ottomans and the British has informed the

Israeli government's ongoing efforts to control and manipulate the self-expression and ethnic identification of its minorities.

Ethnic manipulation

While minoritization refers to the tactic of separating and isolating a group to weaken them – and more easily control them – ethnic manipulation refers to the tactics employed by an external power to manipulate a group's collective identity. These tactics often coexist but are distinct concepts that influence their recipients differently. In the context of Israel, ethnic manipulation accompanies minoritization. As these new 'ethnic communities' emerge, the state works towards minoritizing them to maintain its hegemonic control.

As Ilana Kaufman (2004) notes, the scholarly dialogue around ethnicity and ethnic identity relies heavily on philosophical discussions around homogeneity, cultural boundaries, and the internal struggles for political, religious, linguistic and territorial power. Historically, colonial, post-colonial, and post-industrial states have all used tactics of ethnic manipulation for different purposes, most commonly to maintain control over native communities through the famous 'divide and rule' strategy which entails showing preferential treatment to one group over others (Kaufman 2004). Ethnic manipulation also involves state agents seizing on already-existing values within a targeted 'minority' community and using them as distinctive ethnic attributes (Brass 1991: 292), as Israel has done in treating 'loyalty to the state' as a favoured characteristic of Druze religious leaders (Khnifess 2015: 32). This process has also been named the process of 'ethnicization', as a way of moulding the identities and practices of communal groups to serve the interests of the state (Frisch 1997).

The theory around ethnic manipulation, or ethnicization, is based on an assumption of receptivity from the target community and, without this, the 'success' or 'legitimacy' of state-imposed action is limited. Specifically, Brass (1991) argues that states cannot do whatever they want in manipulating cultural symbols and practices of the culture, for any such action relies on a level of 'popular support' within the target population to have a realistic chance of success. This means that ethnocratic states cannot create minority identities out of thin air but can use their power and resources to reinforce, regroup, and accentuate certain aspects of an identity to make it exclusive and thereby separate it from the majority ethnic group.

Israeli policies towards the Druze

The Druze in Israel have officially been recognized by the Israeli government, through their government-issued identification cards, as 'Druze' by nationality (in 1956) and not just religion (in 1949) (Kaufman 2004). Regionally, this ascription of religious nationality is peculiar. In both Lebanon and Syria, Druze are considered a part of the Arab Lebanese/Syrian nation, religiously holding Druze beliefs (Bennett 1999). Their collective identity as a separate unit in Lebanon/Syria is based on religion, and not a different national identity. Due to their Muslim legacy, Druze continue to celebrate Eid Al Adha (the Islamic holiday that marks the end of the pilgrimages) to this day. It is part of their collective social and religious heritage and is actively preserved in Druze communities throughout the world. In Israel, however, Eid Al Adha is not considered an official holiday for the Druze (Newman 2018: 81). In 1969, the Israeli government actively decided to cancel the Eid from being an official holiday for the Druze and maintain it just for Muslims. Alternatively, Ziyarat Al-Nabi Shuaib (the celebratory visit to the tomb of the Druze Prophet Shuaib) has been officiated as the Druze holiday in Israel. According to the Ministry of Education, Druze holidays also include the visit to Prophet Sabalan and Prophet Al-Khader. Al-Khader's holiday has been celebrated since the 1960s only among the Druze community in Israel. Official holidays in both Syria and Lebanon exclude all three aforementioned holidays.

These policies aim at not just promoting but manufacturing a distinct Druze identity, separate from the larger Arab and Muslim one. Through institutionally disconnecting the Druze from the larger Arab world, the Israeli government proactively alters the collective memory of future Druze generations and their conceptions of a collective identity. For example, compulsory military service is a key mechanism for integrating the Druze into Israeli society. Mandatory conscription was officially implemented for all Druze men in 1967. It has greatly contributed to the development of a 'Druze-Israeli' identity within the Palestinian Arab Druze (Firro 2001). Druze religious figures resisted this enforced conscription. Sheikh Amin Tarif, the spiritual head of the Druze community until his death in 1993, threatened members of the community who joined the Israeli army with excommunication (Nisan 2010). One substantial difference between the Arab Druze in the occupied Golan and the rest of Israel is the fact that they are not required to serve in the Israeli army. This difference could possibly explain why, even when describing a process of ethnic manipulation, Syrian Druze describe a process of 'Israelification' and not 'Druzification' as if one comes before the other.

There are also distinctive legal responsibilities for Israeli education in the occupied Syrian Golan stemming from international humanitarian law. The territory is internationally recognized as an occupied territory under United Nation Security Council Resolutions 242 (1967) and 338 (1973), although Israeli law extends domestic jurisdiction to it under the 1981 Golan Heights Law. Under the Fourth Geneva Convention (Convention IV relative to the Protection of Civilian Persons in Time of War, 1949), 'The Occupying Power shall, with the cooperation of the national and local authorities, facilitate the proper working of all institutions devoted to the care and education of children' (Article 50), which means, alongside international human rights law, that local institutions should be respected (Newman 2018; Office of the High Commissioner for Human Rights 2011: 18). The Israeli government is, therefore, required to take into consideration the implementation of practical steps to advance the right to education to those in the occupied Golan. I discuss next how the educational material serves an Israelification goal, as taught to the Druze community in Israel, and as an extension, the occupied Syrian Golan. The following section analyses educational material from different stages of Druze schools (primary, middle and high school).

Education for the Arab Druze

Arab education is a victim of Israeli pluralism not only in that it is directed and managed by the majority, but it is also a tool by which the whole minority is manipulated . . . [It] is not only an example of the Israeli pluralism by which Arabs are denied power, it is also a means through which the lack of power can be maintained and perpetuated. Arab citizens are marginal, if not outsiders. . . . The Arab Education Department is directed by members of the Jewish majority, and curricula are decided upon by the authorities with little, if any, participation of Arabs. Arab participation does not exceed writing or translating books and materials according to carefully specified guidelines, nor does it extend beyond implementing the majority's policies. (Abu-Saad 2004: 111)

The current schooling system in Israel is divided into five main sectors: state, state-religious, private, Arab and Druze. While the majority of Israel's students are enrolled in state schools, many students receive education in one of the other four sectors. According to the Ministry of Foreign Affairs, this separation allows for the 'multi-cultural nature of Israel's society' to be accommodated.[4] In reality, this is a prime example of what Karayanni (2016) describes as 'tainted pluralism'. To meet these so-called multi-cultural needs, the Ministry of Education has developed and published different textbooks for different sectors, among which are history and language textbooks. While the content of the textbooks might differ from one sector to the other, the Israeli Ministry of Education explains that the purpose of the History curriculum in all sectors is to 'advance a shared responsibility towards the state of Israel'.[5]

There has been extensive academic literature and journalistic coverage exploring general inequalities in education between Arab and Jewish citizens. Inequality and discrimination between Arabs and Jews in the school system have been documented through substantial gaps in annual budgets, frequency of textbook renewal and update, and cultural and linguistic considerations and adaptability (Abu-Saad 2004; Coursen-Neff 2001). According to the education policy professor, Ismael Abu-Saad, this discrimination in education is not a result of bad policy or planning, but rather an expression of the ideological nature of the Israeli state. The 1953 Law of State Education explains that the aim of education in Israel is to 'base [it] on the values of Jewish culture' (Abu-Saad 2004: 106).

Considering these motivations and general consequences of the discriminatory education system, I reflect now on the experiences and challenges the teachers and community share as a result of these curricula. It is important to note that evidence provided is mainly the result of first-hand review of textbooks and multiple interviews with history, geography and civics teachers in Druze schools. Their names will remain confidential, as they requested.

Separate school system

Prior to 1975, the Israeli education system had only four separate sectors (state, state-religious, Arab and private). In 1974, two government committees were formed to discuss possible strategies to strengthen the Druze-Israeli relationship, with no distinction between Palestinian and Syrian Druze communities: the first committee was administered by the Knesset (Schechterman Committee) and the second was a government committee of Arab affairs (Ben-Dor Committee) (Halabi 2018; Khaizaran 2013). The recommendations of the two committees were submitted in 1975 and included, among other things, the separation of Druze schooling from the Arab community in an attempt to improve their socio-economic status and facilitate their integration in the state. The Schechterman Committee specifically recommended:

a. The creation of a Druze-Jewish intellectual committee at the Ministry of Education responsible for managing the Druze school curriculum.

b. The integration of Druze-Israeli awareness in the Druze curriculum.

c. That all teachers in Druze schools should be from the Druze community.

d. The mandatory invitation of Druze veterans and wounded Druze soldiers to give lectures at Druze schools to facilitate the integration of Druze students into the army.

e. Increasing the numbers of Druze university students in the fields of teaching and education.

The Ben-Dor Committee provided further recommendations to separate Druze schools from Arab school curriculum and administration and create and publish History, Arabic and Hebrew books specifically written to meet the aforementioned vision of separation (Khaizaran 2013).

In 2010, a case study investigating the role of Druze high schools in shaping the Israeli-Druze identity quotes the superintendent in charge of Israeli Druze education explaining:

> Our aim is to educate towards deepening the roots of Druze belonging and love of the other based on the principle of 'protecting brethren'. We strive to educate our pupils to be proud of their belonging to the Druze ethnic group and to the State of Israel, such that they will be able to declare their belonging overtly in a strong voice and take pride in their belonging. (Court and Abbas 2010: 149)

This policy indeed manifests itself, as noted below, in the material that is taught in schools, and the extracurricular activities implemented there.

The school in the previous case study is described as clean and well-kept, with images of Israeli political figures hung in the common yard (Court and Abbas 2010: 150).

The physical separation between the Druze and non-Druze Arab students based on their sectarian identity is by itself a major first step towards Druze isolation from the larger Arab community. As the Committee recommended, the teachers and staff in Druze schools are also members of the Druze community. Interactions with non-Druze Arab children and youth, therefore, have been largely limited since 1975 to Druze living in mixed villages like Shefa-Amr or Rameh. Even then, historically, different religious sects lived in different parts of the town, making communal relationships extremely limited. The separation of the schools and the creation of the separate curricula are equally geared towards increasing the sense of loyalty and assimilation that Arab Druze students have towards the State of Israel. Nation states around the world aim at increasing those feelings among their citizens. In this context, however, it is morally and legally questionable that, together with the separation, the school textbooks in different Israeli curricula overwhelmingly depict Arabs as 'hostile, deviant, cruel, immoral, and unfair' (Abu-Saad 2004: 108). These depictions in Israeli textbooks are implemented with goals of the minoritization and ethnic manipulation of Arabs in general, and the Arab Druze in particular. A former advisor of Arab affairs to the prime minister once said that '[the government's education] policy towards Arabs is to keep them illiterate . . . if they were educated, it would be difficult to rule them' (Abu-Saad 2004: 123).

The sterilization of collective memory through the school curriculum

The process of creating a collective memory for a group inherently entails the subsequent formation of boundaries with others (Sorek 2015). It is, indeed, the 'collective concept for all knowledge that directs behavior and experience in the interactive framework of a society' and one that can be strengthened and maintained through 'repeated societal practices and initiation' (Assmann 1995: 126). The collective memory here as well relates to the group's ability to replicate its image again and again, through stories, rituals, anniversaries, and public displays. Furthermore, it has the power to direct one's action both inside and outside the group.

According to Assmann (1995: 130–1), the creation of a collective identity requires the following elements:

1. The concretion of identity; that is, 'what we are' and 'what we are not'
2. The capacity to reconstruct
3. Organization as 'institutionalized communication' or representation.

The Druze collective memory, I argue, has gone through a process of 'sterilization' that prevents it from generating a natural continuity of memory incorporating the above-mentioned elements. The government has manipulated 'who they are', limited their reconstruction of memory, and enacted an isolated, institutionalized representation for the Druze. This sterilization, by definition, has not eliminated the entire collective memory, but rather carefully altered it to create one homogenous narrative that promotes the government's policies.

Within the school system, this sterilization manifested itself initially by the separation (or isolated institutionalized representation – point 3), and then by the selective reconstruction of memory for the Druze (point 2). Just as the Israeli Ministry of Education eliminated any text that includes the word 'Watan' (homeland) from Arabic textbooks during the military rule until 1966, the same government, and government policy, continued to impact the Druze minority in the 1970s.[6] In the Arabic textbooks taught in Druze high schools today, according to one Druze high school teacher interviewed, the only mention of the word 'Watan' is in reference to the Arab world post–First World War.[7] According to Khaizaran (2013), one of the most notable aspects of the Druze textbooks in both history and culture is the fact that any text that would include an allusion to the Druze connection with either Arab or Muslim heritage or culture has been left out. Additionally, Druze writers known for their Arab nationalism, such as Samih Al-Qassim, have either been eliminated from any Druze textbooks or included in a marginal, non-nationalist way. Khaizaran (2013) describes Samih Al-Qassim (1939-2014), one of the most famous writers in the Palestinian community in Israel and abroad, who happened to be Druze, as an author who was 'present by being absent from Arabic textbooks'. Following his review of the Arabic textbooks taught in Druze schools, Khaizaran argues that an author of Al-Qassim's magnitude could not simply be forgotten from Arabic textbooks in a curriculum that arguably aims at highlighting a holistic Druze culture. A simple scan of Al-Qassim's background and writing would explain how advancing knowledge about Druze authors and figures under a notion of Druze particularism distorts community. For example, in his poem 'The Gate of Tears', Al-Qassim refers to the Palestinian Nakba and its aftermath, lamenting the 'rubble of a lost, displaced people' reduced the 'lives of slaves'. Samih Al-Qassim's writing has been characterized as anti-establishment and revolutionary. He was arrested multiple times for his activism and poetry, the earliest of which was his arrest following his refusal to accept the mandatory military service for Druze youth.

The History Curriculum in Druze schools follows the same framework of selective education. The curriculum can be divided into two sections: middle and high school. While middle school history classes do not cover anything pertaining to Israel or the Druze, high school curriculum requires a minimum of thirty hours teaching about the Holocaust, five hours about the unique Druze history, including 'the integration of the Druze in Israel', and seven hours about the socio-religious fabric of the nineteenth and twentieth centuries 'Arab World'.[8] *The History of the Druze* book covers historical aspects of the Fatimid rule in Lebanon and the Levant until early contemporary Lebanon. The book does not cover modern aspects of Druze history. A Druze activist interviewed noted an exaggeration of the role of Druze figures in the history textbook, although the main controversy surrounding the curriculum pertains to what is missing from it.[9] Just as Samih Al-Qassim is missing from the language textbooks, national figures like Shakib Arslan and Sultan Basha Al-Atrash, two of the most influential Arab Druze leaders, are similarly missing from history textbooks in the current curriculum. When asked, high school history teacher E.I explained that 'they know Sultan Basha. They know him as a Druze hero, but not an Arab nationalist.'[10]

In the Civics Curriculum, the government manipulates concretion of identity – the first element of collective memory according to Assmann (1995: 130) – of the Druze community from a very young age. In the civics book for second grade entitled 'Life Together in Israel', there is a chapter about wedding ceremonies; it is divided into four categories: Jewish, Muslim, Christian, and Druze.[11] For the last three categories, wedding traditions vary minimally (beyond the presence of a priest or a Sheikh), and usually due to an urban/country divide, rather than a religious one. But in the book, the elements of the same wedding tradition are divided into three categories and (almost randomly) assigned a sect.[12] In the fourth-grade civics book, there is a chapter about 'Arab *and* Druze Citizens in Israel' (emphasis added).[13] The three-page chapter presents images of different towns and villages across the country that have people from different religions living in them.[14] These efforts of distinguishing the 'us' and 'them' are confusing for the outside readers simply because they are hollow. There is no explanation of how those two categories differ beyond the title.

This confusion is felt accordingly in the various Druze schools and communities. In an interview with a Druze educational content director, W.K. explains that her role includes creating content and overseeing its implementation across thirteen Druze villages, with over 500 Druze participants. Her observation is clear: 'we are confused' she said, 'we do not know who we are. We are in a constant state of perplexity.'[15] W.K. was not the only one. Every teacher that was interviewed for this research noted the same worrisome phenomenon. A.S., a high school history and geography teacher from Yarka, states:

> My students once asked me how I define myself. I said I am an Arab and a Druze. They then asked, 'why did you say Arab if you are a Druze?' and I had to explain that I am an Arab by nationality and a Druze by religion.[16]

According to a Human Rights Watch report on Arab Education in Israel's schools, the government devotes inadequate resources to developing the subjects necessary and unique to Arab education (Coursen-Neff 2001). When asked about the type of knowledge they pass to their students about history, culture, and the region, especially with the limited written material about the topic, high school History teachers had a common response: 'it is extremely restricted . . . there is no place for outside information or sharing our perspective on the issue.'[17] A.S. explains, 'we avoid talking about these [political] issues. We could be fired.'[18] She goes on to reveal that the principal of her high school already gave her a 'final warning' about political discussions with her students and explained that it is unacceptable.[19] In general, there seems to be a constant sense of fear from 'Big Brother' in the education system.

Geography, terminology and law

In all geography textbooks created for different elementary and middle school levels, the borders of the State of Israel include both the occupied Palestinian territories and the occupied Syrian Golan as part of Israel.

In the fourth-grade civics textbook for all Arabic speakers, occupied Buq'atha village is listed as an 'Arab village in the North of Israel close to the Syrian-Israeli borders'.[20]

In the middle school geography textbook *Israel: The Human and the Verizon* (2008), the authors briefly describe the 'significant wars' that Israel has experienced. Under the commentary on the 1967 war, the authors explain:

> The Arab countries did not recognize the state of Israel [. . .] Egypt and Syria attacked Israel. Following the 1967 war, the territory under Israeli control had expanded greatly and had come to include the Golan Heights, the West Bank, the Gaza Strip, and the Sinai Peninsula. Additionally, a part of Jerusalem has come under Israeli control ever since.[21]

Both the biased terminology and the lack of adequate information documented in geography textbooks are noteworthy. In this paragraph, the three Jewish-Israeli authors describe the war, and the subsequent occupation as an 'expansion of land control', as if more land was simply created rather than seized with military force. As recalled by a 25-year-old Syrian activist from occupied Majdal Shams: 'There was never any political knowledge in [our] schools. The word "occupation" was never mentioned. We never had the space to [. . .] identify ourselves as Syrian.'[22]

International human rights and humanitarian law requires occupying powers to actively engage the occupied communities in their own education: '[once] under the control of the enemy, in an occupied territory, [the occupied people's] proper working must be facilitated by the occupying Power and, in the last resort, should local institutions be inadequate, the occupying Power must make arrangements for the maintenance and education, if possible by persons of their own nationality, language and religion' (Office of the High Commissioner for Human Rights 2011: 18). According to the Parental Committee of Majdal Shams, since the 1967 occupation, the Israeli government has been overseeing the processes of hiring and firing principals, teachers and staff.[23] In the early years of the occupation, there were not enough qualified Syrian Arab teachers to teach in the schools, and the several testimonials describe having soldiers teach instead.[24] The Israeli state has in the past dismissed teachers and principals who did not conform to state policy regarding political matters, and multiple teachers have recently received warnings from officials about their activism.[25]

These targeted and oppressive attempts to increase the sense of loyalty of the Druze to the state are morally and legally reprehensible for communities in the Golan who live under occupation. International human rights and humanitarian law require occupying forces to respect the right to education of the communities they rule. This includes the communities' rights to culturally appropriate education that maintains the agency and role of parents in deciding on their children's education, as well as the state's responsibility in educating the students on their history, language, culture, and traditions. For communities in the occupied Golan, this includes the history of the 1967 war and consequent occupation, the illegal annexation, and Syrian cultural and traditional events. The State of Israel has continuously failed to do so, pursuing instead a strategy of reconstructing and sterilizing the collective experiences, memories, and identity of the local Syrian communities, as this strategy fits the political goals of Israelification.

Terminology is powerful. As the previous section illustrated, terminology changes realities, norms and identities. In this case, terminology impacts how residents in the occupied Syrian Golan view themselves – both in terms of ethnicity and citizenship – and how they relate to their surroundings as a whole. The United Nations Group of Experts on Geographical Names (UNGEGN) published a document in 2014 recommending the preservation of Arab geographical names against 'Judaization, changing and distortion' as part of the protection of the cultural heritage of these places (UNGEGN 2014: 11). While still arguably nationalistic in nature, such preservation would safeguard the collective memories, culture, and identity of those living under occupation in the Golan who face the systematic erasure of cultural markers of their Syrian heritage.

The effects of the Syrian war on education and identity

Beyond the school curriculum and the techniques of minoritization that the Israeli government has imposed on the Syrian Druze in the occupied Syrian Golan, there are external factors that have contributed to the shifts in cultural identities, most notably, the Syrian civil war since 2011 (see Reflection 3).

The Syrian war has created tensions in the community, with many younger members alienated from the Syrian regime. In the November 2017 issue of the Hebrew publication of *Globes Magazine*, four young Syrians from the occupied Syrian Golan are interviewed. In the interview, the author describes occupied Majdal Shams as 'Little Tel-Aviv' in its modernity and nightlife – something that distinguishes it from other Druze towns in Israel, he explains. The article describes how the Syrians in the occupied Syrian Golan have 'turned their back to Syria and are becoming more and more Israeli every passing day'. One of the Syrian males interviewed states, 'within five years, we will all be Israeli. Just wait and see.'[26]

Before the eruption of the Syrian civil war, the native residents of the occupied Syrian Golan were allowed limited visitation rights to Syria. According to the amended Nationality Law, these categories included religious Druze men, women over seventy, and students receiving education in Syria. However, in 2012, the Israeli government terminated visitations to Syria for security reasons. This had serious effects on students from the occupied Golan who had previously studied for free at Syrian universities and faced high tuition fees at Israeli universities without benefits available to many Israeli students (Al-Marsad 2017: 4–5).

Due to their physical and emotional proximity to the war, Syrian activists in the Golan also discontinued any cultural and educational activities they used to hold to provide alternative sources of education, most notably, Al-Sham summer camp (see Reflection 2). Al-Sham (meaning Levant) had operated for almost twenty years in the occupied Syrian Golan, providing an environment of cultural and educational enrichment for Arab Syrians separate from the Israeli curriculum. According to Aamer Ibraheem, who attended almost every Al-Sham summer camp since his childhood:

[Al-Sham Summer Camp] was one of most formative experiences on my identity. The Syrian flag was always there. The names of the tents were always names of destroyed Syrian villages. Every year, we would see the police come to take people who are managing the camps, especially after the second day following the [Syrian] flag rising ceremony. And we understood it was because of it.[27]

Ibraheem explains that since the Syrian war, camp activities have been terminated, and no other alternative education framework has taken its place.[28] He describes how the 'cultural and religious centre for the Druze' has shifted from Syria to other Israeli Druze towns and villages, observing that the border closure has accelerated the 'Israelification' process for the Syrian residents.[29] In Majdal Shams since 2017, one could hear a few times a month the town's announcer of local news driving around the village announcing the death of Druze elders from villages and towns around Israel. 'The connection [with the Druze in Israel] is now beyond religion', Ibraheem explains, 'now we see them as the model for our future.'[30]

Conclusion

The Israeli government follows an ethnocratic governing regime. It is a regime that prioritizes a Jewish ethnicity over the ethnicities of all other non-Jewish citizens. The maintenance of this governing system requires directed efforts to weaken the 'others' and attract allies. An old political strategy that has been used to this end is the strategy of 'divide-and-conquer'. The State of Israel has used its authority to divide and conquer non-Jewish communities across several different fields. This chapter focuses on the minoritization and ethnic manipulation of the Arab Druze in order to cause a cultural break between them and other Arabs. This has been done through imposing compulsory army service (except in the occupied Syrian Golan), labelling them as ethnically Druze, and isolating their schools and curriculum from other Arab schools in the system. The separation of the school system was implemented with the intention of strengthening Israeli-Druze relations and advancing an 'Israeli-Druze Identity'. Accordingly, the new Druze curriculum focused on Druze-specific experiences, eliminating any national Arab bonds, and filtering any historical information that may harm the goal of achieving closer Druze-Israeli ties. This policy of separation has resulted in a sense of confusion for some Druze youth about their identity. This confusion should be expected. They speak the same language as other Arabs and share history, traditions, cuisine, and religious holidays with them. The school curriculum that tries to advance this isolated identity has not provided any substantial contextual reference to the alleged differences between Arabs and Druze, thus only magnifying the confusion felt by students.

The Syrian Arab Druze in the occupied Syrian Golan have similarly experienced attempts of cultural suppression within the education system. They have voiced their great concerns about the lack of education about their occupation and history. Importantly, the inaccurate depictions of the state's geography and borders in school curricula have further manipulated their collective identity and culture. In addition to the inadequacy of the education system in the occupied Syrian Golan, the Syrian civil war has significantly contributed to the shifts in the collective identities for the people. The ending of their limited access to Syria has caused their religious and cultural centre to turn to the Palestinian Druze in Israel, further isolating them from their history and particular national traditions. The civil war has also negatively impacted local cultural activities that have been providing Syrian Arab education for generations.

As an internationally recognized occupied territory, the occupied Syrian Golan should receive the protections guaranteed in the various covenants and treaties that Israel has ratified under international humanitarian and human rights law. This includes culturally acceptable education curricula, and the community's agency in protecting its cultural heritage in schools. The State of Israel's continuous refusal to abide by its responsibilities has made it exceptionally difficult to advance such educational freedoms. It is equally challenging to hold the state accountable for its violations when the international documents do not specify the standards for educational 'acceptability' – not to mention that lack of any requirements detailing the importance of historical accuracy. Finally, the power of education is unlimited. It can create, build and empower; and it can also be used to manipulate, suppress and dominate others. This chapter has presented an example of the latter.

HOW TO COUNTER-MAP THE JAWLANI LANDS: VISUALIZING MEMORY, PLACE AND IDENTITY

Jumanah Abbas

In a video about the historical forces behind the formation of Jawlan identity, a resident of Majdal Shams describes the processes and the decisions behind the 1982 strike. Against a scene from the video documenting the crowd protesting in Sultan al-Atrash square, Sheikh Sayigh narrates that 'we [the Jawlani people] collectively decided to strike'. As the video zooms on the crowd, Sheikh Sayigh momentarily pauses but resumes with a reaffirming tone, almost unwaveringly calm, emphasizing that the strike was 'a quest for victory'. The testimony and video stills, extracted from a documentary produced by Al Jazeera, illustrate the many forms of the Israeli unlawful occupation over the Jawlan lands, and reframes political issues linked to the Jawlani identity (Al Jazeera 2009). Screenshots of men, women, young adults and children gathering at the public square are placed against a digital model of the square. The animated videos created for the *Mapping Memories of Resistance* website (http://golan1982.info) present alternative ways of learning about the history of Jawlan. This creative mix of spatial representation and archived in the animation serves not as a definitive representation of a reality and inherited memories but rather helps us to reflect on how visual representations of Jawlanis have become disconnected from their lived experience.

The animated video continues with an account by a resident in Majdal Shams, Sheikh Hassan Sabbagh, who relives moments from the six-month strike in 1982: as he recalls, 'we would go back home, we eat, then go back to the public square.' Towards the end of the animated video, there are images of a mass congregating in the public square. They are demanding liberation, expressing their rejection of the unilateral (annexation) law, throwing Israeli-issued identification cards onto the ground, and burning them. Against the montage of these images gathered from various individuals and from the depths of the internet, one resident of Majdal Shams reaffirms that Jawlan is a unique cultural and political space, a contested site that remains subject to colonial occupation. Such visual medium – an assemblage of 3D digital modelling of Sultan al-Atrash square, video stills from a documentary, urban plans of the four remaining Syrian villages in the occupied Jawlan, audio testimonies, images and videos of the 1982 strike – presents critical ways for understanding identity politics in Jawlan.

Colonial erasure and dispossession continue to unfold under different forms of visual representation, such as colonial maps and their cartographic gaze (Akerman 2017). On one hand, there are traditional cartographies that highlight the Jawlan's strategic geography, resources and geological environment. On the other are maps with reductionist views of the Golan Heights that flatten, if not completely erase, the presence of the Jawlani community. These two-dimensional cartographic views, which can be found in Israeli schoolbooks targeting primary and secondary students, proclaim false histories through cartographic neutrality. As noted in Chapter 5 by Amal Aun, these textbooks include maps of the Jawlan that wipe out the Syrian names of lands and towns, appropriate histories. In the formal and abstracted maps found in these state-authorized books circulating in local schools, the borderlands of the Jawlan are redrawn to be included within the occupied territories of the Israeli state. To that end, as Jawlani activists Aram Abu Saleh (Reflection 3) and Ali Aweidat (Reflection 7) argue, education serves colonial-state logics, notably the intended production of the Jawlani youth as compliant subjects (see also Chapter 5). All Jawlani youth living in the newly annexed lands after 1981 were made stateless first and then subjects of the Israeli state second.

In these textbooks, the reproduction of the Jawlan's spatiality and territoriality is illustrative of a colonial representation of a land excluding the Jawlani people, a territory reconstructed by the colonial authorities as devoid of the stories and the memories of the Jawlani community. Hence, Israel's 'official' mapping of Jawlan is a political practice, which is linked with cementing the settler colonial state's military occupation and official state-sanctioned narratives. But how can we leverage the powers of the cartography to counter this domination? Cartography, as a familiar form of visual representation, is enrolled in Israeli infrastructures of educational knowledge production; that is, schools, their curricula and teaching mechanism (Abbas 2020). Maps are produced by the occupation authorities to showcase the Jawlan as part of the Israeli state. Here, in this reflection, I ask, as I map stories of the Jawlani community: 'is the practice of counter-cartography a way to subvert the cartographic gaze?' Can a visualization mobilize, deploy and influence tools for learning about those under-represented communities and issues in the occupied Jawlan? And most importantly, how do we remodel and narrate stories of the Jawlan without falling into the traps of traditional cartographies?

Through conversation with scholars, activists, students and residents of the Jawlan community, my contribution takes the form of different visuals that counter-map the lands of the Jawlan. The intent is to counter the Israeli representation of land, property regimes and people. Against the settler colonial frontier imaginary, this exercise in counter-cartography begins to sketch, trace, recollect and represent the shared knowledge of the Jawlanis about their homeland. The exercise is a combination of both maps and animated videos. Colonial order is not restructured in these visuals: that is, the Jawlan is not re-territorialized through a conventional map, nor are the lands redrawn to its geo-historical boundaries in the animated videos. Instead, the visuals counter the Israeli representation of land and property regimes: they defy the formality and abstraction of the maps that normalize the occupation of the Jawlan.

For instance, addressing resource politics, one animated video found on the website is a visual response to an account written by the scholar Muna Dajani about the different forms of water infrastructure in the Jawlan. The video begins with a conversation between long-time Jawlani resident, Hayel Abu Jabal, and Muna Dajani, in which he states: 'The battle over water resources has been a longstanding battle with the occupation authorities.' The animation reconstructs scenarios, and narrates different points in history, about the development of formal and informal water infrastructure by the Jawlanis, such as the creation of water ponds, and the construction of tanks, artificial lakes, pipes and networks of pipelines. One scene shifts between aerial footage of Birket Ram and a digital scene of an agricultural landscape. Overall, the video does not present an accurate cartographic depiction of the agricultural landscape, for the land itself is denser, more lively, and populated with local crops and fauna. Instead, the viewer is drawn to the different local responses and relations against Israeli's hegemonic conquest of the Jawlani agriculture systems and economy.

In the video, the interplay between the spatial modelling, videos of Birket Ram, maps and interviews portray the incredibly creative ways in which Jawlanis countered Israel's extraction, exploitation and management of their water resources. Different forms of counter-water infrastructure 'dotted the landscape' as set forth by Dajani (Dajani and Mason 2019). Therefore, the objective was to counter-map, both figuratively and literally, these different forms of resistance against the exploitation of water resources and also confiscation of agricultural land. The animation guided by a counter-map, and informed by the testimonies of the local farmers, reflects the community's self-defined politics of care towards harvesting and preserving the land. Ways of dividing and distributing plot areas, establishing water and agricultural cooperatives, and creating local agricultural methods are all communal efforts portrayed in the animated video.

The conquest over lands and resources also extends to Jabal al-Shaykh (Mount Hermon), which strategically overlooks the territories of Syria and Lebanon. The 'Beyond Jabal al-Shaykh Resort' video begins with Abu Jabal's definition of Mount Hermon as a communal land, which the Israeli state misused the word to extend its ownership over the mountains (see Reflection 8). The video then continues with Abu Jabal's explanation of the physical alteration of Jabal al-Shaykh's landscape, the expansion of military checkpoints, the illegal construction of settler-only roads, and the normalization of the state's occupation over Jabal al-Shaykh, which all lead to refashioning and remodelling of these communal lands as a white, European resort for skiing. Images gathered by the researcher Alaa Iktash shift between aerial views of a digitally modelled mountain and the actual conditions on the ground, revealing this process of 'mimetic spatial production' (Ram 2014) – the projection of a Western leisure space – that has enabled the Israeli settler state to normalize the settler-colonization over communal lands.

At the end of the video, Abu Jabal reveals that he hasn't been to the mountains since the opening of the resort: within Hayel's recollection of the history of Mount Hermon resort is his own determination not to visit it. His oral testimony, alongside the visual illustration of the Jabal al-Sheikh's material and symbolic alteration over the years, is twofold. On one hand, there is not only the depth and breadth of the settler colonial project – the state's control over Jawlan's lands and resources – but also a normalization of colonial projects that continues till the present day. On the other hand, there is the paradoxes between the vestigial digital model of Jabal al-Shaykh/Mount Hermon in the video and the physical alternations of the landscape, the altered past and its current present reality. Both take into account many facets of resistance mobilized and exercised; whether it's through Abu Jabal's own determination not to visit the resort, or through a visual exercise that begins to counter the hegemonic settler colonial representation of Mount Hermon.

Videos are not the only medium used to counter-mapping the lands of Jawlan. A perspectival map (Figure R6.1) showing Jawlan's hilltops and valley at the background, with a constellation of public sculptures that are integral to Jawlan's urban environment, reveals layers of artistic-historical narratives addressing the Jawlani struggle. In the map, each circle is a microcosm of the four remaining Syrian towns in Jawlan, and each surrounded with positions of the sculptures that are produced by the local artists through QR codes of the sculptures' location coordinates on a Google map as a way to disrupt the staticity of a conventional map. For instance, the Jawlani artist Hassan Khater's seminal work, found in Sultan al-Atrash Square, Majdal Shams, includes figures depicting a fighter, a leader, a teacher, a mother and a child. These sculptures are visual artefacts that have asserted their visibility and significance in the spaces they occupy (see Chapter 4). That is to say, different sculptures, monuments and art pieces forge new ways of telling history for the Jawlanis. They are not a representation of history but bring forth historical moments as a central subject to the piece. Visualizing sculptures and monuments together, the map is centred on the inclusion of the local art and countering Israel's settler colonial narrative and legacies.

Another subject concerning place and memory addresses the Jawlani summer camps that took place for young people from 1985 to 1992. Against the spatial and temporal erasure from Israeli representations of the landscape, the counter-cartographic drawing rebuilds the location of summer camps, their spatial imaginary and the inherent memories. In 1985, summer camps began to operate annually and had a communal political agenda to combat the effects of Israeli-controlled educational institutions seen as unreliable, weak and corrupt. Acts of solidarity and resistance were rendered visible in the operation of these summer camps. They became alternative measures to combat the settler colonial state, as well as to resist the indoctrination strategies imposed by the occupation authorities. The drawing (Figure R6.2) visualizes the tent whereby children would learn about the history and the urban geography of the Jawlani villages, as well as the history of those expelled to Syria in 1967

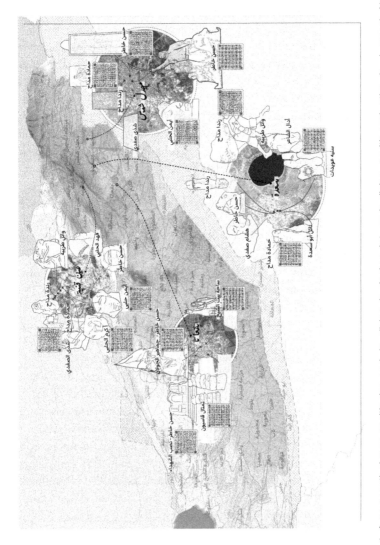

FIGURE R6.1 A perspectival map positioning and visualizing Jawlani sculptures in dialogue with each other, by Jumanah Abbas.

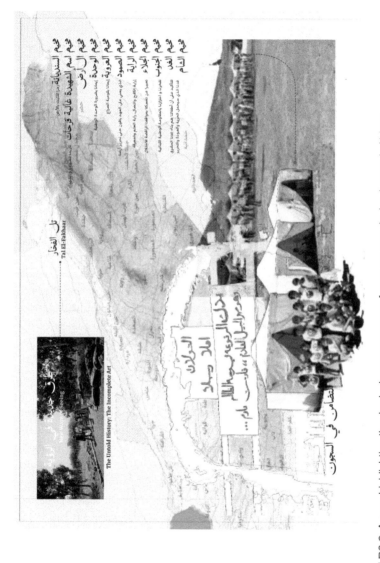

FIGURE R6.2 A map highlighting the Jawlani summer camps for young people, by Jumanah Abbas.

– the families, their roots, traditions, and sociocultural practices. On the right side of the map are the names of the camps: these names reflect certain events and their legacy, such as of the, Camp of Martyr Ghalia Farhat (*mukhaiyym asm alshahida ghālia farhāt*) and Camp of the South (*mukhaiyym aljanub*), in support of the struggles of Lebanon against the Israeli invasion in 1982. The placement of the language, alongside the spatial and temporal relocation of these camps, is a tool to re-imagine a lost space and rethink spatial representations.

In the *Mapping Memories of Resistance* website (http://golan1982.info), an interactive map visualizes the landscapes and people's knowledge of the Jawlan. The names of every destroyed Syrian village and farmland loom in the background, while different representations are illustrative of the lived experience. They form a visual and textual dictionary about the Jawlan. For instance, one drawing situates the Palestinian and Jawlani struggle in a common settler colonial experience, highlighting the shared experiences of solidarity and support recounted also by Muna Dajani, Alaa Iktash, Bassel Rizqallah and Diaaedin Horoub (Dajani et al. 2021). Another map brings to the centre of the drawing the names of agricultural roads that were built by the Jawlan community, but remain outside official Israeli cartographies. These constellations of maps form their own atlas about the Jawlan, and they speak of the human dimension of the long occupation. The drawings are purposefully multi-scalar and eccentric; they manoeuvre through the multiple histories of Jawlan. They guide you through the agricultural landscape, inform you about the arts scene in Jawlan, and teach you ways to learn about, and from, the stories of farmers, activists, artists and educators.

Theoretically speaking, how can a world-making ontology of counter-mapping the Jawlani begin to take shape? If it starts with recognizing the power relations and asymmetries of the occupation – its instrumentality and complicity in the violence of settler colonialism – then the practice of counter-cartography as a tool should not fall within colonial logics, imperial techniques and modes of knowledge (Darwish 2017: 9). Instead, counter-cartography, and the means of counter-mapping Jawlani lands, should be in alignment with emancipatory political practices, and their non-hegemonic and non-representational worldviews.

Hence, the project of counter-cartography is a critical reflection of dominant spatial imaginations. The language of the alternative spatial imaginaries of the Jawlan begin to disturb, refuse, and from there, flip hegemonic narratives and rethink spatial issues anew. Each visual intervention is not a representation of reality but offers an insight on Jawlani memories and the lived experience subject to settler colonialization. Collectively, the maps visualize how societal and political conditions shape the current reality, moving beyond the abstracted and formal cartographies of the occupying power. To map these conditions is to document, re-archive, reshare and narrate stories of shared knowledge about the Jawlan. Here, counter-mapping Jawlan is not means to an end, but mapping for a cause.

THE CONCEPT OF 'JAWLANI YOUTH': BETWEEN COLONIAL POLICIES AND SOCIETY

Ali Aweidat
Translated by Carol Khoury

This reflection is based on, and summarizes, a paper that I wrote, 'The Concept of "Jawlani Youth": Between Colonial Policies and Society',[1] in which I analyse the experiences of groups and movements under different frameworks of 'the Youth'. These groups formed and multiplied recently in the Jawlan and became prominent in the political and social arena. The motivation behind the study was the anxiety and frustration experienced by many of these groups' members, stemming from the failure to realize any of the ideals and expectations from them and intensified with the increasing influences from the Arab milieu and Arab 'youth' groups. Therefore, it was necessary to follow these ideals and narratives throughout the years and to analyse the interactions that shaped them at certain historical turning points, in order to understand more deeply these affective experiences.

In order to trace those interactions, I reviewed historical literature concerning chosen historical points in Jawlan and theoretical literature regarding the 'Youth' concept as a discursive tool in the context of the first Palestinian Intifada (Alazzeh 2020), the performativity of occupied collective identities (Ibraheem 2015) and the concept of conceptual displacement as a colonialist strategy (Ibraheem 2018). In addition, I conducted five interviews with members of the 'Jawlani Youth Movement' (*Hirak*) in June 2019 in Majdal Shams, as well as drawing on my experience as one of the founding activists of the *Hirak*.

The historical reference points chosen for their influence on the Jawlani community are the involvement of the Jawlani 'Secret Underground Cells' in the 1973 war, the popular resistance that was formed in 1981 after the colonial state [Israel] announced its decision to annex the

Jawlan, and the impact of the 2011 Syrian revolution. These historical experiences were analysed through focusing on the dialectic interaction between Jawlani communities, social-economic circumstances, and settler colonialist policies as well as 'internal' social hierarchies and oppression. The analysis traced these dialectical interactions and their roles in shaping and reshaping concepts of Jawlani youth, including deployments of 'the Youth' as a discursive subject and strategy.

The 'Youth' narrative was conceptualized to function as a discursive policing mechanism which delineates the identity category borders and the expectations of who is considered to be part of the political resistance, and who gets a 'pass' from political activism. In this way, 'the Youth' in my paper does not refer to an age-specific identity category, but as a concept intertwined with the dialectical interactions which consist of adopting, questioning or resisting hegemonic colonialist narratives and perspectives.

Finally, colonial structures and influences analysed in this paper do not only refer to a settler colonial perspective but also, and mainly, a broader framework of 'coloniality' – a set of ideals and values that dictate normative lives and experiences, and that originated in a Euro-American colonial epistemology. In this sense, whenever the colonial system is mentioned, it should be taken to include the multifaceted oppressions and systems of power, such as the Assad regime, the patriarchal cultural structures, and other colonial systems of power, in addition to the [Israeli] settler entity.

Central interactions in the shaping of the youth concept: A brief historical narrative

The concept of the Youth began to crystallize in the early days of the 1967 war, wherein people who were able to, armed themselves and participated in the popular resistance (Al Jazeera 2009). At that time, the colonial state's main focus was on completing the occupation of the physical space [terrain] of the Jawlan, as an introductory step to targeting and occupying the cultural and political space from the early 1970s. Cultural colonialism was reflected, among other things, in forcing the Syrian citizens to depend on the occupation's services and economic system, as well as changing the educational curriculum and the teaching staff to force the Jawlani citizens to depend on its schools and universities (Ashtarr News 2019; see Chapter 5).

The functioning of the 'Secret Underground Cells' in 1973 depended mainly on labourers. The members of the cells worked both in areas where the Israeli army had gathered and the already occupied territories in which the colonial state began implementing its project. At that time, the interactions between the colonial policies, the challenging socio-economic situation and Jawlani community resistance to these oppressive policies shaped the youth concept in a way that centred around the exclusionary image of the 'male worker' and symbols like personal sacrifices and struggle, an image that did not reflect many Jawlani citizens' experiences.

The next turning point was the 1982 Great Strike and the popular resistance as an alternative model to the secret cells. This turning point was characterized by widespread popular rejection and resistance that was not subject to any political affiliation or partisanship and where the 'youth' weren't considered as a body separate from society or as a segment in itself (Ashtarr News 2021). A new characteristic that was attributed to the concept of youth in that time stemmed from the 'unidentified nationality' written on the identity cards of the Syrians of the Jawlan (which is used to this day by the Jawlanis as a sign of their rejection of the occupation), which became a key marker of identity in Jawlani society. At that time, the Jawlani youth as a concept was changing to be more inclusive, popular and more rooted in people's experiences. For example, with regard to gender, we can notice that the resistance of frameworks and institutions that characterized these events was also reflected in resisting and challenging the machismo and gender hierarchical structures rooted in the definitions and the hegemonic discourses about 'youth'. However, it continued to focus on educated people as the model for 'the Youth'.

The Jawlani youth concept started shifting again in 2011, after the Syrian revolution started, this time towards popular resistance. The Syrian revolution in 2011 was chosen as one of the historical points analysed, since it is considered a revolution that radically changed the societal taken-for-granted assumptions and concepts (including the concept of 'youth') – assumptions that conflated the concepts of the regime, the homeland and patriotism (Fakher Eldin 2013). This as a result changed the power relations in society, reflected, for example, in the formation of new definitions to the concept of youth, such as rebellion against the family and the patriarchal system.

The 'Youth movement in the occupied Jawlan' (*Hirak*)

After the events of the Syrian revolution intensified, the colonial state invested heavily in the societal rupture and the identity crises forcing the local population into integrating in the 'Israeli community' and colonial projects (Al Jazeera 2012). This led to the deterioration of the cultural and political conditions of Jawlani society (specifically those who weren't dispossessed from their homes and remained in the occupied territory) at all levels, eventually reaching critical levels (Fakher Eldin 2015). At that time, a political and social void formed and limited the definition of the concept of 'the Youth' to include only a group of people of a certain age, thus stripping the concept of its politically subversive properties. At that time, the colonial state announced its decision to hold, during 2018, the first elections for local councils since the occupation of the Jawlan as a final step towards annexing the Jawlan and integrating the local population in its system. These circumstances created an urgent need to organize and confront the elections and what they represent, and all policies of Israelification and colonial projects. In that context a new group called 'Youth Movement in the Occupied Jawlan' was formed and announced its rejection of the colonial-state elections in particular, and state projects in general, and called on the public to resist and not accept the status quo.

The *Hirak* goals were to reduce the societal rupture and void and to oppose the elections. To achieve this goal, the group engaged in a debate about the points of intersection between the different streams and segments of society in order to create a unified and inclusive discourse and organizational model. This strategy was put into action through rejection and protest activities that built up momentum through the months leading up to the elections. In addition to informative content that the *Hirak* published on its social media pages,[2] it also intensified its daily presence in the streets by organizing meetings and demonstrations, including a sit-in tent in a move to reclaim presence in the public space and fill the societal void.

The identity-performative aspect: Resisting colonialism and societal patriarchy

One of the distinguishing features of the *Hirak* relative to its predecessors is the performativity of youth identity, meaning consciously referring to 'youth' in society as a sociopolitical entity, through the analysis and understanding of past experiences aiming to renew the struggle against an oppressive colonial system. The performativity of youth identity led to a societal clash during the weeks of protest. For example, at the outset of the first statement that a representative of the *Hirak* gave to a large public meeting – including clerics and other authoritative personalities – he presented the *Hirak*'s rejection of the norms imposed by gender segregation and the exclusion of women from participating in decision-making, declaring that this matter is a prerequisite for working together. That way, the events of the elections added a new dimension to the concept of youth in terms of decolonial discourse and organizing, and facing the internal challenges that society faces, in particular the patriarchal system.

The birth of a new narrative

The review of the historical experiences analysed shows that the dialectic interactions between the Jawlani community and the context that surrounds it uncovered two hegemonic and contradicting perceptions of the concept of 'youth' in the Jawlan. The first perception emanates from the varying definitions of Syrian Jawlani identity and limits the cultural and political expectations from youth to specific models and norms, through national performative practices (such as annual rituals and popular societal activities) in which the concept of 'youth' is included as the future of the liberation project. The second perception stems from the Zionist (colonial) orientalist vision and aims to erase the definitions that evolve according to the first perception, and to limit the definitions of youth to a specific 'segment' or age-group lacking any differences in class and ideological streams.

In the *Hirak*'s experience, we can see how the two perceptions flow into one discourse that understands the objective reality of these perceptions and models, denaturalizes them and thus is able to reject them. This discourse contributed to regaining the popularity of 'the

Youth' as a concept close to society and the community, moving it away from individualism and from the elitist 'educated youth' model containing patriarchal notions. This discourse and line of thought facilitates the *Hirak*'s and other resistance movements' continuity through the facilitation of members' understanding of their historical context and conditions that generate the available and hegemonic models and narratives of 'the Youth', and hence their ability to reflect upon mechanisms and ways to build different and alternative struggles, to define future goals, and to change political and social reality. In this, it helps the Jawlani people overcome their fatalism and pessimism which stems from the adoption of ready-made colonial and oppressive models and norms, and to regain hope in the future and their ability to self-determination.

Conclusions and recommendations

It is important to remember that the experience of the *Hirak* is a local one, and that any generalization drawn from it must be approached with caution and responsibility. Nevertheless, there are important lessons raised by this reflection. Above all, it is important to analyse and reflect upon the concept of 'the youth' in a broad, complex and multilayered manner, and to forego traditional and limiting lenses in our research. This requires analysing youth in the context of broader political and societal events, and especially the Syrian revolution and the discourses around it, including their impact on resistance movements and activities in the Jawlan. While Jawlani youth have been at the forefront of recent political mobilization against the settler colonial practices (e.g. campaigns against the Israeli municipal elections and wind turbines), we should not treat them as the only bearers of agency and responsibility in opposing colonialism and its projects, but rather work towards intensifying the popular rallying of civil society around their reflective yet radical concept of an inclusive resistance.

As For Me

As for me, the grass of the earth is my hair,
And my eyes are clouds.
The fingers are an awakened river,
And my mouth is a dove crossing the horizons
Searching for doves.

Wheat grew in my navel
When I walked barefoot,
A deer fell asleep on my chest,
It disappeared in the wind for a while,
Then it came back to sleep on my chest.

Be a wave or a forest,
Be arid land,
Be ashes or wreckage,
Be a claw resting in the body of dreams.

As for me, the grass of the earth is my hair,
And my eyes are clouds.

أمّا أنا

أمّا أنا.. فعُشبُ الأرضِ شَعري،
وَعَينايَ غَمام.
أصابِعي نَهرٌ أفاقَ،
وفمي يَمامٌ يَذرُعُ الآفاقَ
بَحثاً عن يَمام.

قَمحٌ نَما في سُرّتي
حينَ مَشَيتُ حافيا،
وَغَفا على صَدري غَزالٌ
غابَ في الرّيح حيناً،
ثُمّ عادَ إلى صَدري يَنام.
كُن مَوجَةً أو غابَةً،

كُن يباساً،
كُن رَماداً أو حُطام،
كُن مِخلَباً يَرتاحُ في جَسَدِ المَنام.

أمّا أنا.. فعُشبُ الأرضِ شَعري،
وَعَينَيّ غَمام.

YASSER KHANJAR

Translated into English by Ghareeb Iksander. Original Arabic poem (2014) published with the kind permission of Raya Publishing House.

SECTION V

A JAWLANI POLITICAL ECOLOGY

FIGURE 6.1 Syrian-flagged Jawlani bulldozers reclaiming land, Mas'ada, 2010. Courtesy of Fares Al Welly archive.

6 BEING IN PLACE

ON THE JAWLAN FORMATION AND THE AGROECOLOGICAL HISTORY OF HIGHLANDS

OMAR TESDELL, MUNA DAJANI AND ALAA IKTASH

Introduction

Standing at the 'top' of Palestine and towering over it, the Jawlan[1] holds a special place in the history of the Levant. While generally seen through its unique cultural history, the Jawlan is also a unique biophysical formation with human communities serving as only a part of its composition. *Hadaba* (highlands) in Arabic can also mean highland plateau. This highland gathers rains that fall upon it to feed Lake Tiberias, the Jordan River and ultimately seep into the Dead Sea where they evaporate slowly. In conventional accounts, human communities are placed at the centre of this agroecological history, yet they play a supporting role to the tremendous biodiversity made possible by the elevation, rains and other beings in the highlands. The biophysical formation as a highland has supported many generations of communities and has been a driving factor for colonization of the area for strategic purposes, yet the role of agroecological processes in that history remains unexplored. Our chapter will examine the diverse agroecological geography of the Jawlani highlands through archival sources, travel accounts and oral history. One of the central challenges of this chapter has been the dearth of sources that discuss the Jawlan as a geographical entity. Lack of sources has inspired us to draw on the experience of other areas, namely Palestine. Through a central conceptual tool, *makaneyyah*, we draw on from a Palestinian agroecological research group (Tesdell et al. 2020).

In the practice of critical geography, humans only play part of the story. In the Jawlan, for example, the volcanic landscape gives rise to plant and animal communities that circumscribe but also make possible certain forms of human habitation. Ranging from the nearly 2,000 metres in elevation above sea level on the slopes of Jabal al-Shaykh (Mount Hermon) to about 200 metres below sea level at the southernmost point on the shores of the Lake Tiberias (Sea of Galilee). Moreover, average annual rainfall amounts range from 1,400 mm to 400 mm at the southern extent. This massive agroecological range in a small area consisting of only 1,800 square kilometres provides a diverse array of microclimates, plant communities, animal communities, soil types and rainfall levels. Moreover, this physical geography is not a stable or static one, with ever-changing climatic shifts, volcanic activity, geologic activity reshaping the surface and the floral and faunal (including human) activity possible.

We propose the consideration of Jawlan as a unique agroecological highland formation. Here 'formation' relates to an Arabic term under development in a new branch of Palestinian critical geography: *makaneyyah* (Tesdell et al. 2022). While this does not directly emerge from the context of the Jawlan, we believe that the conceptual tool enables exploration of the formation of the Jawlan. The central concept we propose for the study of the landscape – *makaneyyah* – (plural, *makaneyyat*) emerges from community-based research, as well as an etymological interpretation of the root-word's origins in Semitic languages.[2]

In line with current thinking in critical geography, we understand the landscape not as a static stage but as a living process, as a *makaneyyah*. Further, it is composed not of individual components but is a formation of ecological and social relations that do not firmly separate between the human and non-human. Here there is an important distinction between formation and system. A system is something understood as governed by rules. A formation is an arrangement that is always emerging and in-formation. *Makaneyyah* comes from *makan* or 'place', ultimately from *kawn* ('being') and *kan* ('to be'). Therefore, the 'process' or *takween* puts an emphasis on the ongoing formation of the landscape's biophysical and social structure.

The Arabic 'to be' emerges from Proto-Semitic languages including Geʿez and Akkadian, meaning 'to be or to exist in place'. Here, emphasis is on being or existing, which is a living form, not a dead or fixed one. In this understanding of place, time is given priority because it is the practice of being in place that is primary to the place itself. This understanding of landscape and space stands in sharp contrast to traditional and even progressive schools in the field of geography (Blomley 2008). In the Arab world in particular, geography has struggled as a field to merge increasingly technical fields of cartography, GIS, geoinformatics with more established fields of historical or political geography, where intellectual production has slowed greatly in recent years. Rather than focus on the fixity of borders, locales, biophysical features, we explore the processes that bring those features into being. Where traditional geography seeks to fix and hold down features on the landscape, we seek to understand the process by which landscape is formed and features come into being and what roles they play. In particular, the *makaneyyah* is an arrangement of features that come together in a particular moment. Here we place an emphasis not only on space but on time as that which organizes space and brings it into being.

For the Jawlan, to be in place as a formation is to acknowledge the overlapping and unstable modes of life in a particular place. As an area with some of the earliest physical evidence of human habitation and settlement over many thousands of years of cultures, it is currently under military occupation by Israel, who severed it from Syria in 1967. From more than 100 Syrian villages comprising over 100,000 people, Israel demolished all but 4 villages and expelled all but about 7,000 people in 1967. Today more than 20,000 Israeli settlers live in 32 colonies with 23,000 Jawlani Syrians living in 5 villages. This political geography underscores the importance of deep historical excavation required to understand what both contains and opens political possibilities for the people who find themselves living under protracted military rule. Yet, at the same time, the occupation of the Jawlan has opened the area to new forms of 'being in place' or *makaneyyat*.

In this chapter, we examine the formation of the Jawlan and how Jawlanis adopted this name as part of their political identification post-1967. We pay particular attention to two manifestations of 'being in place', navigating a new Jawlan post-1967 and the ways in which the Jawlanis have reconfigured their agroecological practices to forge new political configurations to help them remain in place. Growing *tuffah al Jawlan* (apples of the Jawlan) became one such practice where a seemingly economic agricultural activity acquired political subjectivity as it became a tool through which reconfigurations of the agroecological landscape became necessary (Mason and Dajani 2019). Examining nature reserves and their colonial logic of exclusion of Jawlanis from their geography also exposes how these geographical relations were severed and how Jawlanis attempted to reclaim these connections in the face of ongoing dispossession. In the conclusion, we argue that these practices and processes come together in the formation of the Jawlan as a unique political-ecological space.

The history of the present of a name

The name 'Jawlan' was revived by the Israeli authorities based on one of the ancient names of the area. Yet the area also has many other names: Hadaba ('high plateau'); Hauran, which encompasses the basaltic volcanic plains in the eastern part of the Israeli-occupied Jawlan and stretches east nearly to Damascus; and Al Ballan, which generally refers to the southern slopes of Jabal al-Shaykh (Mount Hermon) and includes the Syrian town of Majdal Shams.

One of the first extensive systematic and academic uses of the term comes from the Syrian geographer Adib Suleiman al-Bagh. His 1956 doctoral thesis at the University of Paris explores in detail the historical geography of the Jawlan. In 1983, the volume was published in Arabic translation with the title *Jawlan: A Study in Regional Geography*, with the curious direct usage of the term 'Jawlan' from the Arabic which he attributes to a pre-Islamic Arabic term that is based on an ancient Roman term (al-Bagh 1983: 11). Al-Bagh delimits the borders of the Jawlan as the Jordan River, Lake Tiberias, Mount Hermon, which are very similar to the borders today under Israeli occupation (al-Bagh 1983: 14–15).

One of the first European scholars to posit the name 'Jawlan' is the German scholar Gottlieb Schumacher in 1888. His volume is entitled *The Jaulan: Surveyed for the German Society for the Exploration of the Holy Land* (Schumacher [1888] 2010). Schumacher was part of a group of biblical scholars and archaeologists and surveyed the area, compiling a massive index of place names and their history. Yet, the name 'Jawlan' had very little traction until it was revived by the occupying Israeli authorities in 1967. It has been since co-opted or appropriated by the people of the Jawlan themselves as a distinct identity (Fakher Eldin 2019).

A soil and topographic map of the area clearly distinguishes the basaltic soils of the eastern strip of the area, and they include dormant volcanoes and craters from the famous terra rossa and rendzina soils of the Mediterranean hill region on the slopes of Jabal al-Shaykh. Schumacher distinguishes what he calls the 'northern' and 'southern' Jawlan as, respectively, the 'stony in the northern and middle part' and 'smooth in the south and more cultivated part' (Schumacher [1888] 2010: 12). There were few olive trees or any wild native trees (terebinth, styrax and others are mentioned) due to the need for firewood according to Schumacher ([1888] 2010: 23). Moreover, wheat and other grains were grown in the southern part and pasture in the northern part. Here even Schumacher distinguishes between the 'Jaulan' and the 'slopes of Mount Hermon' ([1888] 2010: 59). Wheat was the lifeblood of peasant society in the Levant as it was in the Jawlan. In line with the entire Levant, meat and rice among other luxuries were not available in any serious way according to Schumacher ([1888] 2010: 45) and vegetables of tomato and cucumber and watermelon were grown in several villages, especially 'Ein Fit, which the author was quite taken with in general. It is there that the author also found the only valley with olive trees and in that village olive oil was produced. This stands in contrast today to the large fruit cash crop-based agroecosystem of apples and cherries in the Jawlan.

Here the importance is not to reach a 'correct' name for the area. In the modern era, colonial authorities had numerous names for the area: Ballan, Hauran, Jawlan. Various Ottoman, French and other authorities ruled from nearby areas including Al-Quneitra and other cities. Yet the people residing in this rough and hilly region also retained a certain autonomy due to their unique geographical formation. Since 1967, they appropriated the term Jawlan (area) and Jawlani (people) as their own. Here, James Scott (2009) in his reading of the difficulty of governing and ruling highland areas of Southeast Asia is instructive. He writes, 'The hills, however, are not simply a space of political resistance but also a zone of cultural refusal . . . hill populations do not generally resemble the valley society culturally, religiously, or linguistically' (Scott 2009: 20). He also notes that both the famed French geographer Braudel and Arab philosopher Ibn Khaldun also wrote on the difficulties ruling over hill regions due to the terrain, population density and difficulty of travel. Therefore, the physical

FIGURE 6.2 A view of the orchards of Majdal Shams and the Jabal al-Shaykh southern foothills, January 2021. Courtesy Wesam Sharaf.

geography of this area, which has come to be known as the Jawlan, has played and continues to play a role in the formation of its unique political and social present under occupation (Figure 6.2).

The layering and appropriation of names adds symbolic complexity to the physical landscape. 'Jawlan', appropriated from 'Golan', was adopted under the Israeli occupation, but this name was also a linguistic appropriation from the numerous previous cultures that inhabited the area. However, under Israeli occupation, the names 'Jawlan' and 'Jawlani' acquired new political valence as, against the intentions of the colonizer, they tied a geographical attachment to an oppositional political identity for those remaining Syrians living in the crucible of Israeli occupation. In this way, the land-based connections emerging from the complex, contested history of the Jawlan as geographical formation allowed the Syrian Jawlanis to forge a new spatial identity as a distinct community rooted in the physical and cultural geography of the foothills of Jabal al-Shaykh.

The question then becomes: how might we trace the agroecological history of the Jawlan from the perspective of its present colonization by Israel? This type of genealogical method made famous by Michel Foucault seeks to 'not confuse itself with a quest for origins, but rather looked to the moment of emergence of a problematic and to trace its descent through all the circuitous paths it may have taken' (Gregory et al. 2011: 270). In this way, we ask, what are the agroecological histories of the present of the Jawlan? The settler colonial present includes expulsion of its people, the destruction of their villages, the building of settlements and the imposition of the spatio-political names 'Jawlan' or 'Golan Heights' and their reappropriation by the remaining inhabitants of Jawlan. However, it also includes an agroecological present that has shaped and reshaped the current political-ecological formations found among the people of what has come to be called the Jawlan.

Agroecological transformations in pre-1967 Jawlan

The geographical location of the Syrian villages at an elevation between 600 and 1,200 metres above sea level, in addition to their position at the headwaters of the Upper Jordan Basin, necessitates agro-development that conforms to these environmental conditions. Under the Syrian government, land was mainly privately owned but while some land was parcelled and distributed to individual owners, other lands were collectively owned as a 'future reservoir for the village and its residents' (ASD 1994; Batatu 1999). Majdal Shams, among other villages in the Golan, carried out land parcellation in the early 1930s, which included a fair distribution of land to each family (mostly Druze and Christian families), according to their needs and the productivity of the land. This was later driven by the Syrian government land reforms (Barnes 2009) and resulted in a situation where most lands in the villages studied were parcelled and ownership was given to local residents. These progressive steps, compared to the feudal system limiting ownership to elite large landholders common in Palestine, secured land ownership to all families within the community and limited state encroachment on their lands and developed, according to Jawlanis, a sense of belonging and attachment to the land.[3]

With land being secured and more equally distributed among the Jawlanis, the potential increased to grow perennial crops, like fruit trees and grape trees, in addition to the traditional seasonal vegetables and grain. According to the Syrian statistics of 1966 regarding agricultural activities in the Quneitra region, most of the crops were rain-fed, with dry or rain-fed farming constituting 370,000 out of 390,000 dunums[4] (cited in Davis 1983: 284), with wheat as the dominant crop. Vegetables on the other hand, like cauliflower and other seasonal varieties, were usually planted around fresh water sources, notably local springs. In the case of Majdal Shams, decentralized collective efforts were carried out to secure water for agricultural development from the nearby springs. Birket Ram or Lake Ram, a unique volcanic pool of 5 million cubic metres capacity, was used for fishing and as a source of drinking water for livestock. These collective efforts of water management were embedded in well-established practices of communal agriculture that pre-dated Syrian rule and were respected by the Syrian state.

This was the case in and around *Marj al Ya'fouri*, the first plain to be planted with apples. Since the 1950s, the Syrian farmers of the region of Jawlan started favouring fruit trees, in particular apple trees, as the most suitable and lucrative crop for these farming communities. The 1960s were also decades of economic prosperity in the region as there was an increasing commercialization of agriculture, evident in the abandonment of growing wheat and a greater reliance on grape vineyards. While the transformation was taking place from wheat to fruit trees, vegetables and other perennial crops were still grown for subsistence purposes. In 1966, the Golan Heights as part of Quneitra province was producing a variety of crops. In the case of fruit trees, apples made up 7,970 dunums of land, constituting 18.5 per cent of total land used, with vineyards dominant at 40 per cent of the land covered by fruit trees. Social infrastructure was also established, with cooperatives and farmers' associations working closely with the Ministry of Agriculture in Damascus to enhance agricultural productivity and marketing (Mara'i and Halabi 1992).

Tuffah al Jawlan: From a lucrative crop to a trope of identity

It can be claimed that prior to 1967, Jawlanis were actively involved in shaping an agroecological landscape under autonomous conditions of resource use and management, adapting and adjusting their cropping selections and patterns based on climatic conditions, elevation and accessibility to water sources. However, the case of the apples of the Jawlan reveal how abrupt changes to their place-based necessitated transformative actions that changed their agroecology and turned apples into tropes for expressing identity.

Majdal Shams farmers were also the first to adopt apple tree planting and begin replacing pulses and seasonal vegetable growing as early as 1946. Apple trees, from Lebanese saplings, were first planted as a fruit crop under flood irrigation in Marj al Ya'fouri, diverting local spring water. Al Marj area was endowed with spring water from *Ras El Nabi'* (Head of the Spring) and therefore was the ideal location for the first orchards. Within ten years, the Jawlani apples (known until today as *Tufah Al Jawlan* – 'Apples of the Golan') were being exported to Egypt. The promise of economic prosperity from growing apples developed what Jawlanis call a *Hajmeh*, or rush to the land. Hayel Abu Jabal, a political activist and veteran farmer narrates:

> The apples have an interesting history in our area. One of the Sheikhs from our region has relatives in Lebanon. On one of his visits, he was introduced to the apple tree and saw how productive it was. He came back and explained to people about the economic value of this crop. People didn't accept this at first . . . but he was a well-known and respected sheikh, so a couple of farmers agreed to go into this venture. A couple of years later in 1950, the apple produce was ready. When people saw the production and the economic value of growing apples, there was a Hajmeh to the land. They planted a large area of land in the Marj. Everybody began planting the apples. I remember clearly in 1953 another Hajmeh, and by then half of the Marj's area was planted. By the end of the 1950s, there were more than 4,000 dunums planted with apple trees. In 1967, the area of apple orchards was 6,400 dunums, and people began considering expanding to rain-fed land.[5]

This account shows how apple growing was already developed and expanding before the Israeli occupation began in 1967 through a *Hajmeh*, a rush to the land. Reliance on springs and collective efforts to bring water to the fields further enhanced local knowledge of available waterways, especially the Sa'ar River and Jabal al-Shaykh snowmelt as a water source. The Jawlanis developed local earthen canals (later replaced by concrete channels) to divert the yearlong flows of the springs to their newly established orchards. Birket Ram was also used for the local irrigation of nearby orchards.

The two *Hajmeh* events in the 1950s reflected a genuine interest by the Jawlanis to invest in an economically profitable crop that suited their climatic conditions and their access to markets in the Arab world.[6]

However, after 1967, a third *Hajmeh* was necessary to counter settler colonial encroachment on their land. As Nazih Abu Jabal, a veteran farmer, recalls:

> Between 1968 and 1970, there was a Hajmeh to reclaim land outside Marj al Ya'fouri: the area of al Khawareet, Al Ballan, Al Qate', Al Hawakeer, the pomegranate orchards, Al Masna'. It was an extraordinary effort of land reclamation ... a strong Hajmeh. The same year that land was reclaimed it was planted with apples and peaches.[7]

This third *Hajmeh* entailed further alternation of the agroecological landscape to secure a place-based Jawlani existence and preserve a society that had become detached from its Syrian core. This transformation placed more emphasis, meaning and value to more-than-human elements such as apples. Ó Cuinn describes, after the sociologist Michel Callon, the apples of the Jawlan acting as an 'obligatory passage point' to allow Jawlanis to secure space and autonomy in their fight to remain in place (Ó Cuinn 2011: 94). Apple planting, therefore, became that entry point to secure their agroecological *makaneyyah*, albeit with compounding challenges that accompany lived experiences under settler colonial rule.

While the Jawlani communities were highly self-sufficient, they still relied economically on marketing their products regionally. Under the occupation, the marketing centres moved abruptly from Quneitra and Damascus to Tel Aviv and Haifa. Under military rule in the Jawlan (1967–81), stringent regulations regarding movement of merchandise in and out of the closed area (the Golan Heights) required a permit from the military governor. Military Order 82 on the transport of agricultural products, issued in December 1967, restricted any transport of agricultural products outside of the Golan Heights unless a permit was issued (IDF 1968). The Jawlani farmers found themselves at the heart of the Israeli agricultural marketing system and enslaved to its rules and regulations. Officially excluded from their means of production and natural resources through military orders and control, they were forcibly integrated into a Jewish-Israeli economy.[8]

Interestingly, the Jawlani collective efforts of land protection and reclamation intersected with the economic conditions and realities of the times. In order to carry out such extensive land reclamation (which was economically costly and technically challenging), machinery, funds, labour and plans were required. All these factors were available because of the economic engagements of the Jawlani with the Israeli economy, which was heavily in need of a workforce in the construction and agricultural sectors. To reclaim lands on hilly slopes, bulldozers were needed and Jawlanis involved in construction work inside Israel volunteered their machinery and time and people also began buying tractors for their personal use.

Since apples trees were the Jawlanis' priority crop, the need for additional water sources also pushed Jawlani farmers to consider small-scale infrastructure construction, such as that of rainwater tanks to irrigate this water-intensive crop, which developed throughout the decades and at present comprises of an irrigation network of pipes, pumps that the Jawlanis manage collectively. This attests that the Jawlanis, now territorially confined, articulated their indigeneity as a separate ethno-geographic community (Mason and Dajani 2019).

For the Jawlanis, apple tree planting became the material expression of a land-based political ontology, countering the systemic misrecognition materialized through displacement, dispossession and strategies of forced citizenship. Compared to historical subsistence focused on vegetables and pulses, apples have become a symbol of the Jawlan, attaching the Jawlanis to the apple crop and, via a new agroecological economy, altering what apples mean to their collective existence on the land. This agroecological transformation, which enables new forms of being in-place and on the land, illustrates how Jawlani farming is in fact a dynamic process of being in-place.

Transformation of the Jawlani landscape: Nature reserves after 1967

This section focuses on the role of nature reserves and parks in the consolidation of land control in the Jawlan and the severing of ties between the Jawlanis and their agroecological *makaneyyah*. Through examining two distinct nature reserves, the 'Banias Nature Reserve' and 'Hermon National Park', this section reveals how nature resources serve to restrict and eliminate Jawlani presence in the extended geography of the occupied and depopulated Jawlan. It also shows how reserves encroach on the limited lands where Jawlani villages and their agricultural enterprises operate today.

The Israeli government has employed many tools in different places in historical Palestine converting Palestinian lands to designated 'green areas' to expropriate the land – what has been called 'green-washing the Nakba' (Masalha 2012: 120). In that sense, nature reserves were replicated in the Jawlan as a tool to restrict accessibility and land use for the indigenous groups. This was carried out immediately following the occupation of the Jawlan as part of a mission established by the Israel Nature and Parks Authority (INPA) to discover, locate and mark potential areas for nature reserves in 1967 (Ram 2014). The military regime forced its jurisdiction over nature reserves and military orders, such as no. 11/67 was issued to conserve natural areas, giving a wide range of authorities for INPA to manage and operate lands that were occupied in the Jawlan as conservation areas (IDF 1968). On 10 November 1967, the first nature reserve was created at al-Bteha valley in the southern Jawlan. After four years of surveying the Jawlan, INPA submitted its proposal for establishing nature reserves in twenty-two sites across the region.

Banias Nature Reserve – Banias as a transformed makaneyyah

The largest waterfall in Israel is in the Nahal Hermon Nature Reserve (Banyas). Above the year-round flow of water there is a 'hanging trail', where unique remains of human legacy can be found (INPA 2021)

This INPA website quotation describes the Hermon Stream (Banias) Nature Reserve. The webpage describes the impressive natural phenomenon of Banias waterfall, dubbing it as 'the most powerful waterfall in Israel'. What the website fails to acknowledge is that Banias was a Syrian village that was occupied and demolished in 1967. The name 'Banias' derives from the karstic spring called Banias, a tributary of the Jordan River that rises from a cave in the mountain (Soffer, Rosovsky and Copaken 1999). Banias was one of 127 villages and sites that were demolished after Israeli archaeologists recommended preserving archaeological sites but to destroy any evidence of populated areas (Ram 2014).

The abrupt transformation and destruction of Banias (the village) is only one case of many sites that have undergone a process of spatial reconfiguration with an intention of destroying the Syrian agroecology.

Before 1967, Banias villagers planted different kinds of agriculture products, especially olive groves, grapes, peas and wheat (Abu Jabal 2019). After 1967, Banias became a nature reserve with tourist paths, hiking trails and archaeological sites. Its rightful owners had become refugees in Syria, some living in refugee camps in Damascus while others live in the Quneitra region and elsewhere (Kiwan 2009).

This spatial elimination not only severed relations between the original inhabitants of the village, who became refugees in Syria, but also systematically cut off the remaining Jawlanis from their previous patterns of inhabitation and living. The Banias Nature Reserve is only 5 kilometres away from the village of Ein Qiniya and around 10 kilometres from Mas'ada. While the Jawlanis who remained in their villages after the occupation are inhabiting the same geographical space, and Banias is an extension of their agroecological *makaneyyah*, their ways of farming and living in these places has been fundamentally transformed: they are only given access to these nature reserves as mere visitors. As Karameh Kanj Abu Saleh, a lawyer from Majdal Shams, explains:

> Our relationship with Banias has changed. Despite the fact that Banias was depopulated and that all its residents became refugees, we kept our relationship with the place, we used to go swimming and walking there but things were different, were don't own the place or run it, we became like visitors.[9]

Encroaching on the remaining makaneyyah: The case of 'Hermon National Park' plan

In recent years, especially since 2013, nature reserves have been increasingly used by the INPA and Israeli environment and agriculture ministries to isolate Jawlani villages and prevent their urban expansion. According to Al-Marsad, the INPA proposed the 'Hermon National Park' plan in 2013, which designates 81,802 dunums of land around Majdal Shams and 'Ein Qiniya as a national park (Al-Marsad 2018). In 2016, Al-Marsad submitted an objection to the park's plan claiming that many of the objectors (Jawlanis) have documents demonstrating private land ownership, while others have documents issued by the commission endowments of Majdal Shams that they own the land, which gives them the right to build on the land (Al-Marsad 2016). The case of Majdal Shams exposes a dilemma faced by Jawlanis whose 'existence in place' is limited due to natural and political delimitations; Majdal Shams sits on the 'border' (see Map 1.1), therefore, cutting it off from expansion to the east. To the north lies the steep slopes of Jabal al-Shaykh Mountain range and to its west lies the destroyed village of Jubbatha Ez-Zeit and the settlement of Neve Ativ (Abu Jabal 2020).[10]

Majdal Shams residents submitted a proposal for a new neighbourhood in the west part of Majdal Shams. However, the INPA opposed the plan and in November 2020 issued a court order to prevent the new neighbourhood from being built. The title of an Israeli news article reporting this case is indicative of how nature reserves are used as a tool for limiting Jawlani presence on the land: 'Winning for nature: there won't be a neighbourhood in the nature reserve of Hermon' (Ynet 2020). It reveals how nature reserves are used as objects of control by the settler state, with Jawlanis and their rightful ownership of the land disregarded. Jawlanis, however, have always designated that area as *mashaa'* (communal) land and have used it extensively for animal herding, especially the local variety of black goats. Since 2013, the INPA prevented Jawlanis from using those lands and declared it as a nature reserve.[11] The INPA's main objection to Jawlani plans for urban expansion is the 'threat' this poses to the unique ecosystem of the area, which contains 650 species of plants, including 10 species of orchids indigenous to the region (Ynet 2021).

The confinement of Jawlanis in enclaves leaves them little room to plan and manage their *makaneyyah* and compels them to prioritize tactics that will eventually erode and completely transform their agroecological system. If the new Majdal Shams project fails to overcome the hurdles mentioned above, the only option remaining for the Jawlanis is to expand on their agricultural lands. The majority of the agriculture lands consist of apple and cherry orchards that hold important significance for the Jawlanis as stated in the previous sections. However, the Jawlani agricultural sector has been facing challenges for decades due to unequal and exclusive marketing competition by Israeli settlement agro-industries and marketing monopolies, in addition to their unequal access to water and land (Dajani 2020). Jawlanis are forced yet again to transform their *makaneyyah* by building on agricultural land which for decades has served not only as a source of income generation but also as signifier of their identity and belonging.

The Jawlani struggle with nature reserves and the power dynamics of settler state institutions (like INPA and other governmental authorities) is part of an ongoing struggle not only to secure rightful access to their resources like water, housing and energy, but also for a dignified and sovereign existence in their *makaneyyah* for present and future generations. This new housing development illustrates how Jawlani people continue to develop new ways of being in their land, in such a way that secures a futurity for these communities despite the relentless settler colonial efforts to make them invisible.

Conclusion

The chapter shows how the Jawlan both emerged as an agroecological formation and how that set of plant-human-animal relations shapes the political options available to the Jawlani people. Based on interviews and archival research, we argue that when viewed through the lens of the *makaneyyah* concept, the area emerges as a complex process and formation rather than a stage upon which political events simply take place. Here we employ a new concept in Palestinian critical geography, *makaneyyah*, which aims to reveal the landscape as a living process rather than as a static stage. A *makaneyyah* is composed not of individual components but is a formation of ecological and social relations that do not firmly separate between the human and non-human.

In this way, we have shown two specific ways that the Jawlani people who remain in the Jawlan after Israeli colonization continue to develop and redevelop the Jawlan as a unique agroecological formation. First, we explored the development of new agricultural crops in the Jawlan preceding and following Israeli occupation. With specific attention to the cash-crop apple industry, we explore how agroecological shifts towards tree fruit production make new ways of 'being in place' or makaneyyat, possible. Second, we explored the ways in which nature reserves both restrict but also enable certain forms of being-in-place for Jawlani people, who conserve traditional knowledge about their land while at the same time opposing the restrictions placed upon them by the establishment of the same reserves. In this way, the reserves both curtail and enable new forms of Jawlani being-in-place for various agroecological futures. We hope that this chapter opens a new set of questions about agroecological transformation and colonization, using new conceptual tools like *makaneyyah* to document ways of agroecological being.

FROM JABAL AL-SHAYKH TO MOUNT HERMON SKI RESORT

Alaa Iktash
Translated by Carol Khoury

And your cold, O Jabal al-Shaykh
It is not the coldness, oh no, no
The coldness is in years rolling
With its diligence and bitterness
And the free soul still in shackles

ZAHER AL RUMMAN, SAMIH CHOUKAIR[1]

Every time these words and melodies play, we remember this mountain, for which the musical icon Fairouz sang, and for which Samih Choukair, the icon of protest singers, dedicated this song. It is the mountain that the Syrians were raised to love, and the Palestinians adored. In the winter they see in it the long-awaited white snow, and in the spring, as the white fragments remain only on its highest peaks, they enjoy its fresh cold water at every waterfall and stream. In summers and autumns, visitors from all walks of life make pilgrimage to it so that they savour the apples and cherries surrounding it. It is Jabal al-Shaykh (Mount Hermon), the mountain historians wrote about, geographers documented and visitors toured.

Regarded as a crucial element in attracting thousands of tourists to the northern part of the occupied Jawlan (which is locally known as the Ballan region), Jabal al-Shaykh is subject to contested, unequally weighted, narratives. There is the narrative of the owners of the land, the Jawlanis, versus the narrative of the colonizers for whom the mountain was a foothold for geopolitical control and resource exploitation. For the latter, 'Mount Hermon' (*Har Hermon*) is a landscape referenced in the Hebrew Bible, justifying the erasure of other stories and narratives. Jabal al-Shaykh has many different names. It's the 'Snow Mountain', or the 'Long Snow' as the Bedouin call it, and 'Mount Shuba' as for the Lebanese. The mountain occupies an important strategic area, be it for the altitude of its towering peaks, or for being a continuum of the eastern Lebanese mountain range, or its connectedness to Wadi al-Ajam (Carob Region) at the northern part, and to the Jawlan Plateau in the south, and the Houran Plain and Palestine to the west. Such a location made it a strategic security target, one that Israel wants to control. The mountain has four main peaks, one of which (at 2,236 metres above sea level) is located within the occupied part of the Syrian Jawlan, and is permanently controlled by the Israeli army. The lands of the mountain itself are mostly non-agricultural, thus the people of region used it for cattle grazing for years, until this practice began to disappear (in the occupied part) for many reasons, with the Israeli occupation being one of them. Jabal al-Shaykh is the principal source of freshwater for the Jawlan, serving as the main feeder for Lake Tiberias, the Jordan River and the Barada River which flows close to the Syrian capital, Damascus (Berney et al. 1994).

This reflection recovers the narrative of the owners of this stolen homeland, focusing on the development of 'Mount Hermon ski resort' – one of the first settler colonial projects to be established after the Israeli occupation of the Golan Heights. Large areas of communal land belonging to Majdal Shams were seized for this project, preventing the local owners of the land from accessing it, unless they purchased an entry ticket, just like any other 'visitor'. The reflection draws on an extended conversation with Hayel Abu Jabal, a political activist and veteran farmer from Majdal Shams, and a review of historical documents on the ski resort history.[2]

Neve Ativ settlement on the ruins of the village of Jubbatha Ez-Zeit

Established in 1971, the Neve Ativ settlement (see Map 1.2) is not a single and isolated settlement project, but part of a wider process of Jewish settler colonization in the Jawlan. What distinguishes this project is its proximity to the remaining Jawlani villages and in particular to Jabal al-Shaykh. After a number of state officials visited the mountain, a governmental body called the Hermon Authority was established to investigate the potential of developing a ski resort (Ram 2014). As Ram (2014) states, this new authority's sole focus to realize the ski resort was to demolish the Syrian village of Jubbatha Ez-Zeit. The settlement of Neve Ativ was established on the lands of Jubbatha Ez-Zeit and assigned the management of the new ski project.

Israeli government deliberations regarding settlement in Jubbatha Ez-Zeit began right after the 1967 war. During the Israeli cabinet session on 8 September 1968, new immigrants from the United States of America were approved to settle in the area of Jubbatha Ez-Zeit adjacent to Jabal al-Shaykh. The decision required coordination with the Ministry of Security, the Ministry of Agriculture and the Ministry of Immigrant Absorption. Perhaps the most prominent issue with the decision was the thirty immigrant families who insisted on settling in this particular area.[3] Since it opened in 1971, the Jabal al-Shaykh resort, 'Mount Hermon ski resort', has been managed by Neve Ativ settlement, which receives all its financial profits.[4] The utilization of the area for commercial skiing began at a small scale, alongside the creation of the settlement itself. This was followed shortly by road networks construction, although the significant expansion of the resort took place a decade later, following the unilateral decision to annex the Golan Heights and the issuing of the Golan Heights Law.

Colonizing Jabal al-Sheikh and Jawlani lived realities

In addition to the extensive investment in the ski resort, agricultural activities were prioritized for economic investment by the Settlement Division, an implementation unit of the World Zionist Organization (WZO). According to a Settlement Division document published in 1981, Neve Ativ had a population of only 100 persons controlling 1,050 dunums of land, of which 250 dunums were built on and rest was agricultural land. Apple orchards occupied 390 dunums and avocados 200 dunums. According to the same document, provision was made in the settlement's budget to expand land use, including establishing an additional 300 dunums of apple orchards, 300 dunums of avocado orchards and 60 dunums to expand tourism land use.[5] These plans for settlement expansion of Neve Ativ's agricultural lands had detrimental impacts on the Jawlanis, whose agricultural activities were already severed after the occupation, including from the loss of access to critical water sources and the abrupt disconnection from Syrian markets. As Hayel Abu Jabal recalls:

> Neve Ativ started as a tourist village built by an American Jew. The residents of Neve Ativ, just like us, relied on agriculture after they reclaimed the land of the area. By competition, they influenced us – their produce competed with ours. When their produce entered the Tel Aviv and Haifa markets, ours filled the markets of the West Bank. According to market rules: the greater the supply, the lesser the demand. The settlements' produce soon invaded all markets. The markets of the West Bank were soon closed before us, although we had good relations with people in the West Bank. But when the product tag says 'Golan', one wouldn't know any more if it is from us or from the settlements.[6]

Not only did Neve Ativ encroach on Jawlani land and contribute to stifling of the already severed Jawlani agricultural activities, it also materially cut it off from its surroundings. As the British journalist Helena Cobban reflects in a series of articles published in 1998 entitled 'Golan Days', the settlement with its Alpine-style wooden cabins on the slopes of Jabal al-Sheikh stood in stark contrast to its surroundings and cut the Jawlani villagers from free movement because of its inconvenient location by the mountain road:

> 'Neve Ativ' is the settlement closest to the ski slope. Its 'cute', stylized-Alpine-style houses cling to the south slope of Jebel al-Sheikh, and it has many guest-cabins available for summer or winter tourism. Because there is so little flat terrain up here, the settlement has been built on land that straddles the little mountain road. And if that means that the heavy iron gates at each end of the settlement are rolled closed each night for the settlers' security – why, in their view, that probably does not matter since it is 'only' the villagers of Majdal Shams just round the hill who are badly inconvenienced.[7]

She continues to reflect on how the whole settlement is built on Jubbatha Ez-Zeit's land and that part of the lodge is even built on part of the village's cemetery, in a blatant manifestation of settler colonialism's quest for elimination and replacement of the native population (Wolfe 2006). The Mount Hermon ski resort reflects Israeli efforts to normalize its military occupation of the Golan Heights by transforming 'the mountain into an "ordinary" ski resort' (Ram 2014: 737). It did so after decades of framing the Jawlan as a military war zone, denying the existence of hundreds of thriving Syrian villages and communities there and justifying the illegal occupation.

Conclusion

Jabal al-Shaykh for the Jawlanis goes further than its depiction as an Alpine-style touristic site and exposes existential struggles for Jawlanis who are severely confined in terms of their access to land. Hayel Abu Jabal talks about how lands of Jabal al-Shaykh have been subject of confrontation between the people of Majdal Shams and the Israeli occupying authorities since 1967. These confrontations have surfaced again in the last few years as Majdal Shams residents require lands to expand on for urgently needed housing projects.[8] The Jawlanis emphasize that land ownership in Jabal al-Shaykh is *mashaa'* (common property) and therefore belongs to the people of the area, whereas the occupying authorities classify it as state-land. In his own words:

> Ard mashaa' (communal land) is the kind of land that belongs to the people at large. Why mashaa'? Since it's not arable, it was made communal so it can be used for common grazing. Anyone who has animals, cattle that is, can use it. It belongs to everybody – anyone who has cows, goats, sheep. Nowadays there isn't any grazing, we are trying to make it a land for construction. We have a Waqf (Endowment) Committee that is responsible of the land in Jabal al-Sheikh. This Waqf Committee, along with the Popular Committee of Majdal Shams residents, are confronting Israel who is misusing mashaa' and consolidating the ownership of the land to the State. We say to Israel 'no!'. This land belongs to the people, and the people nowadays need it and want to construct here, and by people, I mean the people of Majdal Shams.[9]

After more than fifty years of the establishment of the ski resort, the Jawlanis relate to Jabal al-Shaykh through contrasting practices and connections. For many Jawlanis, the ski resort, while signifying land theft from its original inhabitants, has also been a source of income generation for permanent and seasonal work. Others – like Karameh Kanj Abu Saleh, a lawyer and activist from Majdal Shams – seek a different relation with Jabal al-Shaykh. Karameh organizes hiking and walking trips to discover the mountain from a different perspective to break the cultural hegemony imposed by a settler colonial state.[10]

Untitled poem

In the name of the rose that I gave to my love.
And also, because a gazelle is now running in the pasture,
And the wind carries the clouds so that it rains in my heart.
Because I call the apple tree my mother
I never knew a lover from my country
Who didn't steal a kiss in its shadow.
Because the soil is my body, and grass is my hair.
Because the trees are my eyelashes, and the river is my blood.
Because the soldiers killed my grandfather while he was guarding the field,
And because I want my daughter to be among the apple trees on the day I die.

باسم الوردة التي أهديتها لحبيبتي.
ولأن غزالة تركض الآن في المرعى،
والريح تحمل الغيم كي يمطر في قلبي.
لأني أسمّي شجرة التفاح أمّي
وما عرفت عاشقاً من بلادي،
لم يسرق قبلةً في ظلها.
لأن التراب جسمي، والعشب شعري.
لأن الأشجار رموشي، والنهر دمي.
لأن الجنود قتلوا جدّي وهو يحرس الحقل،
ولأني أريد لابنتي أن تكون بين أشجار التفاح يوم أموت.

YASSER KHANJAR
Translated into English by Ghareeb Iksander

7 CONCLUSION

THE JAWLAN AS COUNTER-GEOGRAPHY

MUNA DAJANI, MUNIR FAKHER ELDIN AND MICHAEL MASON

The enduring life of the 1981 National Document

For over half a century, the Jawlani communities remaining in the occupied Syrian Golan Heights have lived under occupation: in December 1981, with the move from military rule to Israeli civil law and administration, the territory was effectively annexed. This has not altered the position of the United Nations Security Council (Resolution 497, 1981), and the rest of the international community, which treats Israel as an occupying power and thereby subject to the obligations of international humanitarian law, including the 1949 Geneva Convention Relative to the Protection of Civilian Persons in Time of War. Most Security Council members reasserted this position in March 2019, following the unilateral decision of the United States to recognize Israel's sovereignty over the occupied Syrian Golan (United Nations Security Council 2019). However, the affirmation by Security Council members of their commitment to a rules-based international order rang hollow in the context of decades of inaction over the deepening settler colonization by Israel, with impunity, of the occupied Syrian Golan and occupied Palestinian territory. Protracted occupation has in both cases facilitated the dispossession, segregation and exclusion of indigenous Arab communities, although the ethnic cleansing of the Golan Heights is less well known than the case of Israel/Palestine.

In this volume we focus on the period since 1981, highlighting Jawlani experiences of, and reactions to, annexation. When they released the National Document in March 1981 (People in the occupied Syrian Golan 1981), the remaining Syrian communities publicly rejected the 'forceful integration' of the territory by Israel, including measures to erase their Arab Syrian nationality. As contributors to this book reveal (e.g. Chapter 3 and Reflection 1), the National Document became a wellspring for the Jawlani political imaginary in the 1980s, motivating diverse forms of non-violent resistance to annexation and strengthening solidarity with Palestinians in their struggle for national liberation. It has been revisited on multiple occasions, whether on an annual basis during the anniversary celebrations held by the Jawlanis or through recent youth activism (Reflection 7). Ties with Syria were also revived at the same time, whether opportunities in higher education in Syria or Eastern Europe, economic exchanges (particularly the export of Golan apples to Damascus), and religious and family visits. These interactions became more difficult as Israel tightened border restrictions: they completely collapsed when the Syrian civil war broke out in March 2011, exposing divisions within the Jawlani communities over loyalty to the regime of Bashar al-Assad. From 2015, the destabilizing effects of this long, bloody conflict on the Jawlanis encouraged the Israeli right-wing Zionist government to seek to consolidate the 'normalization' of the Golan through economic development plans and the imposition of municipal elections to the four annexed Syrian villages (instead of the Israeli Interior Ministry directly appointing mayors and councillors in these villages).

The election of Donald Trump as US president gave a major boost to this normalization project when he signed the presidential proclamation on 25 March 2019 recognizing Israeli sovereignty of the Golan Heights. Netanyahu expressed his thanks by announcing a new Jewish settlement in the northern Golan to be named 'Trump Heights' (Ramat Trump). However, plans to turn the Jawlanis into a 'permanent minority' within the occupied Syrian Golan Heights corresponded with a new wave of protests: the contributions to this volume convey the diverse forms of insurgent politics and cultural expression articulating visions of Jawlani self-determination. Recent oppositional activity has included the boycotting of the municipal elections in 2018, protests against multinational companies (sanctioned by the state) siting wind turbines on Jawlani land, and cultural efforts to resist linguistic assimilation to Hebrew-dominated media. The National Document remains a political touchstone: in a coincidence of history beyond his grasp, Trump signed the presidential proclamation on Israeli sovereignty over the Golan Heights on the 38th anniversary of the signing of the National Document by the Syrian citizens in the occupied Golan Heights. The Golan Youth Movement seized on this coincidence to release on Facebook a digitally manipulated image, replacing the proclamation in Trump's hands with the 1981 National Document, received with happy applause by Benjamin Netanyahu and David Friedman, US ambassador to Israel (Figure 7.1). In this imagined alternative universe, the ceremonial erasure of the occupied Jawlan by the supreme wielders of military power morphs into their celebration of Syrian Arab identity. Such deft acts of satire on social media are characteristic of younger Jawlani activists, opening up new channels of political communication and mobilization.

In this Conclusion, we consider further the idea of the Jawlan as a *counter-geography*; that is, the imaginative construction of an ethno-geographic community that contests or even bypasses spatial Judaization

FIGURE 7.1 Donald Trump 'presents' the 1981 National Document of the People of the occupied Syrian Golan. Digitally manipulated image, Golan Youth Movement, 26 March 2019. Courtesy of the Golan Youth Movement.

and other power effects of the Israeli occupation. What does it mean to represent such a counter-geography – both to depict the lived experiences and aspirations of the Jawlanis, and to imagine the social, political and ecological conditions of possibility for a just future? Informed by the contributions to the book, we offer preliminary comments that are properly part of a much wider political conversation about Jawlani (and Palestinian) futures for those living under settler colonialism. To do so, we first revisit the central conceptual themes of the book – *everyday colonization* and the *politics of the governed* – to offer analytical conclusions that advance a critical understanding of the effects of, and political reactions to, settler colonialism. We then discuss a *counter-cartography* of the Jawlan (supplementing the counter-maps presented in Reflection 6) as emblematic of the imaginative work possible to sketch a decolonial future.

Everyday colonization in the occupied Jawlan

From the comparative perspective of settler colonial studies, Israeli settler colonialism has several historical parallels with the creation of European settler societies across 'New World' contexts. In these terms, settler colonization is a social formation founded on the control of land, which is realized coercively by the dispossession and displacement of indigenous inhabitants. Settler colonialism's irreducible element, according to Patrick Wolfe, is this territoriality, whatever the racial, religious and civilizational grammars enrolled to legitimate its practice (2006: 388). Not surprisingly, many critical studies of Israeli settler colonialism have focused on the multiple modes by which land is appropriated, confiscated, segregated, militarized and otherwise controlled by the settler state (e.g. Makdisi 2008; McKee 2016; Weizman 2007). The territorial expansion of Zionist settler colonialism operates through an expansive and intricate spatial Judaization that uproots the land-based ties of the non-Jewish native, yet at the same time uses the perceived threat of this repressed Arab 'other' to maintain emergency laws and other measures justifying a securitized state. While Palestinians living in Gaza and the West Bank often experience the full force of this security apparatus, the institutionalized discrimination also faced by 1948 Palestinians (Palestinians with Israeli citizenship) over access to land and other resources exposes the structural inequality of Israel as a Jewish settler state. As shown throughout this book, land-based and other injustices against non-Jewish inhabitants are replicated in the occupied Jawlan.

Chapter 2 applies the thesis of lifeworld colonization, formulated within European critical theory, to Israeli settler colonialism in the occupied Syrian Golan. As discussed in the chapter, lifeworld colonization posits that major pathologies experienced in everyday lives as a loss of meaning and/or lack of autonomy are a systemic result of runaway capitalism (commodification) and state authority (bureaucratization): in other words, expanding structures of economic and political power overwhelm the world of lived experiences. A key motivation for this analytical framing was to consider settler colonial processes in relation to the wider circuits of production and liberal rule associated with Western capitalist states – a model of statehood that informs the self-representation of Israel as the 'only liberal democracy' in the Middle East. While Israel has in recent decades embraced an export-oriented neoliberalism and continues to affirm a rights-based culture, this official narrative is sharply contradicted by the protracted regime of occupation in the Golan Heights, which was intensified by the normalization of Israeli rule after the 1981 annexation. Israeli settler colonialism in the occupied Syrian Golan has employed state-driven market and political logics that deracinate Jawlani lifeworlds in a manner that would be unrecognizable to a European citizen. However, even applied only to Europe, a theory of lifeworld colonization that does not register the after-effects of settler colonial violence would be analytically blind; for European capitalism, like North American capitalism, was founded on extractivist colonial economies displacing and eliminating indigenous peoples, and the concentrations of wealth and power generated historically by these activities still deform the lives and life opportunities of entire populations.

Everyday colonization invites scrutiny of the daily experiences of Israeli occupation, as manifest in Jawlani society, culture and ecologies, in a way that acknowledges settler colonialism as an *unexceptional* variant of the constitutive violence of capitalist market relations – a variant that, historically, typically begins from a destructive baseline of ethnic cleansing and primitive accumulation. This conceptual shift disrupts the provincial, largely metaphoric use of 'lifeworld colonization' as applied by Habermas and others to the objectifying effects of late European capitalism, instead opening up analytical space for a more comprehensive account of the violence of settler colonialism, both its material and symbolic harm. The Zionist settler colonial doctrine of *terra nullius* (land belonging to no one) justifies the return to the land of Israel an exiled Jewish people by denying indigenous Arab populations an authentic history and territory. Terra nullius informs ethno-racial processes of land dispossession and social segregation that, alongside material uprooting, assault the inner sense of belonging of populations living with belligerent occupation. The principal symbolic violence of Israeli settler colonialism in the occupied Syrian Golan Heights is thus the social reproduction of a dominant reality that attempts to strip the Jawlanis of their historical-geographic memory and their Syrian Arab identity, while constructing a non-Arab Druze nationality – as the Druze in Israel are recognized (Firro 1988: 196). At the same time, through capital investment (e.g. in green energy) and the spread of Israeli culture (e.g. Hebrew social media), that dominant reality promises material and psychological rewards for those who embrace it, sowing generational and other social divisions throughout Jawlani communities.

Lifeworlds of everyday experience and meaning are more-than-human: they are enmeshed in, and sustained by, numerous biophysical processes. In its dispossession and displacement of indigenous peoples, Israeli settler colonialism also radically transforms native landscapes and ecologies, remaking nature in its own civilizational image (Braverman 2014; Salih and Corry 2022). The damage to indigenous lifeworlds wrought by settler colonial violence in the Jawlan is *biopolitical* in the sense that the settler state forecloses the survival and flourishing of socio-ecological communities incompatible with Zionism. The comprehensive erasure, in 1967, of a Syrian terrain of villages and farms, followed by comprehensive land expropriation, created a geographical palimpsest for Jewish settlements, agricultural use and extensive military zones. Settler landscapes in the north bear little resemblance to the pre-1967 Jawlan and its highland plateau agroecology (Chapter 6), whether they feature capital-intensive, state-supported settlement agriculture (commercial fruit orchards and large livestock ranches) or the production of Alpine ski resort experiences (Mount Hermon ski resort and Neve Ativ settlement). They also produce 'wild natures', whether Jewish National Fund forests or nature reserves showcasing 'biblical' animals, such as the Nubian ibex. These settler ecologies serve to naturalize occupation, masking its injustices – past and present – of resource dispossession and the elimination of other forms of life.

The colonization of everyday lifeworlds moves through and beyond their immediate affective settings to the wider *hydrological* and *geophysical* fields within which they occur. A geostrategic driver for continued Israeli occupation of the Golan Heights is that it secures access to key surface and groundwater sources draining directly or indirectly towards the Jordan River (Dajani 2018: 229–33). For two decades from 1967, Israeli geologists conducted mapping of the volcanic layers in the Golan, which were labelled part of the 'Bashan Group' of rocks (Mor et al. 1997: 17), after a term for the area from the Hebrew Bible. Similarly, Israeli hydrologists began detailed studies of the Golan aquifer shortly after the conquest of the territory. In March 1968, a military order established Israeli authority over all water resources in the occupied Golan Heights. Israeli hydrological surveys informed the first attempts in the same year to drill deep water wells, with high volume extraction from multiple wells delivered by the 1980s, mostly in the vicinity of Allone Habashan settlement (Dafny et al. 2003: 142). Development of the Salukia wellspring near Katzrin facilitated the growth of Israeli mineral water company, Mey Eden. In the north, Birket Ram (Lake Ram), the only open natural water reservoir in the Golan Heights, was confiscated in 1968 under a military order and subsequently used to provide irrigation water for Israeli settlers: the remaining Syrian communities were given limited access in 1977, at higher water prices than charged to the settlers (Dajani 2018: 234; Wessels 2015a: 608). Such details are important for grasping the depth of everyday colonization in the occupied Jawlan: far from being innocent or neutral, the survey, classification and division of earth materials (minerals, rocks, soil and water) are at the heart of settler colonial dispossession (Yusoff 2018: 15).

Politics of the governed

We use 'politics of the governed' as a term to account for the diverse ways in which the Jawlanis engage with the political field of settler colonial power. Most visibly, this has involved them confronting land dispossession, social segregation and the symbolic violence wrought by the Zionist devaluation of non-Jewish ways of knowing and living. However, Israeli authority is not only coercive and, particularly in the period since 1981, the strategy of normalization has drawn Jawlanis ever more deeply into the mesh of everyday living, and coping, with annexation. It is therefore a remarkable indicator of the robustness of the anti-colonial position sustained over decades by the Jawlanis that these Israelification measures conferring tangible benefits – for example, greater civil freedoms than under military rule and access to Israeli health and social services – have still failed to convince the majority of the Jawlani population to give up their indeterminate citizenship status as 'undefined nationals' and renounce their Syrian Arab identity. To explain this recalcitrance, which is often written off by Israeli authorities as susceptibility to 'extremism' or misinformation, we will briefly note the significance of at least four elements of Jawlani mobilization supporting an anti-colonial politics: (i) a resilient Syrian Arab identity, (ii) a collective defence of land, (iii) a politics of solidarity with Palestinians and (iv) the maintenance of autonomous associations for communal decision-making.

The 1981 National Document remains the most important political statement of the *self-identification of Jawlanis as Syrian Arabs*: this nationality is asserted as passing from generation to generation regardless of Israeli attempts to negate it. At the same time, the declaration affirms the distinctive religious and cultural heritage of the people in the occupied Syrian Golan, which features the boycott (*hirm*) as a potent mechanism of social control, for the National Document declares that anyone who becomes an Israeli national, or otherwise violates the declaration, shall be expelled from the community. The boycott threat, which can be permanent or temporary, covers the possibility of exclusion (even excommunication) from Druze religious rituals and/or the exclusion of community members from social events. From the general strike in 1982 to the boycott of the Israeli-run municipal elections in 2018, communal boycotts issued by the Druze congregation houses (*khalwat*) in the Jawlani villages have played a pivotal part in the political mobilization against occupation and annexation (Fakher Eldin 2019). Importantly, the use of the boycott as a political tool has united religious and more secular members of the Jawlani villages, who have otherwise diverged over communal rulings on some social issues (e.g. women's access to higher education, the consumption of alcohol). The resilience of the Syrian Arab identity of Jawlanis is, in short, sustained by a strong Druze tradition of unifying in self-defence against external aggressors.

Jawlani political subjectivity is also telluric ('of the earth') for its core anti-colonial strategy is the *collective defence of land*. Orchards of apple trees and, more recently, cherry trees have symbolized Jawlani resistance against land dispossession by Israeli authorities. From the 1950s, initially for economic reasons, the coordinated planting of apple trees followed communal appeals to develop land, expressed as a *hajmeh* ('rush'). At the onset of occupation in 1967, the remaining Syrian Druze villages invoked a hajmeh to protect their common land (*mashaa*') and also develop local areas of Syrian state land, both vulnerable to Israeli expropriation without evidence of cultivation. Similarly, a hajmeh took place in the early 1980s as a collective response to the imposition of Israeli citizenship. Again, the strategy was to expand agricultural land use – including by the reclamation of marginal lands – although Jawlani orchards were sometimes uprooted by Israeli state actors and settlers, mirroring the destruction of Palestinian olive groves in the West Bank. From the late 1980s, the Jawlanis created agricultural cooperatives to scale up a collective 'counter-infrastructure' for the supply and distribution of irrigation water (Chapter 6; see also Dajani and Mason 2018). These land-based projects are inherently political as they struggle for permanence in the face of an occupational regime that not only favours settler agricultural enterprises through subsidies, land allocations and agricultural support services but also actively undermines Jawlani farmers through arbitrary cycles of land confiscation and property destruction.

The *political solidarity* forged by Jawlanis with the Palestinian liberation movement has solidified the anti-colonial framing of their opposition to Israeli occupation. As Diaaedin Horoub discusses (Reflection 2), this encompasses associations forged by Syria and Palestinian political prisoners in the 1970s to student solidarity networks in the 1980s and more recent coalitions. Historically, an important ideological and organizational source for this solidarity politics was the Israeli Communist Party (Rakah), including its newspaper, *Al-Ittihad*, and affiliated groups, such as the Democratic Arab Women's Movement. In 1967, the Democratic Women's Movement coordinated early political mobilization against occupation both in Palestine and the Jawlan, which included the participation of Jewish leftists. Twenty-five years later, Palestinian writer Salman Natour founded a Committee for Solidarity with the Golan with *Al-Ittihad* co-founder Emile Touma: during the 1982 general strike, the committee organized solidarity visits to the Jawlan and gathered political, medical and other material support from Gaza, the Galilee and the West Bank (Dajani et al. 2021). The Jawlanis reciprocated during the First Intifada (1987–93) with political mobilization in support of the Palestinians, including annual commemoration of landmark events such as Land Day (30 March) and Nakba Day (15 May), and the Jawlani co-development of idea of steadfastness (*sumud*) to articulate the defence of their orchards has drawn on these long-established networks of solidarity. When possible, Palestinian merchants from Jenin, Nablus, Nazareth and Gaza have helped to market Jawlani agricultural crops.

Finally, the Jawlanis have, since the start of the long occupation, demonstrated a capacity for creating and sustaining *autonomous associations for communal decision-making*. As Fakher Eldin observes in Chapter 2, in the remaining Syrian villages after 1967, the Druze congregation house (*khalwa*) survived as a key space for collective decision-making. Over time, there has been a decline in the communal authority of spiritual leaders within the congregation houses, yet they have fostered broad-based support for anti-colonial political struggle by bringing together religious and secular members of society. This shift became more pronounced after 1981 as the Jawlani communities resisted Israelification. While the *khalwat* have faced internal criticism when they have failed to stop or limit the negative effects of Israeli rule – notably over ownership of, and access to, land – they have nevertheless remained vital bodies for expressing, and protecting, communal autonomy. They have been supplemented, from the 1980s, by the emergence of formal civil society organizations, including the Golan Academic Association (now the Arab Association for Development) and the Women's Committee in the Golan, and also the creation of agricultural cooperatives to represent and assist farmers – for example, in negotiations over water access with Mekorot, the Israeli National Water Company. All these organizations require continual maintenance within a strongly asymmetric associational field in which Israeli state actors (e.g. directly appointed municipal councils), corporations (e.g. social media companies) and Jewish settlements colonize Jawlani lifeworlds.

Mapping Jawlani futures

How to map a landscape or territory that exposes relations of domination; a mapping that historicizes and therefore denaturalizes settler colonial spaces? Against the overwhelming geopolitical weight of 'facts on the ground' – the settlements and settlement enterprises, the territorial grip over natural resources, the infrastructure systems and services locked into national networks of control, the forbidding military zones – the Jawlani communities uphold a survival culture. The stubborn refusal of the majority of the population (over 85 per cent) to adopt Israeli citizenship, or to be classified only in religious terms as a 'Druze minority', speaks to their lived experiences of the injustices of occupation, which flare up as grievances and antagonistic protests directed at the Israeli authorities. In this way, their assertion of a Syrian Arab identity is, regardless of the violent breakdown and fragmentation of Syrian state sovereignty, fed by the unceasing denial by Israel of their self-determination and dignity.

A *counter-geography* is already present, therefore, in the myriad ways across everyday life in which Jawlanis embody and emplace their own sense of community, performing a society, culture and ecology against the grain of the Israeli occupation. Of course, these daily practices of living are invariably compromised and fractured by dominant settler colonial interests, and there is currently greater freedom for imaginative work rather than the material flourishing of a Jawlani community. Counter-cartography, the production of spatial imaginaries that make domination visible, is one means to disrupt sovereign cartographies of calculation and control (Mesquita 2018). At a first level of critical reflection, this can use conventional geographic coordinates to map networks of settler colonial power, such as Jewish settlements in the Jawlan, which we counter-map within the boundaries of Syria's Quneitra Governorate alongside more familiar borders (see Map 1.2). It can also, still with standard spatial projections, visualize the effects of settler colonial violence, such as showing the Syrian communities destroyed by Israeli forces after July 1967 (see Map 1.3). In this way, Al-Marsad's production of a comprehensive map that includes all places of inhabitation pre- and post-1967 performs a Jawlani counter-geography that denaturalizes the cartographic world of settler colonialism (Al-Marsad 2021). As Quiquivix (2014) explains in her work on map-making in Palestine, Palestinians developed maps as a necessity only after Oslo and their nation-state-building endeavour. Similarly, it was in response to the geographical violence of settler colonialism that the Jawlanis embarked on an endeavour to mark through maps their territorial dispossession and remaining presence on the land. Such cartographic efforts represent a 'remapping' by indigenous collectives to reclaim recognition, not just in opposition to settler colonial logics but also a remapping 'that privileges kinship and memory in interpretation of the landscape' (Iralu 2021:14).

Remapping allows the spatial visualization of alternative pasts and futures by communities subject to protracted domination. At this second level of critical reflection and practice, indigenous activists and scholars have devised more subversive modes of mapping to deconstruct settler colonial geographies and reclaim those identities, place attachments and ecological relations erased or eroded by ethnic cleansing. These mapping projects seek to convey anthropological facets of the lived experience of a landscape rather than the abstract, objectifying gaze of a conventional state-centred cartography (Barnd 2017; Iralu 2021).

In Reflection 6, Jumanah Abbas shows some of the ways in which, counter to an Israeli cartography of spatial domination, there can be alternative visual representations of ordinary and insurgent Jawlani practices, including the mapping of memories. Jumanah draws from the extensive and rich experiences of Jawlanis and their multi-sited, diverse education with its key role in counter-hegemonic political processes (Hawari et al. 2019: 162). Counter-cartography can take multiple shapes and forms from oral history accounts to videos, murals, community events and actions with an objective of decolonizing cartography and spatial knowledge production. Can we produce a map that is situated in local knowledge, produced solely for collective purposes of documenting and narrating local histories and experiences and still deem it significant, relevant and useful to wider audiences, especially in the Western world? Figure 7.2 is an example of such a map, which moves to communicate a counter-cartography of Jawlani identity politics, both mixing Arabic and English and rightfully making demands on an Anglophone audience to make sense of visual iconography that may well be unfamiliar (e.g. 'The March' statue in Majdal Shams) – to have to learn more, with respect, to uncover the various layers of meaning that will be legible to a Jawlani audience.

Can we develop such emancipatory mapping, regardless of its legibility to outsiders and people less familiar with the Jawlan? Even at the risk of illegibility, the act of engaging with mapping, or unmapping indigenous spatialities, has in itself an emancipatory potential to challenge our perceptions on meanings and situated knowledges of indigenous existence in space, place and time. The Jawlan is a unique sociopolitical formation that is rich in culture, political and social resistance embedded in quotidian daily acts of existing and persisting despite the ongoing settler colonial reality.

It also pushes us to go beyond mapping as geographically bounded and invites us to include experiences and stories of places, people and memories transcending those borders. Counter-mapping as an act

FIGURE 7.2 A counter-cartography of Jawlani identity politics and resistance, by Jumanah Abbas.

of resistance is also carried out by those who were expelled from the geography of the Jawlan: for example, in Adam Shapiro's compelling documentary, *Al-Joulan: A Guarded Palace* (2011), in which Rasha Elass, a Syrian journalist and a descendant of a displaced Jawlani, takes us on a journey of return to her father's village of Jubbatha Ez-Zeit. Can counter-mapping create inclusive narratives of homeland and belonging that serve not just the Jawlanis that remain but also the families of those that were forced to flee? We can only hint at the forms and practices of such collective imagining, which is anyway properly part of the self-determination by Jawlanis of their social and political futures. Our hope is that this volume at least provides a resource for understanding, and critically engaging with, settler colonial practices that, for far too long, have written the Jawlanis out of their own history and geography.

Dawn

He closed the door tightly
And let the curtains down on all windows.
He filled the holes with old fabrics
Until darkness prevailed.
It was enough for a visitor or one who lost the way
To knock on the door
So that light returns to me,
It was enough for you to cross my imagination
So that the sun climbs on my eyelashes
And the dawn pours out.

فجر

أقفل البابَ بإحكامٍ
أسدلَ الستائرَ على النوافذِ كلّها
سدّ الثُقوبَ بأقمشةٍ قديمةٍ
إلى أن سادَ العتم.
كانَ يكفي أن يطرقَ البابَ زائرٌ
أو تائةٌ ضلّ الطريقَ
كي يَعودَ الضوءُ إليّ،
كان يكفي أن تَعبرَ في خيالي
كي تتعربشَ الشمسُ على رموشي
وينسكبَ الفَجر.

YASSER KHANJAR

Translated into English by Ghareeb Iksander. Original Arabic poem (2019) published with the kind permission of Al Mutawassit.

NOTES

Reflection 1

1 Najah al-Wali, 2004. Interviewed by Fawzi Wahbeh and Munir Fakher Eldin.

2 Marches with widespread participation took place in the Jawlan on the day of Gamal Abdel Nasser's death (28 September 1970). Nasser was president of the United Arab Republic which, from 1958 to 1961, included a union with Syria.

3 Hala Fakher Eldin, 2004. Interviewed by Munir Fakher Eldin.

4 Ibid.

5 Ibid.

6 Hayel Abu Jabal, Afif Mahmoud and Hammoud Mir'I, 2004, Majdal Shams. Interviewed by Fawzi Wahbeh and Munir Fakher Eldin.

7 Ibid.

8 *Al-Ittihad* newspaper, 20 April 1982.

9 *Al-Ittihad* newspaper, 14 May 1982.

10 *Al-Ittihad* newspaper, 19 March 1982.

11 Hayel Abu Jabal, Afif Mahmoud, Hammoud Mir'I, 2004, Majdal Shams. Interviewed by Fawzi Wahbeh and Munir Fakher Eldin.

12 Ibid.

13 *Al-Ittihad* newspaper, 12 February 1982.

14 *Al-Ittihad* newspaper, 9 March 1982.

15 *Al-Ittihad* newspaper, 4 June 1982.

16 Hala Fakher Eldin, 2004, ibid.

17 Hayel Abu Jabal, Afif Mahmoud, Hammoud Mir'I, 2004, ibid.

18 In her testimony about the Great Strike, Najah al-Wali says that, before 1982, women did not have a prominent role in Jawlani political activism. In 1986, she took part in founding the Women's Union in the Jawlan. She adds that the strike experience and the political activism generated by it resulted in the birth of the Women's Union. Najah al-Wali, 2004. Interviewed by Fawzi Wahbeh and Munir Fakher Eldin.

19 Testimony by Amira Ibrahim on the TV show 'Under Focus – al-Jawlan, part 2', June 2009.

20 Hala Fakher Eldin, 2004, ibid.

21 Najah al-Wali, 2004, ibid.

22 *Al-Ittihad* newspaper, 6 April 1982.

23 *Al-Ittihad* newspaper, 9 March 1982.

24 *Al-Ittihad* newspaper, 11 May 1982.

25 Hala Fakher Eldin, 2004, ibid.

Chapter 3

1 See Amal Aun's contribution in this volume (Chapter 5).

2 Personal communication with the late Syrian film-maker Omar Amiralay and director Usamma Muhammad. In 2006, Fatih Al-Mudarris Cultural Center organized a festival called the Syrian Cinema Week, in which canonical works by Syrian film-makers were screened, and the two film-makers were hosted in an online session from Beirut, where they spoke for the first time to a Syrian audience in the occupied Golan. The event was highly emotional.

3 This history was narrated by several activists to the author in recorded interviews in 2004. Contacts were established with the high-ranking leaders of the communist party, such as Tawfiq Zayyad, Tawfiq Toubi and poet Samih al-Qasim, and also, there were strong connections with other factions of the Palestinian activists, especially progressive Arab nationalist lawyers such as Muhammad Mi'ari and later the Abna' al-Balad Movement.

4 See Diaaeddin Horoub's reflection in this book (Reflection 2).

5 Documentation of this episode is found in Hamoud Mare'i's private papers, Majdal Shams.

6 See the contributions to this volume by Aram Abu Saleh (Reflection 3) and Ali Aweidat (Reflection 7).

7 The *hirm* is of two types: religious and social. The religious *hirm* is imposed on religious men or women who commit moral offences that contradict key social ethics and civilities (such as if one engages in unnecessary quarrels, drinks alcohol, attends a wedding with music and dance, etc.) or religious rules. The social is when someone is excommunicated or expelled from the

community. The *hirm* of both types is mostly temporary; it is issued with a temporal effect for days or months, but it can also take a permanent form or made conditional upon repentance. In the religious life, murder and adultery are causes for permanent *hirm*, which allows one a lesser religious life with no access to the secret sacred books and prayers of the Druze faith. The *hirm* against Israeli citizenship was conditional upon one retracting his/her status as Israeli citizen and asking forgiveness from the community.

8   There is much writing on this topic in Arabic, but for a useful recent review, see Paul Tabar's article 'Sectarianism in Lebanon: Thinking with Bourdieu against Marx' (in Arabic), published online by the Arab Center for Research and Policy Studies, Doha, Qatar. 30 Augustus 2021. https://www .dohainstitute.org/ar/ResearchAndStudies/Pages/Sectarianism-in-Lebanon -Bourdieus-Thought-on-Marxist-Critique.aspx

Reflection 2

1   Jamal Al-Salqan, former president of the Birzeit University Student Council, 19 August 2019, Ramalla, interviewed by Diaaeddin Horoub.

2   Salman Fakhr Eldin, 27 July 2020, Majdal Shams, interviewed by Diaaeddin Horoub.

3   Al-Salqan interview, ibid.

4   See the campaign website at: http://right2edu.birzeit.edu/

5   Ali Hassouna, 6 May 2019, Ramallah, interviewed by Diaaeddin Horoub and Hanan Hussein

6   Fakhr Eldin interview, ibid.

7   Ibid. Editors' note: The 'Jerusalem Group' or 'Matzpen Jerusalem' was a political faction within Matzpen, the Israeli Socialist Organization. On Matzpen, see Fiedler (2020).

8   Ibid.

9   Al-Salqan interview, ibid.

10   Ibid.

11   Hassouna interview, ibid.

12   Ibid.

13   Al-Salqan interview, ibid.

14   Hassouna interview, ibid.

15   Ibid.

16 An annual tradition, held by the Student Union Council at Birzeit University, which contains a huge book exhibition, involving publishing houses in occupied Palestine, an exhibition of national manufactures and national heritage, Okaz market and an exhibition of Palestinian plants, and ends with a celebration of Palestinian folklore.

Reflection 3

1 Some refer to the start of the revolution on 18 March 2011.

2 For the full statement, see http://www.ahewar.org/debat/show.art.asp?aid =252088&r=0

3 For example, watch a video of supporters of the Assad regime attacking opposition protestors on July 21, 2012, in the village of Majdal Shams: https://www.youtube.com/watch?v=jjc660y05d4&t=159s. Also watch the video 'Confrontation between the Loyalists and the Opposition in the Golan Heights' on 23 December 2011: https://www.youtube.com/watch?v =CWrLDQXmh0s&t=302s

4 It should be noted that, in this conflict, there is no role for the 'Israelized' segment or inclined segment of the population to adopt an identity that is compatible with the Israeli presence in the Golan Heights. In other words, this conflict has been and continues to be, a conflict between the Syrian patriots or the Syrian 'National Movement' in the occupied Golan and independent of the Israeli occupation. This makes it a Syrian internal conflict.

5 Syrian 'National Movement' is used here for writing purposes only and does not refer to a set organizational movement.

6 This means that the conflict in Syria was no longer a fully Syrian conflict, due to the terrible violence that the Assad regime has practiced from the outset on Syrians and their revolutionary centres – through the use of various types of weapons and methods of repression without any moral or international deterrent, the widespread use of arrest and concealed imprisonment, murder under torture, and sectarian massacres, and also from the regime introducing non-Syrian military forces into Syrian territory, starting with Lebanon's Hezbollah and Iranian and Afghan Shiite militias and ending with the Russian military intervention to help the regime in 2015. In addition to this, the rise of the counter-revolutionary forces was also represented by armed jihadists and Islamists who joined the anti-regime side and fought with non-Syrian forces.

7 That belonging to a state means full and inevitable belonging to its ruler and ruling regime. Thus, belonging to Syria means we necessarily belong to Bashar Al-Assad, hence the validity of the term 'Syria Assad'.

8 Another significant transformation of the Jawlani society has been the move from a peasant society to a semi-urban society. While this is an important factor to mention, it requires separate research and analysis.

Chapter 4

1 Details about the story of *al-Masirah* here and below were collected in an interview with the artist, conducted by Munir Fakher Eldin on December 2002 in the artist's home in Majdal Shams. However, much of the interpretation of the work, unless otherwise stated, is the authors'.

2 One should by no means read the miraculous here as a distinct feature of a 'subaltern' world. See Edwards (1989).

3 See, for example, report on Dr Alaa Abu Saleh dated 9 February 2022. https://emek.mynet.co.il/health/article/rk008dz111q?fbclid =IwAR1GdOm7CSc3m_QYAFsuXd2Mb0NTAeKBScIyOnidaZJnK-ZGeO -TGW97JOA.

4 https://israelscouts.wordpress.com/, https://www.israelscouts.org/

5 https://noal.org.il/english/

6 https://rothschildcp.com/english/

7 https://www.facebook.com/waheeb.ayoub

8 https://jawlany.com/الاعتداء-على-وتحطيم-تمثال-الفنان-أيمن/

9 http://ashtarr.net/?p=9805

10 Al-Khadir is venerated in popular religion, by Muslims and Christians, as a warrying saint, known in the Christian traditions as Saint George.

11 https://www.facebook.com/search/top?q=rushdie%20braek

12 https://www.facebook.com/saleem.awad2

13 https://www.facebook.com/rami.ayoub.501

14 https://www.facebook.com/alkadamani

Reflection 4

1 'The Bombing of the Statue of the March, the Statue of Sultan Basha al-Atrash, in Majdal Shams' (1987).

2 Hassan Khater, 2002. Interviewed by Munir Fakher Eldin on 13 December.

3 Wael Tarabieh, 2020. Interviewed online by Abdel Qader Thweib on 8 February.

4 Randa Maddah, 2018. Interviewed online by Abdel Qader Thweib on 29 September.

5 Fahad Al-Halabi, 2018. Interviewed online by Abdel Qader Thweib on 29 September.

6 Tarabieh 2020, ibid.

7 Ibid.

8 Ibid.

9 Maddah (2012).

Reflection 5

1 See, for example, this rendition of the poem 'Apple of Golan Heights' by Suleiman Samara: https://www.youtube.com/watch?v=PM0GAsGVV0Y

2 *Golan Times* website, Available at: https://cutt.us/5ybI4

3 See: https://www.youtube.com/watch?v=stFYOCK63r4

4 See: https://www.youtube.com/watch?v=_eq7pFiz15s

5 *Al-Mudun* newspaper website, Available at: https://cutt.us/Tp1tb

6 Monte Carlo International Website (2015).

Chapter 5

1 Translated from official government letter titled 'Subject: Bar-Yehuda's Letter Regarding the Druze in Isfiya' dated 14 June 1950.

2 'Arab-Jewish Love Story Rejected for Israeli Schools' (2015).

3 Aamer Ibraheem, 2017. Interviewed online by Amal Aun on 3 October.

4 Israeli Ministry of Foreign Affairs (2013).

5 Israeli Ministry of Education (2016).

6 This refers back to the Millet System and separate school system.

7 'L.H', a Druze high school teacher from Daliat Al Carmel, 2017. Interviewed by Amal Aun.

8 Israeli Ministry of Education (2017) Druze and Circassian schools. The Manual for Core Curriculum for History.

9 'S.F', a Druze activist, 2017. Interviewed by Amal Aun on 21 September.

10 'E.I', a Druze high school teacher, 2017. Interviewed by Amal Aun on 25 November.

11 Sawaed and Safir (2009).

12 Ibid.

13 Yousef (2017).

14 Ibid.

15 'W.K', a Druze education content editor, 2017. Interviewed by Amal Aun on 24 November.

16 'A.S', a Druze high school teacher, 2017. Interviewed by Amal Aun on 25 November.

17 'E.I.' interview, ibid.

18 'A.S.' interview, ibid.

19 Ibid.

20 Yousef (2017), ibid., p. 23.

21 Faiba et al. (2008).

22 Ibraheem (2017), ibid.

23 In early 1980s, teachers who protested against the Israeli annexation plan were dismissed from schools without compensation. Israeli courts deemed these arbitrary procedures 'legitimate' (Al-Marsad 2005).

24 Majdal Shams Parental Committee, 2017. Interviewed by Amal Aun on 20 September. Also, Ibraheem (2017), ibid.

25 Ibid. The Parental Committee also gave an example of one teacher who expressed an objection to an activity taking place in a Majdal Shams school and consequently had Israeli intelligence contact him and ask him to refrain.

26 Foyer (2017).

27 Ibraheem (2017), ibid.

28 Ibid.

29 Ibid.

30 Ibid.

Reflection 7

1 Aweidat (2020).

2 Golan Youth Movement Facebook page: https://www.facebook.com/golanyouthmovement

Chapter 6

1 Here we use the spelling 'Jawlan' rather than 'Golan' to tie it more closely to the soft 'g' of the Arabic rather the more common Israeli spelling 'Golan'.

2 See Makkaneyyat website for more information: https://makaneyyat.org/en-gb/

3 Interview with Salman Fakher Eldin, political activist, January 2017 in Majdal Shams.

4 A dunam was the Ottoman unit of area equivalent to 0.247 English acres and is still commonly used in the Levant.

5 Interview with Hayel Abu Jabal, farmer and political figure, 17 December 2016 in Majdal Shams.

6 Interview with Nazih Abu Jabal, farmer, 7 September 2017 in Majdal Shams.

7 Interview with Nazih Abu Jabal, farmer, ibid.

8 At first, Jawlani farmers economically benefited from an open and demand-hungry Israeli market for its unique product: the apples. By the 1960s, the apple trees which had been planted in the first *Hajmeh* in the 1950s were now fully mature and at the peak of productivity, especially as the farmers had acquired skills in maintaining and enhancing the productivity of the apple trees. However, the settlement enterprises were also developing competition with the Jawlanis in apple production and were soon monopolizing the production and marketing of apple crops.

9 Interview with Karameh Kanj Abu Saleh, lawyer and activist, 16 October 2021, via WhatsApp.

10 Interview with Hayel Abu Jabal, ibid.

11 See Reflection 8 by Alaa Iktash.

Reflection 8

1 Samih Choukair (1990) *Zaher Al Rumman* ('Pomegranate Blossom') song. Lyrics and music by Samih Choukair, used by permission of Samih Choukair.

2 Interview with Hayel Abu Jabal, Majdal Shams, 19 June 2020.

3 Document from the State of Israel Archives, File No. א- 7913/48, titled Neve Ativ file, Cabinet sessions in 1968 (in Hebrew).

4 Haaretz (2006).

5 Document from the State of Israel Archives, File No. א-4145/24, titled Neve Ativ file, the World Zionist Organization/Settlement Division. dated 27 September 1981 (in Hebrew).

6 Abu Jabal interview, ibid.

7 Cobban (1998).

8 Proposed Israel Nature and Park Authority of a 'Hermon National Park' plan threatens to surround Majdal Shams from the north and west. See Brik (2018).

9 Abu Jabal interview, ibid.

10 Interview with Karameh Kanj Abu Saleh, Majdal Shams, 20 June 2020.

REFERENCES

Abbas, J. (2020), 'Landscapes of Education in the Golan Heights', *Arab Urbanism*. Available online: https://www.araburbanism.com/magazine/landscapes-of-education (accessed 18 September 2021).

Abu Jabal, A. (2019), 'Banias: The Pearl of the Jawlan', *Ashtarr News*, 5 February (in Arabic). Available online: http://ashtarr.net/?p=3879 (accessed 3 November 2021).

Abu Jabal, A. (2020), *Lost Dreams between the Syrian Al-Awda Neighbourhood and Israeli 'New Majdal Shams' Neighbourhood*, Harmoon Center for Contemporary Studies (in Arabic). Available online: https://www.harmoon.org/reports/و-السورية-العودة-ضاحية-بين-ضائعة-أحلام/ (accessed 3 November 2021).

Abu Jabal, A. (2021), 'Do We Have to Rehabilitate Our Souls and Minds?', *Ashtarr News*, 5 May (in Arabic). Available online: http://ashtarr.net/?p=11070 (accessed 19 February 2022).

Abu Jabal, J. and N. Ayoub (2009), *Seizing Land and Water Resources: A Tool to Strengthen Israeli Settlements in the Occupied Golan*, Majdal Shams: Al-Marsad – Arab Human Rights Centre in the Golan Heights.

Abu Libdeh, H., L. Hajjar and B. Tarabieh (1994), *A Survey of the Syrian Population in the Occupied Golan Heights: Demography and Health*, Majdal Shams: Arab Association for Development.

Abu-Saad, I. (2004), 'Separate and Unequal: The Role of the State Educational System in Maintaining the Subordination of Israel's Palestinian Arab Citizens', *Social Identities*, 10 (1): 101–27.

Abu Sharar, H. (1982), 'Israeli Facts on the Golan's Steadfastness', *Palestinian Affairs*, 127: 209, Beirut: PLO Palestine Research Center (in Arabic).

Abu-Sitta, G., O. Dewachi, V.-K. Nguyen and J. Whittall (2016), *Conflict Medicine – A Manifesto*, Beirut: Global Health Institute, American University of Beirut. Available online: https://msf-analysis.org/conflict-medicine-manifesto/ (accessed 19 February 2022).

Akerman, J. R. (2017), *Decolonizing the Map: Cartography from Colony to Nation*, Chicago: The University of Chicago Press.

Alaawar, S. (2018), 'A Statement Issued by People in the Occupied Golan after the Meeting of Yafouri Regarding the Decision of the Israeli Minister to Hold Elections for the Local Councils in the Golan Villages', *Golan Times*, 11 July. Available online: http://golantimes.com/news/22135 (accessed 21 March 2021).

Alazzeh, A. (2020), 'The Illusion of Youth', *Assafir*, July (in Arabic). Available online: http://palestine.assafir.com/Article.aspx?ArticleID=3348 (accessed 29 October 2021).

Al-Bagh, A. (1983), 'Al-Jawlan: A Study in Regional Geography', Arabic translation of 1956 doctoral thesis, University of Paris, Paris.

Al-Batheesh, N. (1987), *The Jawlan: Confronting the Occupation 1967–1986*, Majdal Shams: Union Press (in Arabic).

Al-Batsh, J. S. (2013), 'Volunteering in the Thinking of Palestinian Mass Organizations in the West Bank and Gaza Strip 1981–1994', *University of Palestine Journal*, 5: 230 (in Arabic).

Al-Hasan, A. (2011), *Beyond a Day: Al-Zaftiya Notebooks*, Damascus: The Arab Writers Union (in Arabic).

Al Jazeera (2009), 'Under the Microscope: The Golan', [two-part documentary], 9 June (in Arabic). Available online: https://www.youtube.com/watch?v=PDnVY6PxzLU (accessed 29 October 2021).

Al Jazeera (2012), 'Education in the Golan: A Struggle of Will and Identity', 10 June (in Arabic). Available online: https://www.aljazeera.net/news/rep ortsandinterviews/2012/6/10/التعليم-بالجولان-صراع-إرادات-وهوية (accessed 29 October 2021).

Al-Joulan: A Guarded Palace (2011), [Documentary] Dir. Adam Shapiro. Available online: Vimeo (accessed 1 August 2021).

Al-Marsad (2005), *The Occupied Syrian Golan Background*, Majdal Shams: Al-Marsad – Arab Human Rights Centre in the Golan Heights.

Al-Marsad (2008), *The Forgotten Occupation: Life in the Syrian Golan after 50 Years of Occupation*, Majdal Shams: Al-Marsad – Arab Human Rights Centre in the Golan Heights.

Al-Marsad (2014), *Israeli Agricultural Settlement in the Occupied Golan Heights during the Syrian Conflict*, Majdal Shams: Al-Marsad – Arab Human Rights Centre in the Golan Heights.

Al-Marsad (2016), *Al-Marsad Submits Objection to 'Hermon National Park' Plan*, Majdal Shams: Al-Marsad – Arab Human Rights Centre in the Golan Heights. Available online: https://golan-marsad.org/al-marsad-submits -objection-to-hermon-national- park-plan/ (accessed 3 November 2021).

Al-Marsad (2017), *Human Rights Violations Committed by the State of Israel in the Occupied Syrian Golan*, Majdal Shams: Al-Marsad – Arab Human Rights Centre in the Golan Heights.

Al-Marsad (2018), *Forgotten Occupation: Life in the Syrian Golan after 50 Years of Israeli Occupation*, Majdal Shams: Al-Marsad – Arab Human Rights Centre in the Golan Heights.

Al-Marsad (2021), *Destroyed Residential Communities by Israel after Occupying the Golan in 1967*, Majdal Shams: Al-Marsad – Arab Human Rights Centre in the Golan Heights.

Arab-Jewish Love Story Rejected for Israeli Schools (2015), *Aljazeera*, December. Available online: http://www.aljazeera.com/news/2015/12/arab -jewish-love-story-rejected-israeli-schools-151231102739368.html (accessed 21 November 2017).

ASD (1994), *Land Confiscation Policy in the Occupied Syrian Golan Heights*, Majdal Shams: Arab Society for Development.

Ashtarr News (2019), 'The Reality of Education in the Golan before the Occupation' (in Arabic). Available online: http://ashtarr.net/?p=3263 (accessed 29 October 2021).

Ashtarr News (2021), 'On the Anniversary of the General Strike in the Occupied Syrian Golan' (in Arabic). Available online: http://ashtarr.net/?p=3578 (accessed 29 October 2021).

Aweidat, A. (2020), 'The Concept of "Jawlani Youth": Between Colonial Policies and Society'. Available online: http://golan1982.info.

Assmann, J. (1995), 'Collective Memory and Cultural Identity', *New German Critique*, 65: 125–33.

Aun, A. (2018), 'Israeli Education Policies as a Tool for the Ethnic Manipulation of the Arab Druze: Israel and the Occupied Syrian Golan', MPA diss., Cornell University, Ithaca.

Bailey, T. (2013), 'Introduction', in T. Bailey (ed.), *Deprovincializing Habermas: Global Perspectives*, 93–105, New Delhi: Routledge.

Barakat, R. (2018), 'Writing/Righting Palestine Studies: Settler Colonialism, Indigenous Sovereignty and Resisting the Ghost(s) of History', *Settler Colonial Studies*, 8: 349–63.

Barnd, N. B. (2017), *Native Space: Geographic Strategies to Unsettle Settler Colonialism*, Corvallis: Oregon State University Press.

Barnes, J. (2009). 'Managing the Waters of Ba'th Country: The Politics of Water Scarcity in Syria', *Geopolitics*, 14 (3): 510–30.

Batatu, H. (1999), *Syria's Peasantry, the Descendants of Its Lesser Rural Notables, and Their Politics*, Princeton: Princeton University Press.

Bennett, M. A. (1999), 'Reincarnation, Marriage, and Memory: Negotiating Sectarian Identity among the Druze of Syria', PhD diss., University of Arizona, Tucson.

Berman, M. (1983), *All That Is Solid Melts into Air: The Experience of Modernity*, New York: Verso.

Berney, K. A., T. Ring, N. Watson, P. Kulling, C. Hudson and S. La Boda (1994), *International Dictionary of Historic Places, Volume 4: Middle East and Africa*, Chicago and London: Fitzroy Dearborn.

Bin, D. (2018), 'So-called Accumulation by Dispossession', *Critical Sociology*, 44 (1): 75–88.

Blomley, N. (2008), 'The Spaces of Critical Geography', *Progress in Human Geography*, 32 (2): 285–93.

Bourdieu, P. and A. Sayad (1964), *Le Déracinement: La Crise de L'agriculture Traditionelle en Algérie*, Paris: Les Éditions de Minuet.

Bourdieu, P., L. J. D. Wacquant and S. Farage (1994), 'Rethinking the State: Genesis and Structure of the Bureaucratic Field', *Sociological Theory*, 12 (1): 1–18.

Brass, P. (1991), *Ethnicity and Nationalism: Theory and Comparison*, Newbury Park: Sage Publications.

Braverman, I. (2014), *Planted Flags. Trees, Lands and Law in Israel/Palestine*, Cambridge: Cambridge University Press.

Brik, N. (2018), 'Building Up: Housing and Planning Policies in the Occupied Syrian Golan', in Al-Marsad (ed.), *The Forgotten Occupation: Life in the Syrian Golan after 50 Years of Occupation*, 106–15, Majdal Shams: Al-Marsad – Arab Human Rights Centre in the Golan Heights.

Castells, M. (1997), *The Power of Identity*, Oxford: Blackwell.

Chatterjee, P. (2004), *The Politics of the Governed: Reflections on Popular Politics in Most of the World*, New York: Columbia University Press.

Choi, S. E. (2016), *Decolonisation and the French of Algeria*, London: Palgrave Macmillan.

Cobban, H. (1998), 'Golan Days', Part 1: Golan and the Human Dimension. Available online: http://helenacobban.com/golan.html (accessed 28 October 2021).

Cohen, S. B. and N. Kliot (1992), 'Place-names in Israel's Ideological Struggle over the Administered Territories', *Annals of the Association of American Geographers*, 82 (4): 653–80.

Cohen, Y. and N. Gordon (2018), 'Israel's Biospatial Politics: Territory, Demography, and Effective Control', *Public Culture*, 30 (2): 199–220.

Coursen-Neff, Z. (2001), *Second Class: Discrimination against Palestinian Arab Children in Israel's Schools*, New York: Human Rights Watch.

Court, D. and R. Abbas (2010), 'Role of Druze High Schools in Israel in Shaping Students' Identity and Citizenship', *Education, Citizenship and Social Justice*, 5 (2): 145–62.

Dafny, E., H. Gvirtzman, A. Burg and L. Fleischer (2003), 'The Hydrogeology of the Golan Basalt Aquifer, Israel', *Israel Journal of Earth Science*, 52: 139–53.

Dajani, M. (2018), 'Water Struggles as Struggles for Recognition: The Lived Geographies of Farming Communities in Sahl al-Battuf and the Occupied Golan Heights', PhD diss., London School of Economics and Political Science.

Dajani, M. (2020a), 'Danger, Turbines! A Jawlani Cry against Green Energy Colonialism in the Occupied Syrian Golan Heights', *Jadaliyya*, 22 April. Available online: https://www.jadaliyya.com/Print/41010 (accessed 21 March 2021).

Dajani, M. (2020b), 'Thirsty Water Carriers: The Production of Uneven Waterscapes in Sahl al-Battuf', *Contemporary Levant*, 5 (2): 97–112.

Dajani, M., A. Iktash, B. Rizqallah and D. Ali Hroub (2021), 'Palestine is Southern Syria: On Palestinian Solidarity with Jawlani Communities', *Palestine In-Between*. Available online: https://palestineinbetween.com/Palestine-is-southern-Syria (accessed 24 August 2021).

Dajani, M. and M. Mason (2019), 'Counter-infrastructure as Resistance in the Hydrosocial Territory of the Occupied Golan Heights', in F. Menga and E. Swyngedouw (eds), *Water, Technology and the Nation-State*, 131–46, Abingdon: Routledge.

Darwish, M. (2017), 'Introduction', in A. Soueif and O. R. Hamilton (eds), *This Is Not a Border: Reportage and Reflection from the Palestine Festival of Literature*, 7–9, London: Bloomsbury.

Davis, U. (1983), 'The Golan Heights under Israeli Occupation 1967–1981', Working Paper, Durham: University of Durham, Centre for Middle Eastern and Islamic Studies.

Delforno, A. (2019), *More Shadows than Lights: Local Elections in the Occupied Syrian Golan*, Majdal Shams: Al-Marsad – Arab Human Rights Centre in the Golan Heights.

Edwards, D. B. (1989), 'Mad Mullahs and Englishmen: Discourse in the Colonial Encounter', *Comparative Studies in Society and History*, 31 (4), 649–70.

Elkins, C. and S. Pedersen, eds (2005), *Settler Colonialism in the Twentieth Century: Projects, Practices, Legacies*, New York: Routledge.

Eqeiq, A. (2013), 'Writing the Indigenous: Contemporary Mayan Literature in Chiapas, Mexico and Palestinian Literature in Israel', PhD diss., University of Washington, Seattle.

Faiba, T., M. Segev and S. Lapi (2008), *Israel: The Human and the Spatial*, Tel Aviv: Center for Educational Technology, 9.

Fakher Eldin, M. (2013), 'A Reading of Political Mobilization in the Occupied Golan', *Jadaliyya*, 1 May (in Arabic). Available online: https://www.jadaliyya .com/Details/28536/ (accessed 29 October 2021).

Fakher Eldin, M. (2015), 'Syrians in the Occupied Golan: Between the Revolution, the Regime and the Occupation', *Journal of Palestine Studies*, 104: 27–32 (in Arabic).

Fakher Eldin, M. (2019), 'Power, Politics and Community: Resistance Dynamics in the Occupied Golan', *Journal of Palestine Studies*, 49 (1): 77–92.

Falah, G. (1996), 'The 1948 Israeli-Palestinian War and Its Aftermath: The Transformation and De-signification of Palestine's Cultural Landscape', *Annals of the Association of American Geographers*, 86 (2): 256–85.

Fiedler, L. (2020), *Matzpen: A History of Israeli Dissidence*, trans. J. Schneider, Edinburgh: Edinburgh University Press.

Firro, K. (1988), 'The Druze in and between Syria, Lebanon and Israel', in M. J. Esman and I. Rabinovich (eds), *Ethnicity, Pluralism, and the State in the Middle East*, 185–97, Leiden: Brill.

Firro, K. (1999), *The Druzes in the Jewish State: A Brief History*, Leiden, Boston, and Cologne: E. J. Brill.

Firro, K. M. (2001), 'Reshaping Druze Particularism in Israel', *Journal of Palestine Studies*, 30 (3): 40–53.

Foyer, D. (2017), 'We Got Together – The Most Common Words in Majdal Shams: The Golan in Tension', *Globes Magazine*, 18 November. Available online: https://www.globes.co.il/news/article.aspx?did=1001211807 (accessed 21 October 2021).

Fraser, N. (1985), 'What's Critical about Critical Theory? The Case of Habermas and Gender', *New German Critique*, 35: 97–131.

Frisch, H. (1997), 'State Ethnicization and the Crisis of Leadership Succession among Israel's Druze', *Ethnic and Racial Studies*, 20 (3): 580–93.

Geertz, C. (1973), *The Interpretation of Cultures: Selected Essays*, New York: Basic Books.

Gordon, N. and M. Ram (2016), 'Ethnic Cleansing and the Formation of Settler Colonial Geographies', *Political Geography*, 53: 20–9.

Gregory, D., R. Johnston, G. Pratt, G. M. Watts and S. Whatmore (2011), *The Dictionary of Human Geography*, Chichester: John Wiley & Sons.

Haaretz (2006), 'Group Accuses Mt. Hermon Ski-area Owner of Charging Illegal Fees', 28 November. Available online: https://www.haaretz.com/1 .4933874 (accessed 28 October 2021).

Habermas, J. (1987), *The Theory of Communicative Action Volume 2: Lifeworld and System: A Critique of Functionalist Reason*, Cambridge: Polity Press.

Hage, G. (2009), 'Hating Israel in the Field: On Ethnography and Political Emotions', *Anthropological Theory*, 9 (1): 59–79.

Halabi, R. (2018), 'The Education System as a Mechanism for Political Control: The Education System for the Druze in Israel', *Journal of Asian and African Studies*, 53 (7): 1018–31.

Halabi, U. R. (1992), 'Life under Occupation in the Golan Heights', *Journal of Palestine Studies*, 22 (1): 78–93.

Halon, E. (2020), 'Israel Green Lights Hundreds of Wind Turbines in North', *Jerusalem Post*, 1 January. Available online: https://www.jpost.com/israel -news/israel-green-lights-hundreds-of-wind-turbines-in-northern-israel -612757 (accessed 21 March 2021).

Harel-Shalev, A. and I. Peleg (2014), 'Hybridity and Israel's Democratic Order: The End of an Imperfect Balance?', *Contemporary Review of the Middle East*, 1 (1): 75–94.

Harvey, D. (2003), *The New Imperialism*, Oxford: Oxford University Press.

Hawari, Y., S. Plonski and E. Weizman (2019), 'Seeing Israel through Palestine: Knowledge Production as Anti-colonial Praxis', *Settler Colonial Studies*, 9 (1): 155–75.

Heinich, N. (2011), *La Sociologie de l'Art*, trans. H. Qubeisi, Arab Organization for Translation, Beirut: Lebanon (in Arabic).

Hitti, P. K. (1928), *The Origins of the Druze People and Religion with Extracts from Their Sacred Writings*, New York: Columbia University Press.

Ibraheem, A. (2015), 'The Forced Definition of National Identity Practices', *Jadal Magazine*, Issue 24, Mada al-Carmel – Arab Centre for Applied Social Studies (in Arabic). Available online: http://alqaws.org/ckfinder/userfiles/ files/JDL24- (accessed 29 October 2021).

Ibraheem, A. (2018), 'Elimination and Displacement in the Occupied Golan Heights: Policies of Colonized Settlement and Conceptual Transfer', *Nakbafiles*, 5 June (in Arabic). Available online: https:// nakbafilesarabic.org/2018/06/05/الم-السوري-الجولان-في-والترحيل-المحو/ (accessed 29 October 2021).

IDF (1968), 'Pamphlets, Orders and Announcements Published by the Israeli Defense Forces in the Golan Heights'. No. 6. Jerusalem: National Library of Israel.

Ince, O. U. (2018), 'Between Equal Rights: Primitive Accumulation and Capital's Violence', *Political Theory*, 46 (6): 885–914.

Inglis, D. and J. Hughson (2005), *The Sociology of Art: Ways of Seeing*, London: Palgrave.

INPA (2021), 'Hermon Stream (Banias) Nature Reserve', Available online: https://www.parks.org.il/en/reserve-park/hermon-stream-banias-nature -reserve/ (accessed 19 February 2022).

Internal Displacement Monitoring Centre (2007), *Syria: Forty Years On, People Displaced from the Golan Remain in Waiting*, Oslo: Norwegian Refugee Council Internal Displacement Monitoring Centre.

Iralu, E. (2021), 'Putting Indian Country on the Map: Indigenous Practices of Spatial Justice', *Antipode*, 53 (5): 1485–502.

Israel State Archives (1982), 'Folder Name: Education – Druze – Golan Heights', Ref. no. Gal 17727/11. Military Government letter to the population of the Golan Heights dated 6/9/1981 (in Hebrew).

Israeli Ministry of Foreign Affairs (2013), 'Education: Primary and Secondary'. Available online: http://www.mfa.gov.il/mfa/aboutisrael/education/pages/education-%20primary%20and%20secondary.aspx (accessed 15 November 2017).

Israeli Ministry of Education (2016), 'The Core Program for Teaching History in the Israeli Education System'. Available online: https://cms.education .gov.il/EducationCMS/Units/Mazkirut_Pedagogit/AgafHevraRuach/ TochniyotLimudim/liba_history.htm (accessed 20 October 2021).

Jahshan, J. and H. Yahya (2014), *Palestinian Volunteer Work: A Memory of a Homeland that Refuses to be Forgotten*, Ramallah: Rosa Luxemburg Stiftung and Palestinian Voluntary Work Committee (in Arabic). Available online: https://www.rosalux.ps/wp-content/uploads/2015/06/ كتاب-العمل-التطوعي-الفلسطيني-ذاكرة-وطن-تابى-النسيان.pdf (accessed 19 February 2022).

Jawlany (2020), 'The New Artwork of Ayman Al-Halabi at Al Nafoura Plaza Is Destroyed by Vandals', (in Arabic). Available online: https://jawlany .com/مجهولون-يخربون-العمل-الفني-الجديد-لأي/ (accessed 2 November 2021).

Johnson, P. (2019), *Companions in Conflict: Animals in Occupied Palestine*, New York: Melville House.

Karayanni, M. M. (2014), *Conflicts in a Conflict: A Conflict of Laws Case Study on Israel and the Palestinian Territories*, Oxford: Oxford University Press.

Karayanni, M. M. (2016), 'Tainted Liberalism: Israel's Palestinian-Arab Millets', *Constellations*, 23 (1): 71–83.

Karkabi, N. (2018), 'Electro-Dabke: Performing Cosmopolitan Nationalism and Borderless Humanity', *Public Culture*, 30 (1): 173–96.

Karkabi, N. and A. Ibraheem (2020), 'On Fleeing Colonial Captivity: Fugitive Arts in the Occupied Jawlan', *Identities*, https://doi.org/10.1080/1070289X .2020.1851006

Kastrinou, A. M. A., S. Fakher El-Deen and S. B. Emery (2021), 'The Stateless (Ad)vantage? Resistance, Land and Rootedness in the Israeli-occupied Syrian Golan Heights', *Territory, Politics, Governance*, 9 (5): 636–55.

Kaufman, I. (2004), 'Ethnic Affirmation or Ethnic Manipulation: The Case of the Druze in Israel', *Nationalism and Ethnic Politics*, 9 (4): 53–82.

Kedar, A. (2003), 'On the Legal Geography of Ethnocratic Settler States: Notes Towards a Research Agenda', *Current Legal Issues*, 5: 401–41.

Khaizaran, Y. (2013), *The Arabic Language in the Service of Teaching: A Critical Review of Arabic Textbooks in Druze Schools*, Nazareth: Dirasat – the Arab Center for Law and Policy (in Arabic).

Khaizaran, Y. (2020), 'On the State's Education Apparatus: Zionization and Minoritarianism of Druze Consciousness in Israel', *Arab Studies Journal*, 26 (2): 76–107.

Khalidi, R. (2020), *The Hundred Years' War on Palestine: A History of Settler Colonialism and Resistance, 1917–2017*, New York: Macmillan.

Khanjar, Y. (2018), 'The Movement to Reject the Local Council Elections in the Occupied Golan: A Victory over the Occupation and Preservation of the Unity of the Nation', *Al-Quds Al-Arabi*, 11 March 2018 (In Arabic).

Khanjar, Y. (2019), *It Is Not Midway*, Milan: Al Mutawassit (in Arabic).

Khnifess, A. (2015), 'Israel and the Druze Political Action: Between Politics of Loyalty and Politics of Violence', PhD diss., SOAS, London.

Kipnis, Y. (2013), *The Golan Heights: Political History, Settlement and Geography since 1949*, London: Routledge.

Kirrish, F. N. (1992), 'Druze Ethnicity in the Golan Heights: The Interface of Religion and Politics', *Institute of Muslim Minority Affairs Journal*, 13 (1): 122–35.

Kiwan, M. (2009), 'Syrian Refugees from the Jawlan: Between the Nightmare of Suffering and the Dream of Return', *Al Hayat*, 2 April. Available online: https://elaph.com/Web/NewsPapers/2009/4/425429.html (accessed 4 November 2021).

Krampf, A. (2018), *The Israeli Path to Neoliberalism: The State, Continuity and Change*, London: Routledge.

Lee, S. S. (2008), 'The De-minoritization of Asian Americans: A Historical Examination of the Representations of Asian Americans in Affirmative Action Admissions Policies at the University of California', *Asian American Law Journal*, 15: 129–52.

Limone, N. (2012), 'Germany's Most Important Living Philosopher Issues an Urgent Call to Restore Democracy', *Haaretz*, 16 August. Available online: https://www.haaretz.com/germany-s-most-important-philosopher-issues-an-urgent-call-for-democracy-1.5285348 (accessed 19 February 2022).

Maddah, R. (2012), 'Light Horizon'. Available online: https://randamaddah.com/?page_id=96.

Maddison, S. (2013), 'Indigenous Identity, "Authenticity" and the Structural Violence of Settler Colonialism', *Identities*, 20 (3): 288–303.

Majalli, N. (1982), *Al Jawlan: Epic of Steadfastness*, Akko: Arabesque Publications (in Arabic).

Makdisi, S. (2008), *Palestine Inside Out: An Everyday Occupation*, New York: W.W. Norton.

Mamdani, M. (2020), *Neither Settler Nor Native: The Making and Unmaking of Permanent Minorities*, Cambridge: Belknap Press.

Mandelkern, R. and M. Shalev (2021), 'The Political Economy of Israeli Neoliberalism', in R. Y. Hazan, A. Dowty, M. Hofnung and G. Rahat (eds), *The Oxford Handbook of Israeli Politics and Society*, 653–71, Oxford: Oxford University Press.

Ma'oz, Z. U. (2010), 'Jews and Christians in the Ancient Golan Heights', *Israel Exploration Journal*, 60 (1): 89–93.

Mara'i, T. and U. R. Halabi (1992), 'Life under Occupation in the Golan Heights', *Journal of Palestine Studies*, 22 (1): 78–93.

Masalha, N. (2012), *Expulsion of the Palestinians: The Concept of 'Transfer' in Zionist Political Thought*, Beirut: Institute for Palestine Studies.

Mason, M. (2011), 'An Application of Warfare Ecology to Belligerent Occupations', in G. E. Machlis, T. Hanson, Z. Špirić and J. E. McKendry (eds), *Warfare Ecology: A New Synthesis for Peace and Security*, 155–73, Dordrecht: Springer.

Mason, M. and M. Dajani (2019), 'A Political Ontology of Land: Rooting Syrian Identity in the Occupied Golan Heights', *Antipode*, 51 (1): 187–206.

Mason, M., M. Dajani, M. Fakher Eldin and O. Tesdell (2021), 'The Occupied Jawlan: An Online Open Curriculum', *Middle East Centre Paper Series*, 58, London: LSE, Middle East Centre.

Massad, J. (2007), 'Permission to Paint: Palestinian Art and the Colonial Encounter', *Art Journal*, 66 (3): 126–33.

Mbembe, A. (2003), 'Necropolitics', *Public Culture*, 15 (1): 11–40.

McKee, E. (2016), *Dwelling in Conflict: Negev Landscapes and the Boundaries of Belonging*, Stanford: Stanford University Press.

Mesquita, A. (2018), 'Counter-cartographies: Politics, Art and the Insurrection of Maps', in Kollectiv Orangotango (eds), *This is Not an Atlas: A Global Collection of Counter Cartographies*, 26–35, Bielefeld: transcript Verlag.

Mohammed, A. A. (2014), *Golan Heights in Literature*, Damascus: Arab Writers Union (in Arabic).

Monte Carlo International Website (2015). Available online: https://www.mc-doualiya.com/programs/histoire-chanson-mcd فرقة-نص-تفاحة-أغنية-محل-صغير-ومسكر -الفنان-مضاء-المغربي-ال-20150811/

Mor, D., H. Michelson, Y. Druckman, Y. Mimran, A. Heimann, M. Goldberg and A. Sneh (1997), *Notes on the Geology of the Golan Heights*, Report GSI/15/97, Jerusalem: Geological Survey of Israel.

Murphy, R. and D. Gannon (2008), 'Changing the Landscape: Israel's Gross Violations of International Law in the Occupied Syrian Golan', *Yearbook on International Humanitarian Law*, 11: 139–74.

Muslih, M. (1993), 'The Golan: Israel, Syria, and Strategic Calculations', *Middle East Journal*, 47 (4): 611–32.

Natour, S. (1982), 'Thirteen Thousand Political Prisoners Are Appealing to all the Free People of the World', *Al-Ittihad*, 12 March (in Arabic).

Neep, D. (2012), *Occupying Syria under the French Mandate: Insurgency, Space, and State Formation*, Cambridge: Cambridge University Press.

Newman, A. (2018), 'Education under Occupation: Israeli Educational Policies in the Occupied Syrian Golan', in Al-Marsad (ed.), *The Forgotten Occupation: Life in the Syrian Golan after 50 Years of Occupation*, 80–6, Majdal Shams: Al-Marsad – Arab Human Rights Centre in Golan Heights.

Nisan, M. (2010), 'The Druze in Israel: Questions of Identity, Citizenship, and Patriotism', *The Middle East Journal*, 64 (4): 575–96.

Ó Cuinn, G. (2011), 'Land and Space in the Golan Heights: A Human Rights Perspective', in S. Egoz and G. Pungetti (eds), *The Right to Landscape: Contesting Landscape and Human Rights*, 85–98, Farnham: Ashgate.

Office of the High Commissioner for Human Rights (2011), *International Legal Protection of Human Rights in Armed Conflict*, Geneva, OHCHR.

'On the Anniversary of the Colonial Defeat: The Largest Demonstration in the History of the Golan', *Al-Ittihad*, 20 April, 1982: 1 (in Arabic).

People in the occupied Syrian Golan (1981), *The National Document for the Syrian Citizens in the Occupied Golan Heights*, Majdal Shams: People in the occupied Syrian Golan (in Arabic). Available online: http://archive.palestine-studies.org/ar/node/1080 (accessed 24 August 2021).

Phillips, J. C. (2015), 'The Anti-Assad Campaign in the Golan Heights 2011–2012: Reimagining Syrian Nationalism in a Contested Borderland', *L'Espace Politique*, 27: 3.

Qassem, A. S. (1984), *The Golan Heights 1967–1984*, Beirut: Dar Al Ummah Publishing (in Arabic).

Quiquivix, L. (2014), 'Art of War, Art of Resistance: Palestinian Counter-cartography on Google Earth', *Annals of the Association of American Geographers*, 104 (3): 444–59.

Ram, M. (2014), 'White But Not Quite: Normalizing Colonial Conquests through Spatial Mimicry', *Antipode*, 46 (3), 736–53.

Ram, M. (2015), 'Colonial Conquests and the Politics of Normalization: The Case of the Golan Heights and Northern Cyprus', *Political Geography*, 47: 21–32.

Rouhana, N. and A. Sabbagh-Khoury (2016), 'A Settler Colonial Citizenship: The Essence of the Relationship between Israel and Its Palestinian Citizens', in A. 'Azm et al. (eds), *The Question of Palestine and the Future of the Palestinian National Project. Part II: Settler Colonialism and the Re-imagining of the Future of the Palestinian National Movement*, 163–201, Beirut: The Arab Center for Research and Policy Studies (in Arabic).

Rowe, N. (2011), 'Dance and Political Credibility: The Appropriation of Dabkeh by Zionism, Pan-Arabism, and Palestinian Nationalism', *The Middle East Journal*, 65 (3): 363–80.

Russell, H. (2018), 'Breaking Down the Fence: Addressing the Illegality of Family Separation in the Occupied Syrian Golan', in Al-Marsad (ed.), *The Forgotten Occupation: Life in the Syrian Golan after 50 Years of Occupation*, 28–37, Majdal Shams: Al-Marsad – Arab Human Rights Centre in the Golan Heights.

Saba-Sa'di, S. and A. H. Sa'di (2018), 'State Power and the Role of Education in the Constitution of Natives' Subjectivities: The Druze in Israel', *Social Identities*, 24 (6): 817–35.

Salih, R. and O. Corry (2022), 'Displacing the Anthropocene: Colonisation, Extinction and the Unruliness of Nature in Palestine', *Environment and Planning E: Nature and Space*, 5 (1): 381–400.

Samara, S. (1999), *Jawlan: A Mission of Belonging*, Damascus: Arab Writers Union (in Arabic).

Sawaed, S. A. and B. Safir (2009), *Life Together in Israel*, Jerusalem: Israeli Ministry of Education, Culture and Sports (in Hebrew).

Schumacher, G. ([1888] 2010), *The Jaulân: Surveyed for the German Society for the Exploration of the Holy Land*, Cambridge: Cambridge University Press.

Scott, J. C. (1985), *Weapons of the Weak: Everyday Forms of Peasant Resistance*, New Haven: Yale University Press.

Scott, J. C. (2009), *The Art of Not Being Governed: An Anarchist History of Upland Southeast Asia*, New Haven: Yale University Press.

Sezgin, Y. (2010), 'The Israeli Millet System: Examining Legal Pluralism through Lenses of Nation-Building and Human Rights', *Israel Law Review*, 43: 631–54.

Shai, A. (2006), 'The Fate of Abandoned Arab Villages in Israel, 1965–1969', *History & Memory*, 18 (2): 86–106.

Shalhoub-Kevorkian, N. (2012), 'The Grammar of Rights in Colonial Contexts: The Case of Palestinian Women in Israel', *Middle East Law and Governance*, 4 (1): 106–51.

Shamir, J. (2021), 'For the Druze in the Golan Heights, the Syrian Civil War Opened a New Door to Israel', *Haaretz*, 15 March. Available online: https://www.haaretz.com/israel-news/.premium.HIGHLIGHT.MAGAZINE-for-the-druze-in-the-golan-heights-the-syrian-civil-war-opened-a-new-door-to-israel-1.9621144 (accessed 2 November 2021).

Sharaf, W. (2020), 'The Syrian Golan Facing the Fans of Israel', *Metras.co*, 18 January (in Arabic). Available online: https://metras.co/الجولان-السوري-في-مواجهة-مراوح-إسرائ/ (accessed 19 February 2022).

Shields, C. M., R. Bishop and A. E. Mazawi (2005), *Pathologizing Practices*, New York: Lang.

Shihadeh, M., ed. (2014), *The Palestinians in Israel and the Civil Service Plan: Preliminary Readings*, Haifa, Mada Al-Carmel: Arab Center for Applied Social Research (in Arabic).

Shokair, M. (2021), 'Remembering the Syrian Revolution through Song', *Syria Untold*, 9 April. Available online: https://syriauntold.com/2021/04/09/remembering-the-syrian-revolution-through-song/ (accessed 19 February 2022).

Simpson, L. C. (2019), 'Race', in A. Allen and E. Mendieta (eds), *The Cambridge Habermas Lexicon*, 364–6, Cambridge: Cambridge University Press.

Soffer, A., M. Rosovsky and N. Copaken (1999), *Rivers of Fire: The Conflict over Water in the Middle East*, Lanham: Rowman & Littlefield Publishers.

Sorek, T. (2015), *Palestinian Commemoration in Israel: Calendars, Monuments, and Martyrs*, Stanford: Stanford University Press.

Southlea, A. and D. Nezh Brik (2019), *Windfall: The Exploitation of Wind Energy in the Occupied Syrian Golan*, Majdal Shams: Al-Marsad – Arab Human Rights Centre in the Golan Heights.

Srinivasan, A. (2018), 'The Aptness of Anger', *Journal of Political Philosophy*, 26 (2): 123–44.

Streit Krug, A. and O. Tesdell (2021). 'A Social Perennial Vision: Transdisciplinary Inquiry for the Future of Diverse, Perennial Grain Agriculture', *Plants, People, Planet*, 3 (4): 355–62.

Suiliman, G. and R. Kletter (2022). 'Settler-Colonialism and the Diary of an Israeli Settler in the Golan Heights: The Notebooks of Izhaki Gal', *Journal of Holy Land and Palestine Studies*, 21 (1): 48–71.

Talfah, F. (2010), 'Abdul Majid Al-Faouri: The Jawlan Features Prominently in My Poetry', *eSyria website*, 28 April (in Arabic). Available online: https://www.esyria.sy/2010/04/عبد-المجيد-الفاعوري-للجولان-حيز-كبير-في-شعري (accessed 19 February 2022).

Tatour, L. (2019), 'The Culturalisation of Indigeneity: The Palestinian-Bedouin of the Naqab and Indigenous Rights', *The International Journal of Human Rights*, 23 (10): 1569–93.

Tesdell, O., Y. Othman, Y. Dowani, S. Khraishi, S. Alkhoury, M. Deeik, A. Streit Krug, B. Schlautman and D. Van Tassel (2020), 'Envisioning Perennial Agroecosystems in Palestine', *Journal of Arid Environments*, 175: 104085. https://doi.org/10.1016/j.jaridenv.2019.104085

Tesdell, O. and Editors (2022), 'An Open and Ingrained Method for Studying Landscape', *Jadaliyya*, 19 January (in Arabic). Available online: https://www.jadaliyya.com/Details/43780/مكانيات-طريقة-مفتوحة-ومتأصلة-لدراسة-المشهد-الطبيعي (accessed 1 May 2022).

The Bombing of the Statue of the March, the Statue of Sultan Basha al-Atrash, in Majdal Shams (1987), *Ashtarr News*, 10 April. Available online: http://ashtarr.net/?p=4582.

Tsibiridou, F. (2011), 'Multiplying Minoritization Processes for New Migrants: From Legal Positivism to Creative Hermeneutics', *Annuaire International des Droits de L'Homme*, 6: 294–313.

UNEGN (2014), *The Arab Division for Experts on Geographical Names*, New York: The United Nations Statistics Division.

United Nations Security Council (2019), 8495th Meeting, Wednesday 27 March, 2019, S/PV8495, New York: United Nations.

Urman, D. (1995), 'Public Structures and Jewish Communities in the Golan Heights', in D. Urman and P. V. M. Flesher (eds), *Ancient Synagogues: Historical Analysis and Archaeological Discovery*, 373–618. Leiden: Brill.

Veracini, L. (2010), *Settler Colonialism: A Theoretical Overview*, New York: Palgrave Macmillan.

Weber, M. (1978), *Economy and Society: An Outline of Interpretive Sociology*, Berkeley: University of California Press.

Weizman, E. (2007), *Hollow Land: Israel's Architecture of Occupation*, London: Verso.

Wessels, J. I. (2015a), 'Challenging Hydro-hegemony: Hydro-politics and Local Resistance in the Golan Heights and the Palestinian Territories', *International Journal of Environmental Studies*, 72 (4): 601–23.

Wessels, J. I. (2015b), 'Down to the River: Identity, Citizenship, Security, Borders and Water in the Occupied Golan Heights', *Middle East Critique*, 24 (3): 269–87.

White, B. T. (2011), *The Emergence of Minorities in the Middle East: The Politics of Community in French Mandate Syria*, Edinburgh: Edinburgh University Press.

Wolfe, P. (1999), *Settler Colonialism and the Transformation of Anthropology: The Politics and Poetics of an Ethnographic Event*, London: Cassel.

Wolfe, P. (2006), 'Settler Colonialism and the Elimination of the Native', *Journal of Genocide Research*, 8 (4): 387–409.

Yiftachel, O. (1997), 'Israeli Society and Jewish-Palestinian Reconciliation: "Ethnocracy" and Its Territorial Contradictions', *The Middle East Journal*, 51: 505–19.

Yiftachel, O. (2006), *Ethnocracy, Land and Identity Politics in Israel/Palestine*, Philadelphia: Penn Press.

Yiftachel, O. and A. Ghanem (2004), 'Towards a Theory of Ethnocratic Regimes: Learning from the Judaization of Israel/Palestine', in E. Kaufmann (ed.), *Rethinking Ethnicity: Majority Groups and Dominant Minorities*, 179–97, London: Routledge.

Ynet (2020), 'Winning for the Nature: There Won't be a Neighborhood in Hermon Nature Reserve', *Ynet*, 29 November (in Hebrew). Available online: https://www.ynet.co.il/cnvironment-science/article/B1H1BeWjP (accessed 19 February 2022).

Ynet (2021), 'Hermon Nature Reserve in Danger of Extinction', *Ynet*, 1 July (in Hebrew). Available online: https://www.ynet.co.il/environment-science/article/SyzTwT93u (accessed 19 February 2022).

Yousef, M. (2017), 'I Love My Home', For Grade 4, Jerusalem: Israeli Ministry of Education.

Yusoff, K. (2018), *A Billion Black Anthropocenes or None*, Minneapolis: University of Minnesota Press.

INDEX

permanent minorities 10, 56, 88, 184, *see also* minoritization
politics of the governed 6, 14–15, 19, 51–67, 186, 189–92
primitive accumulation 29–33, 36, 39, 187
Purple Line (ceasefire line) 1–2, 4–5

Qadamani, Majeed 101
Qans, Hasan 116
Qassem, Abdul Sattar 12
Qassim, Samih al- 133–4
Quiquivix, Linda 193
Quneitra
city 2, 7, 34, 60, 89, 165, 170
Israeli destruction of (1974) 34
Syrian governorate 6–7, 115, 167–8, 173, 193
A Quote (artwork) 86

Rabitat al-Jami'iyyin, *see* Golan Academic Association
resistance
and art 94, 106–7, 111, 114, 117–18, 141, 148
general strike (*see* general strike)
identity-based 28, 36–9, 58, 63, 89
Jawlan commune 46
Jawlani 5–6, 12–18, 36–41, 57–8, 61, 69, 78, 88–90, 94, 144–5, 155–6
non-violent 6, 12, 37, 91, 184, 191, 194–6 (*see also sumud*)
underground cells 69, 150–2
and volunteering 15, 68, 70–6, 92, 95–6
and 'weapons of the weak' 57
resource dispossession 3, 6, 12, 24, 32–7, 115, 142, 164, 171, 184–93
Rizqallah, Bassel 14, 148

Sahita 3, 30
Salqan, Jamal al- 72–3
Samara, Suleiman 116
Schechterman Committee 131

Schumacher, Gottlieb 9, 164–5
Scott, James 57, 165
semiotics 15, 53–8, 66–7
settler colonialism
Israeli 11, 14, 24, 27–36, 41, 115, 149, 186–8, 193
theory 12, 14, 24–36, 55–7, 66–7, 180, 186–8
violence of 11, 24–5, 31–2, 35, 40, 67, 148, 187–9, 193
Shams, Jamila 47
Shapiro, Adam 196
Shouting Hill 1–4, 59
social pathologies 26–7, 35
sovereignty 30, 32, 40, 44, 54–6, 60, 87, 97, 102, 183–5, 193
Soviet Union 58, 63
sumud ('steadfastness') 4, 12, 37, 73, 116, 192
Syria, *see also* Assad
border crossings with 17, 28, 59–61, 89, 124, 138, 140, 184
community separation 42, 60–1, 78–82, 97, 138–40
conflict in 15, 17, 29, 37, 61, 77–8, 90, 124, 137–40, 184
national identity 12, 43–8, 57, 97, 115–18, 128, 190–3 (*see also* National Document)
peace negotiations with Israel 29, 32, 59–60
prisoners 12, 58, 68–9, 73, 191
property 16, 32–3, 167
state of 1–2, 6, 10–11, 28, 32, 123, 136, 144

Tarabieh, Wael 16–17, 105, 108–9
Tesdell, Omar 18
Thweib, Abdel Qadir 17
Toot Ard 95, 118
Touma, Emile 191
Tsemel, Lea 71

United Nations Disengagement Observer Force (UNDOF) 1, 3, 89